T0328000

Published by Semiotext(e)
PO BOX 629, South Pasadena, CA 91031
www.semiotexte.com

Special thanks to Robert Dewhurst and John Ebert.

Cover Design: Lauren Mackler
Back Cover Photograph: Robert Giard, "Andrea Dworkin," 1992
Layout: Hedi El Kholti

ISBN: 978-1-63590-080-4

Distributed by The MIT Press, Cambridge, Mass. and London, England
Printed in the United States of America

10 9 8 7 6 5 4

Last Days *at* Hot Slit

The Radical Feminism of **ANDREA DWORKIN**

Edited by
**JOHANNA FATEMAN AND
AMY SCHOLDER**

semiotext(e)

Contents

introduction by Johanna Fateman

LAST DAYS AT HOT SLIT:
The Radical Feminism of Andrea Dworkin

Black-and-white photos show a hippie couple in a city-hall ceremony in Amsterdam. The bride is not the Andrea Dworkin we know, who wore a uniform of denim overalls and sneakers, militant and unmitigated by a single capitulation to feminine beauty standards. This one is very young, just twenty-two, with black-rimmed eyes and a chin-length hair cut with bangs. In a letter from April 1969, she writes to her parents in New Jersey about her wedding, "no one gave me away. in the ceremony we promised to respect each other."[1] In a group shot, the newlyweds, dressed in embroidered robes (hers Turkish, his Tibetan), stand seriously at the center of their long-haired friends. Oddly, the groom's hand isn't around Dworkin's shoulder or waist, but gripping her neck. It's also on her neck in the photo of them standing before a canal kissing.[2]

In New York, the women's movement was charging forward, still in its first exhilarating years. Just two months before Dworkin said "I do," Ellen Willis and Shulamith Firestone founded the action-oriented radical-feminist group Redstockings. And soon after, Willis reports, from a fly-on-the-wall perspective for the *New Yorker*,[3] a group of some thirty women wreaked havoc on an abortion-law hearing of the all-male New York State Joint Legislative Committee on Public Health, demanding to testify as the "real experts" on illegal abortion. Though one day Willis would become Dworkin's enemy, Firestone would first become her hero for writing *The Dialetic of Sex* (1970). And the Redstockings' winning tactic—of which their disruption that day was just one early example—would become Dworkin's guiding principle, her religion: The advance guard of the second wave showed that by casting off stigma and shame, by forcing their stories into the public record, they could open the floodgates of women's rage to change the culture and the law.

In September 1971 Dworkin writes home in tall, fast cursive.[4] It's her handwriting, but not the writer we know. Composed in the aftermath of a cataclysmic visit from her parents—during which they witnessed her husband's rage and saw him hit her; during which she begged them to take her away and they refused—the long letter is an excruciating document of concealments, excuses, and apologies—all things she would eradicate from her prose shortly. By November, she's living as a fugitive. At her husband's hands she's been disabused—almost fatally—of her faith in the male-led Left. Now she hides from him on a farm, on a freezing houseboat, or in the basement of a nightclub, with the help of a new lover. Ricki Abrams brings her books—Firestone's, which introduces the concept of the sex-class system, Robin Morgan's anthology *Sisterhood is Powerful* (1970), and Kate Millett's *Sexual Politics*, from the same year—and together the two women begin to work on one of their own.

In between her letters home, in which she puts on a brave face and asks for money until she can get back on her feet, Dworkin writes with Abrams about fairy tales, foot binding, witch burning, and porn. Until finally, in 1972, desperate and destitute, she agrees to carry a briefcase of heroin through customs in exchange for a thousand dollars and a ticket to New York. The dope-smuggling plan falls through, but Dworkin keeps the money and gets away, carrying with her a ticket to a writer's life—an unfinished manuscript she's thinking of calling *Last Days at Hot Slit*.

The draft she arrived in New York with would ultimately become *Woman Hating*, published in 1974 (Abrams would decide not to be part of the final version), and this collection is titled for her abandoned idea—chosen to memorialize her escape, the high stakes of her literary debut, and the apocalyptic, middle-finger appeal of her prose. It opens with a postcard written four years after her wedding.[5] In New York with Gringo, the beloved German shepherd she somehow rescued from Amsterdam, she's divorced and ecstatic, working as an assistant to the poet Muriel Rukeyser. Dworkin thanks her parents for their money and solicits their pride, brazenly demanding to be loved for who she really is—now, the author of a truly incendiary feminist text.

———

Through chronological selections from Dworkin's lifetime of restless output—excerpts from her most infamous nonfiction works and examples of her overlooked fiction, as well as two previously unpublished works—*Last Days at Hot Slit* aims to put the contentious positions she's best known for in dialogue with her literary oeuvre.[6] An iconic figure of so-called anti-sex feminism, Dworkin still looms large in feminist demands for sexual freedom. In her singular scorched-earth theory of representation, pornography is fascist propaganda, a weapon as crucial to the ever-escalating war on women as Goebbels's caricatures were to Hitler's rise. In her analysis of the sex-class system, prostitution is a founding institution, the bottom rung of hell. And in her vision of sexual liberation, there's no honor in squeezing pleasure from the status quo—s/m is nihilistic playacting founded on farcical consent or craven collaboration, "Dachau brought into the bedroom and celebrated."[7]

And so, in the feminist insistence that women have the right to make and use pornography, to choose sex work, to engage in every kind of consensual act without shame, and to do so as revolutionaries, Dworkin is the censorial demagogue to shoot down. But nearly four decades after the historic Barnard Conference on Sexuality, which drew the battle lines of the feminist sex wars—pro-sex feminists staking out territory for the investigation of pleasure, while Women Against Pornography protested outside—and nearly three decades since the ascendance of the third wave signaled her definitive defeat, we hope it's possible to consider what was lost in the fray.

This collection is the product of years of conversation. When Amy Scholder, my co-editor, invited me to contribute to *Icon* (2014)[8]—a collection of nine personal essays, for which each author chose a public figure who influenced, intrigued, or haunted her—she reignited a teenage obsession of mine, which proved to be contagious. By choosing Dworkin as my subject, I returned to a moment in the 1990s, when my discovery of her militant voice fueled my nascent feminist rage, and when I quickly disavowed her politics with the kind of clean, capricious break that youth affords. But for Amy and me both, in reading Dworkin's books with fresh eyes—measuring them against her lingering presence in feminist discourse as a symbol, frozen in time at the helm of a failed crusade—we found much more than the antiporn intransigence she's reviled or revered for.

Dworkin was a philosopher outside of and against the academy, one of the first writers to use her own experiences of rape and battery in a revolutionary analysis of male supremacy. With astonishing vulnerability and searching rigor, she wrote of fucking, whoring, and the atrocity of rape; she wrote without apology, wielding the blunt, ugly language most appropriate to the bitter subject matter of her life. And while her work is by no means all autobiographical, her lifelong, unflinching inquiry into women's subjugation was founded on a simple desire: "I wanted to find out what happened to me and why."[9]

———

Born into a lower-middle-class Jewish family in Camden, New Jersey, in 1946, Dworkin was raised under the specter of the Holocaust, in the hushed home of a frequently bedridden mother. Sylvia Dworkin's heart condition is prominent in Andrea's portrayal of her childhood. She and her brother Mark are separated and sent to live with relatives during Sylvia's hospital stays; Harry, their father, is often absent, working two or more jobs so his wife can see the best doctors. Andrea keeps Sylvia alive through psychic vigilance and peaceful conformity, she thinks. Conversely, she makes her sicker with the disruptive force of her true personality.

Childhood is a long, drawn-out loss of girlish illusions, as it becomes clear, through a series of painful lessons, that her ambitions—to be a poet, to obey only her instinct for adventure—are categorically male. There's a mythic dimension to this narrative: The female hero's journey is a search for greatness and meaning, in which rebellion and naiveté alike are punished by stunning sexual cruelty. And there is no home to return to, transformed or not.

Her life comes into focus through the overlapping accounts of her essays and fiction. At age nine, left alone for the first time to see a movie, a paperback of Baudelaire in her pocket, she is sexually assaulted in the dark of the theater. "The commitment of the child molester is absolute," she writes, regarding the incident in *My Life as a Writer* (1995), "and both his insistence and his victory communicate to the child his experience of her—a breachable, breakable thing any stranger can wipe his dick on."[10] Her novel *Mercy* (1990) complements that cold indictment with the flustered anguish of a child. Narrated by her first-person protagonist, also named Andrea, it opens with a long scene in which the trauma of that day is defined by the twin horrors of the molester's violation and her mother's shame-tinged panic to confirm that "nothing happened," i.e., that he only wiped his dick on her daughter, didn't force it inside.

Dworkin has a book with her when she's jailed in 1965, too—a volume of Charles Olson's poetry. While a freshman at Bennington, participating in the college's work program as a volunteer for the Student Peace Union in New York, she's arrested protesting the Vietnam war outside the U.N. and held at the Women's House of Detention for four days, where she is subjected to a sadistic pelvic exam, a gynecological rape. Upon her release, bleeding, she writes outraged letters to the papers about her ordeal. Her efforts lead to a highly publicized grand jury hearing about the jail's conditions, at which she testifies. In a *New York Times* article—one of the many reports that would mortify her parents—Dworkin is a "plump girl with black hair and dark eyes," who describes how the leering, brutal doctor questioned her. "He asked me where I went to school. Then he wanted to know how many Bennington girls were virgins."[11] In an apt foreshadowing of what's to come—at age eighteen, before her feminist awakening is even on the horizon—she's willing to brand herself with an image of sexual shame in the name of justice.

Fleeing her parents' humiliation and disapproval, Dworkin exiles herself to Crete, arriving almost penniless. The trip marks the start of a period of sporadic survival sex and prostitution. There she writes poetry, self-publishing a number of chapbooks, including such seething juvenilia as *Notes on Burning Boyfriend*,[12] a surreal homage to the Quaker activist Norman Morrison, who set himself on fire below Secretary of Defense Robert McNamara's office window. Her teenage poetry is antiwar, anticapitalist, and sexually explicit, influenced by the dramatic landscape of her surroundings and the intensity of the love affair that consumed her during this sojourn. Though she returns to Bennington to finish her course work, she's gone again before commencement—to Amsterdam, to write about the Dutch-anarchist movement Provo. She falls in love with one of its members—but now we can skip to a better beginning.

————

"This book is an action, a political action where revolution is the goal. It has no other purpose," Dworkin writes in *Woman Hating*— a sentiment that might preface every one of her works. The book is steeped in the anti-imperialist, socialist vision of her countercultural milieu, informed by the tactics and rhetorical style of the Black Power movement, and profoundly indebted to Firestone and Millett. Dworkin writes with palpable hope, believing that the women's movement can build upon the radical ideas of the day, bring new truths and momentum to global struggles. Among the five short excerpts included here is a portion of the introduction, which lays out Dworkin's planetary agenda for revolution and makes explicit her expectations of the reader. "One cannot be free, never, not ever, in an unfree world, and in the course of redefining family, church, power relations, all the institutions which inhabit and order our lives, there is no way to hold onto privilege and comfort. To attempt to do so is destructive, criminal, and intolerable."

Dworkin presents a vision of *American*—or rather Amerikan—feminist history as one inextricable from Black liberation, beginning with "prototypal revolutionary models" such as of Sojourner Truth and Harriet Tubman. And while her account of the first wave and the Seneca Falls convention in 1848 glosses over the rift between its white organizers and Black suffragists, we find her grappling with the importance of class and race in a revolutionary analysis of her own time. She names the biases of the women's movement as its "most awful failure"—even as she echoes the mistakes of her white feminist peers. Readers will find a simplification of the thorny issues, a comparison of (implicitly white) women's degraded social role to that of a "shuffling" caricature of minstrelsy, and a jarring deployment of racial slurs to make a point. Dworkin's concept of "primary emergency" though, a rudimentary, intersectional distinction that acknowledges a woman's most acute oppression may not be *as a woman*, while not groundbreaking, represents a challenge to the arrogant myopia of many of the white second wave's loudest voices. Her antiracist ethos is rooted in her upbringing—her parents' vocal support for the civil rights movement—and informed by her own work to end the war, but Dworkin's evolving attunement to race, apparent in her subsequent writing, will arise from her close study of pornography's favorite tropes—its sexualization of skin color, dependence on ethnic caricature, and interest in enslavement.

She writes in the fresh tradition established in *Sexual Politics* by Millett, whose literary analysis of the male canon illuminates the political character of sex. Dworkin will use it as a model throughout her career, expanding its application to systematically dissect patriarchal artifacts, whether canonical works such as Flaubert's *Madame Bovary* or the unacclaimed novels *Black Fashion Model* and *Whip Chick*. "Woman as Victim: *Story of O*," is emblematic of her sensibility. Her treatment of Pauline Réage's 1954 classic of sado-masochistic literature in *Woman Hating* obviates the need to debate its status as art or pornography—either way, *Story of O* is allegorical, the distinguishing details of its story easily boiled off to reveal its essence as a perniciously instructive schema of sexual metaphysics. Dworkin uses the word *cunt* and refers to fucking, cocksucking, gangbanging, and rape without relent, in a rebuke to Réage's vocabulary of erotic euphemism as well as the official language of philosophical abstraction. Though she refines her execution of such analyses over the years—and calibrates them with varying degrees of artistic reverence and castrating bravado—the strategy is fully formed in her seductively rough-hewn first book.

Her afterword, "The Great Punctuation Typography Struggle," is a rebuke of standard punctuation, offering an alternate vision of her text—a glimmer of how she had wanted it to appear on the page. "Ive attacked male dominance, thats ok," she writes of her fight with the publisher, "Ive attacked every heterosexual notion of relation, thats ok. Ive in effect advocated the use of drugs, thats ok . . . lower case letters are not. it does make one wonder." Though she was prevented from delivering the body of *Woman Hating* in an overtly experimental form, we have included her concluding, unconventionally punctuated statement, in hopes that it will draw out the formally innovative qualities of subsequent works, too—her scant commas, never-ending sentences, her use of repetition, about-face confrontations, and deadpan absurdism. She cared about style.

Though it found an appreciative feminist audience, *Woman Hating* didn't earn enough to support her, nor did it result in paid writing opportunities. "I was convinced that it was the publishing establishment—timid and powerless women editors, the superstructure of men who make the real decisions, misogynistic reviewers—that stood between me and a public particularly of women that I knew was there," she reflects. "The publishing establishment was a formidable blockade, and my plan was to swim around it."[13] Speaking gigs became a way to survive, and to reach women.

Of the many talks Dworkin gave, at feminist conferences, colleges, and for women's groups that passed a hat around after Q&A's, we've included "Renouncing Sexual 'Equality,'" from 1974, in which she calls for "an absolute transformation of human sexuality," a demand in line with her expanding understanding of patriarchy's incursions into every aspect of life, the institutional nature of even our most intimate dynamics and acts. Here, she introduces a vision of sex that would rankle and repel many, a scenario of ostensible liberation that came to represent, as feminist debates around pleasure and desire unfolded, a sharply constrained and prescriptive menu of behavior. Speaking of the profound changes required to realize a just society, she says, "For men I suspect that this transformation begins in the place they most dread—that is, in a limp penis. I think that men will have to give up their precious erections and begin to make love as women do together." Such presumptions regarding how women do or should make love together would cause her trouble—though not as much as her perceived threats to male orgasm. But if she left hazy the controversial specifics of revolutionary sex at this juncture, her understanding of the ancient, hidden epidemic of male sexual violence was achieving a level of devastating precision.

Dworkin had some stability by now. She lived with the writer John Stoltenberg, a gay man who would be her partner until she died in 2005. (They married in 1998.) Polaroids from this period show a life of pets and books—Gringo with a Frisbee in the sun; Stoltenberg with a kitten on his chest; Dworkin armored in overalls, reading in an armchair, a tuxedo cat and an orange tabby standing guard at the window. In another image, they lounge with her on the bed, a SMASH PATRIARCHY poster on the wall behind them.[14] After seeing Lily Tomlin perform at Lincoln Center, Dworkin sent her a copy of *Woman Hating* and a note ("I feel so shy about writing to you. I love your work enormously. It means so much to me").[15] Looking through the writer's papers, I was always happy to find evidence of joy, because by all accounts, the terror and numb despair of her past were always close, constantly brought to the fore by the nature of her work.

"The Rape Atrocity and the Boy Next Door,"[16] a longer speech, which she wrote in 1975, the same year that Susan Brownmiller's landmark book *Against Our Will* was published, is a striking document from a time when marital rape was legal in all fifty states, and when women's radical candor was still just beginning to reveal the depth and ubiquity of sexual violence. The title—the word *atrocity*— underscores Dworkin's insistence on reframing the commonplace and infrequently prosecuted act of rape as not just a tool of political control, but as a *war crime*, committed on dates, in respectable households, and everywhere else you can imagine. "I am here tonight to try to tell you what you are up against as women in your efforts to live decent, worthwhile, and productive human lives," she explained to her college audiences. "Once you understand what rape is, you will be able to resist all attempts to mystify and mislead you into believing that the crimes committed against you as women are trivial, comic, irrelevant." Dworkin labored against a backdrop of naturalized, normalized, invisible misogyny to illuminate the genocidal character of violence against women, and while there were legions that would charge her with hyperbole, there was also a growing feminist army who found, in her electrifying indictments of male supremacy, the truth at last. Delivering a talk like "Rape Atrocity," came at a great cost, though.

> I heard about rape after rape; women's lives passed before me, rape after rape; women who had been raped in homes, in cars, on beaches, in alleys, in classrooms, by one man, by two men, by five men, by eight men, hit, drugged, knifed, torn, women who had been sleeping, women who had been with their children, women who had been out for a walk or shopping or going to school or going home from school or in their offices working or in factories or in stockrooms, young women, girls, old women, thin women, fat women, housewives, secretaries, hookers, teachers, students. I simply could not bear it. So I stopped giving the speech. I thought I would die from it. I learned what I had to know, and more than I could stand to know.[17]

Knowing more than she could stand became a default state, because Dworkin was morally compelled to speak out about the most difficult, the most painful things for the rest of her life. Just as women, to win the right to abortion, had spoken out about facing death in motel rooms and back alleys to terminate pregnancies, or of being forced as teenagers to carry their rapists' babies to term, she would have to talk about the violence of her marriage in order to help other women. "A Battered Wife Survives" is her first public account of that time in Amsterdam, and we preface it with her letter to her parents, in which she warns them of their cameo appearance in her story.

At the same time, her focus on pornography intensified. In the late 1970s, her thundering speeches—delivered at conferences and colleges, also rallies and marches—named porn as terrorism, as material created to demonstrate women's inferiority through the unrelenting depiction of them as whores hungry for violation and punishment, designed to make men sexually reliant on such portrayals and to teach them to act out the scenarios. "Images of women bound, bruised, and maimed on virtually every street corner, on every magazine rack, in every drug store, in movie house after movie house, on billboards, on posters posted on walls, are death threats to a female population in rebellion," she explained to a small group of students at the University of Massachusetts in the winter of 1977. "Female rebellion against male sexual despotism, female rebellion against male sexual authority, is now a reality throughout this country," she continued, perhaps too optimistically, assessing the state of the women's movement. "The men," she accused, "meeting rebellion with an escalation of terror, hang pictures of maimed female bodies in every place."[18]

To put such a dramatic pronouncement in context: In 1975, the producer of *Snuff*, a low-budget film about a Manson Family–like satanic biker gang had courted publicity with the claim that the movie showed the real dismemberment and murder of a woman; and the next year a Sunset Boulevard billboard advertising the Rolling Stones' new album *Black and Blue* showed model Anita Russell in bondage, her legs spread, a dark mark on her inner thigh, and beside her, the text, "I'm 'Black and Blue' from the Rolling Stones—and I love it!" A new group called Women Against Violence Against Women (WAVAW) organized letter-writing campaigns and consumer boycotts, initiating a model of feminist media critique and action that caught on. More groups would soon form, specifically focused on porn, and interested in legal interventions.[19]

The Equal Rights Amendment was still on the table, and with nearly a decade of feminist cultural and legislative victories adding up, it wasn't crazy to view such violent material, particularly its new mainstream presence, as dangerous political retaliation—especially if you were suffocating in women's stories of sadistic abuse and rape while writing through the night, night after night, as Dworkin was. In 1978, she addressed a packed auditorium before the first national "Take Back the Night" march, in which thousands of women walked through San Francisco's red-light district after dark, their protest banners mingling with the neon signs. "If a woman has any sense of her own intrinsic worth, seeing pornography in small bits and pieces can bring her to a useful rage," she said. "Studying pornography in quantity and depth, as I have been doing for more months than I care to remember, will turn that same woman into a mourner."[20]

Pornography: Men Possessing Women (1981) is the sophisticated descendant of *Woman Hating*, a more intricate argument that does not stop with the dissection of patriarchal artifacts. In it, porn is formulated as propaganda on a par with that of any genocidal regime, relying as it does on an identical vocabulary of dehumanizing racial, ethnic, and sexual stereotypes to justify the persecution of a group. It is also *evidence* of persecution—a literal documentation of abuse and degradation in some cases, and a faithful representation of commonplace practices, such as rape, in others. "The force depicted in pornography is objective and real because force is so used against women," Dworkin writes. "The debasing of women depicted in pornography and intrinsic to it is objective and real in that women are so debased. The uses of women depicted in pornography are objective and real because women are so used. The women used in pornography are used in pornography." In her logic, the production of the image, the image itself, and the sexual-ideological use of the image in white-male supremacist society are folded together in pornography as a cultural practice. The book is difficult to excerpt—and difficult to read—because much of its power is derived from what it asks you to weather as a reader, tracking the progression of her argument through a punishing, cumulative process of rhetorical extremes and unsparing descriptions of cruelty.

While the instinctual response to Dworkin's central argument is the procurement of real or theoretical counter-examples to her generalizations about pornography as a genre rooted in the debasement of women, such efforts are futile—debasement is baked into her definition. At one fell swoop in her preface, with a characteristically startling and pointed transhistorical flourish, she damns both Ancient Greece and the ACLU by invoking porn's etymology— its origin in the word *pornai*, which denotes the lowest caste of prostitute, the brothel slave. "This is not a book about the First Amendment. By definition the First Amendment protects only those who can exercise the rights it protects. Pornography by definition— 'the graphic depiction of whores'—is trade in a class of persons who have been systematically denied the rights protected by the First Amendment and the rest of the Bill of Rights." Sexually explicit images portraying true equality, made by choice under fair working conditions—should they exist—are not pornography, but something else. The feminist pornography movement would emerge later, in the mid-1980s, with such endeavors as Candida Royalle's woman-centered film production company or the lesbian magazine

On Our Backs. And though Dworkin would be hostile to their material too, it wasn't what she was talking about in 1981.

While it may be possible now to read *Pornography* in a number of ways—as experimental literature, durational cultural criticism, a provocation dramatizing the representational crises posed by a rapidly expanding porn industry—in its day Dworkin's book was anchored in a vocal and prominent antipornography faction of the feminist movement, defined by dogged grassroots action and an uncompromising view of media that depict sexual subordination. Linda Marchiano, known as Linda Lovelace, star of *Deep Throat* (1972), had, in 1980, come out with a shocking account of her abuse and coercion during its filming, and the slogan "Pornography is violence against women" had become doctrine. Dismayed feminist detractors felt antipornography activism had sucked the air out of discussions of sexuality and added to the prohibitions on women's behavior, while also flirting dangerously with pro-censorship positions. Any chance of a substantive discussion of *Pornography's* innovative structure, Dworkin's aesthetics of rage, or theoretical nuance was lost—the text was inextricable from her public persona within the rancorous melee of the women's movement, splintering as it entered the Reagan era.

The author of the book's negative *New York Times* review is none other than Ellen Willis. She opens with a pointed rhetorical question: "Who would have predicted that just now, when the far right has launched an all-out attack on women's basic civil rights, the issue eliciting the most passionate public outrage from feminists should be not abortion, not "pro-family" fundamentalism, but pornography?"[21] To Willis, unmoved and alarmed by Dworkin's polemic, the "peculiar confluence" of the feminist antipornography movement and the cultural agenda of the Right was "evidence that feminists have been affected by the conservative climate and are unconsciously moving with the cultural tide." In her view, both religious moralism and Dworkin's metaphysical absolute of male power offered no path forward for women's sexual liberation. And while "The misogyny Andrea Dworkin decries is real enough," she grants, the author's vision is, Willis writes, "less inspiring than numbing, less a call to arms than a counsel of despair."

The next year, Willis participated in the Barnard Conference on Sexuality, an event organized by Columbia University professor Carole S. Vance, who was explicit in her mission to critique the feminist antipornography movement and to regroup around such open-ended questions as, "How do women get sexual pleasure in patriarchy?" Outside, protestors stated one way women should *not* get it: Their t-shirts read FOR A FEMINIST SEXUALITY on the front and AGAINST S/M on the back. In general, Dworkin's writing does not directly engage with the positions of her feminist adversaries; she might argue that her rebuttals are implicit in her broader critique of male supremacy. And publicly, her allies took up for her. (Women Against Pornography leader Dorchen Leidholdt responded to Willis's review in a letter to the editor.)[22] But this is not to say that the opposition of pro-sex feminists did not enrage and grieve Dworkin, that she was above private attacks and demands for ideological fealty, or that accusations of political and sexual conservatism escaped her notice.

In the unpublished manuscript *Ruins* (1978–83), a novel structured as a series of letters to people from her past, there is one piece titled "Goodbye to All That." Published here for the first time, it was written in 1983, calling out, with livid sarcasm, the biggest names associated with the antipornography counter-movement, skewering them as false renegades. "Goodbye, Ellen, baaad

baaad Ellen," she writes. Though she addresses her critics by first name only, they are, undoubtedly, in addition to Willis, sex radical Patrick Califia, queer activist Amber Hollibaugh, and Gayle Rubin, a cultural anthropologist associated with queer BDSM groups. More generally, Dworkin bids adieu to "all you swastika-wielding dykettes, all you tough dangerous feminist leatherettes, all you sexy, nonmonogamous (it does take the breath away) pierced, whipped, bitten, fist-fucked and fist-fucking wild wonderful heretofore unimaginable feminist Girls." And in heartbroken half-resignation to the changing tides, she also says goodbye to her friends and comrades. "Goodbye to the dummies who thought sex could express reciprocity and equality and still be sexy. Goodbye to the dummies who thought this movement could change the world."[23]

But these rifts, and the academic trends precipitating the emergence of gender studies programs and queer theory, could not distract her from the real war for long. That same year, she addressed an audience of hundreds of men, at a National Organization for Changing Men conference. "I Want a Twenty-Four-Hour Truce During Which There is No Rape" is a rare appeal to the unfair sex, illustrating her vivid sense of women's unrelenting emergency. "We don't have forever. Some of us don't have another week or another day for you to discuss whatever it is that will enable you to go out into those streets and do something. We are very close to death. All women are. And we are very close to rape and we are very close to beating. And we are inside a system of humiliation from which there is no escape for us."

She didn't broker a détente that day or ever, but the Antipornography Civil Rights Ordinance that she coauthored later in 1983, with feminist legal scholar Catharine MacKinnon, represented a new battlefield strategy. It was an attempt to reframe pornography as a form of sex discrimination, a civil rights violation, allowing those harmed by it to sue for damages. High profile but doomed campaigns to enact the law in various cities throughout the eighties took Dworkin beyond the polarizing skirmishes of the women's movement, and put her at the center of a larger public debate. The 1986 Meese Commission's report on pornography included a transcription of thirty minutes of her brutal, poetic testimony; her image would never recover from this strategic alignment with anti-obscenity conservatism.

Dworkin's apparent—or suspected—sympathy for the Right was perhaps, more accurately, a profound resentment of the progressive pretensions of the Left, dating back to her teen experiences with the radical lip-service of men who'd fucked her over. The booming porn industry of the 1970s was rooted in a fraternal counterculture, she often pointed out, led by cynical entrepreneurs of the so-called sexual revolution. Her book *Right Wing Women*, published that same pivotal year—1983—explores women's fate at the other end of the political spectrum. What is perhaps most notable about the book in the context of her career at this point is her use of the misogynist cruelty of the Right as a foil to the sexist betrayals of the civil-libertarian Left—each side harbors a virulent strain of antifeminism, and she doesn't really have a preference. Her position is, in some ways, a confrontational for-the-sake-of-argument pose. Dworkin was functionally, on all other issues, left of the Left. But her involvement with proposed antipornography legislation made her bipartisan disdain suspicious.

The book, expanded from a 1977 article published in *Ms.*, is a compassionate exploration of mostly white, Evangelical women. Dworkin's chapter on abortion and anti-abortion women is brutally thorough; another titled "The Coming Gynocide" is, as the title suggests, a harrowing presentation of her predictions for the near future, where male supremacist ideology realizes its logical extreme. We've included her first chapter, "The Promise of the Ultra-Right," in which she looks at women's embrace of religious absolutism and conformity as a savvy calculation made to better their chances of physical and social survival. It is some of Dworkin's funniest writing, as she acerbically summarizes the positions of her right-wing sisters and their instructions for how to love and submit—or, to look at it another way, how to use a career of antigay activism (Anita Bryant) or born-again therapy (Ruth Carter Stapleton) to escape forced childbearing and the prison of the home.

Right Wing Women gets a backhanded compliment in the paper of record four years after its release, in a double pan of Dworkin's nonfiction work *Intercourse* and her first novel *Ice and Fire*, published simultaneously in the United States in 1987. Dworkin writes her own letter to the editor this time:

> I despair of being treated with respect, let alone fairly, in your pages. The review of "Ice and Fire" and "Intercourse" (May 3) is contemptuous beyond belief. In an adjacent column, Walter Kendrick, who has written a pro-pornography book and has equated me with Hitler in the pages of The Village Voice, is congratulated for insulting me. Thirteen years after its publication, your reviewer comments that "Woman Hating" is brilliant—thanks. And only four years after the publication of "Right-Wing Women," it too is called brilliant. Don't get ahead of yourselves. Neither book, by the way, was reviewed by The New York Times.[24]

Carol Sternhell's review reflects the cultural forces working against Dworkin's legibility as a thinker by this time. "Sexual intercourse should be abolished. It's the cause of many (most? all?) of women's problems. It's a lousy idea for the human race," she glibly mischaracterizes the argument of *Intercourse* (and, as she sees it, the implicit message of *Ice and Fire* as well). "Besides, men are such creeps—all they want to do is 'occupy,' 'violate,' 'invade' and 'colonize' women's bodies,"[25] she mocks. Dworkin's untempered prose, her focus on the extremes of sexual violence and the exploitation of women in the sex industry—and arguably, her failure to make crystal clear at every possible opportunity the distinction between the social construction or metaphysical definition of male power and actual men—had earned her a reputation as a man hater and a gender essentialist. Her sweeping descriptions of patriarchy's toxic viscera were taken as evidence of a conviction that men are irredeemable; heterosexuality is hopeless, and, most famously, all sex is rape. But the bedrock of Dworkin's feminism was, to the contrary, a repudiation of the essentialist, biological determinist logic that undergirds fascism and genocide. She believed that men, women, and sex could be different than they are now.

That her lifelong, most fundamental position was consistently construed as its opposite was no doubt demoralizing. And yet Dworkin did not cater to the Sternhells of the world, trying to get them to understand. The formal daring and dirge-like excavations of *Intercourse* rendered it incomprehensible to those indifferent or hostile to her project—and though that bothered Dworkin, it wasn't enough to change the way she wrote.

Fucking is subject to radical skepticism in her book. She explores its meaning as an act and an institution by inhabiting male writers' perspectives and portrayals of it, in works by Leo Tolstoy,

Kobo Abe, James Baldwin, Tennessee Williams, Isaac Bashevis Singer, and Gustave Flaubert. (Ironically, critics, in egregious misunderstandings of the text and Dworkin's strategy, frequently took Tolstoy's pessimistic view of sex as hers.) Reading *Intercourse* now, I find it lucid and almost uncontroversial in its denaturalization of the act; Dworkin's exposure of intercourse as the linchpin of heterosexuality, as its emblem and climax, rings true. Intercourse is socially and legally regulated to create and enforce sex difference and male supremacy—who can deny it? Many contemporary readers will have already wandered to this place, or somewhere nearby, through Foucault or Butler.

As Dworkin points out in her introduction to the 1995 edition, which we have included, skepticism, with regard to something as precious as intercourse, is not allowed—not from a woman author and certainly not from a harridan like her. We've also included a particularly skeptical chapter, "Occupation/Collaboration," that moves dangerously back and forth between the metaphysics of fucking and women's physical experience of it, provoking readers with an intentional blurring of worlds. "How to separate the act of intercourse from the social reality of male power is not clear, especially because it is male power that constructs both the meaning and the current practice of intercourse as such," she writes. "But it is clear that reforms do not change women's status relative to men, or have not yet. It is clear that reforms do not change the intractability of women's civil inferiority," she adds grimly. "Is intercourse itself then a basis of or a key to women's continuing social and sexual inequality?"

That question, which throws the viability of intercourse into doubt should equality ever be realized (fat chance), and which demonstrates Dworkin's unencouraging agnosticism on the issue, somehow raises the stakes unbearably high for many readers. She doesn't threaten (emptily) to take fucking away, but she does issue a serious challenge: "If intercourse can be an expression of sexual equality, it will have to survive—on its own merits as it were, having a potential for human expression not yet recognized or realized—the destruction of male power over women. . ."

Again, Dworkin's notoriety foreclosed any possibility that her work would be recognized or contended with *as art*. Stoltenberg— an antipornography and antirape writer in his own right, focusing on the socialization of men—describes, in a 1994 article about their life together, finding safety under siege. "Over time, 'home' has been seven different places, including an apartment in Northampton, Massachusetts, where we scraped by on food stamps; a mold-growing bunker on a buggy island in the Florida Keys; and a rat-ridden, fumy walk-up on Manhattan's Lower East Side," he recalls. "We are now fortunate to own our own house, a Victorian brownstone in Brooklyn, filled with warm colors and woodwork and walls full of books. We feel almost blissfully happy here—partly because this is our snug harbor against the storm. . ." Dworkin was an object of derision for writers like Sternhell, ostensibly a feminist, while also facing death threats and more dangerous ridicule, such as a series of antifeminist, anti-lesbian, anti-Semitic caricatures in *Hustler*. She sued for libel, and the court ruled against her in 1989. Speaking to the difficulties of those years, Stoltenberg writes, "Andrea's and Larry Flynt's lawyers deposed me, and I found I could not get through the interview without breaking down in sobs."[26]

Dworkin wrote novels because she wanted to; she wrote them for a tiny readership, for a future audience, or to cast them into the void. Certainly, their reception was disappointing for an author who still harbored an aching literary ambition. We have included a short section from *Ice & Fire*, an excerpt that could be read as a fictionalized snapshot of her life, post-jail, post-Crete and pre-Amsterdam. She takes drugs and turns tricks with her best friend, as they try to be artists together in New York. "We are going to make a movie, a tough, unsentimental avant-garde little number about women in a New York City prison," Dworkin writes, laughing a little at her young self, "I have written it. It strangely resembles my own story: jailed over Vietnam the woman is endlessly strip-searched and then mangled inside by jail doctors." The novel is tragic, but this part isn't. At the Woolworth's photo booth they "pose and look intense and avant-garde," she writes, "We mess up our hair and sulk, or we try grinning, we stare into the hidden camera. . ."

Mercy (1990) is more explicitly autofictional, a pointed mirroring of Dworkin's own life events, though one that spins off into the kind of unhinged hallucination her nonfiction was often accused of. Never cited as a work on a par with *Pornography* or *Intercourse*, the unsung magnum opus is a revelatory foil to those works, just as formally complex, but uninhibited by the demands of traditional argumentation. "My narrator, who is a character in my book, knows less than I do," Dworkin reflects, writing of her final novel. "She is inside the story. Deciding what she will see, what she can know, I am detached from her and cold in how I use her."[27] It's a telling observation, as the opposite might be assumed—that *Mercy*'s unpunctuated stream-of-consciousness or diaristic style constitutes a loosening of her rhetorical grip.

In the first-person novel, Dworkin chronicles—or grieves—the life of Andrea, who writes of her name, many times throughout the book, with anger or disbelief, that "it means manhood or courage." Of her childhood home, she notes, also in a mournful refrain, that it was just down the street from Walt Whitman's house in Camden.

The historic site's proximity fuels dreams of *Leaves-of-Grass* greatness; and for the anti-imperialist teen poet she becomes, Whitman is a symbol of an alternate, mythic nation. "I'm from his country, the country he wrote about in his poems, the country of freedom, the country of ecstasy, the country of joy of the body," she insists, "not the Amerika run by war criminals."

Mercy is indisputably a tale of horrific sexual violence, beginning with Andrea's molestation at the movies, and never pausing for long in its depictions of abuse. But contrary to Dworkin's reputation—to the image of her as a prudish, perennial victim—she also offers a passionate account of the adventures of a sexual rebel. In her fiction, depictions of sex, good and bad, with men and women, begin to answer the questions that she raised throughout her career about the possibilities of pleasure under patriarchy, to represent her vision of a liberated sexuality—not through the example of a superhuman revolutionary who practices a squeaky-clean reciprocity, but through the trial-and-error journey of an imperfect protagonist.

At age twenty, living in New York, she sees a woman she desperately wants. "The room's empty but she sits at the table next to me, black leather pants, black hair, painted black, like I always wanted." They're at a Kosher restaurant downtown. "I can't go with her now because she has an underlying bad motive, she wants to eat," she wryly observes, "and what I feel for her is complete sex." Encounters with women provide fleeting reprieve from male violence; they're trapdoors to Whitman's ecstatic country. "Your life's telling you that if you're between her legs, you're free—free's not peaceful and not always kind, it's fast," she writes. "There's not many women around who have any freedom in them let alone some to spare, extravagant, on you, and it's when they're on you you see it best and know it's real."

Mercy also tells of a marriage in Amsterdam, much like Dworkin's it would seem, offering a level of detail not present in her nonfiction. The relationship begins as a profound romance between radicals, the couple's shared drive to sow antiauthoritarian chaos fueling a gender-transcending sexual bond. Dworkin describes it as "a carnal expression of brotherhood in the revolutionary sense, a long, fraternal embrace for hours or days, in hiding." Sex affirms their freedom and sustains their underground life of righteous crime. "I liked fucking after a strike, a proper climax to the real act—I liked how everything got fast and urgent; fast, hard, life or death; I liked bed then, after, when we was drenched in perspiration from what came before; I liked revolution as foreplay; I liked how it made your supersensitive so the hairs on your skin were standing up and hurt before anything touched you." Pleasure and pain are entangled, sensitively, in her accounts of their relationship before it turns. "I liked to be on top and I moved real slow," she writes, "using every muscle in me, so I could feel him hurting—you know that melancholy ache inside that deepens into a frisson of pain?" But Andrea is not always on top, and doesn't mind ("there wasn't nothing he did to me that I didn't do to him"), until, somehow, she finds herself always on the bottom—tied to the bed, and then, beaten almost to death.

How do we reconcile this Andrea—desirous, self-critical, principled, the author's obvious self-portrait—with the antisex villain invoked in third-wave defenses of sexual empowerment? And how can we understand this Andrea next to the ruined monster of *Mercy*'s end? Her blood runs green, she has nothing left to lose, and at last she summons the courage and manhood suggested by her name to visit arbitrary nighttime vigilante injustice on the city's most unlucky men.

This time, the *Times* review makes the stunning claim, regarding *Mercy*, that "Ms. Dworkin advocates nothing short of killing men."[28] However outlandish its author Wendy Steiner's interpretation may be, it's perhaps an accurate measure of the public perception of Dworkin's politics. And she insightfully credits her with a "new representational strategy," "risking the prurience of the pornography she deplores," written in a style combining "the repetition of the early Gertrude Stein and, ironically, the unfettered flights of Henry Miller." But in a misreading that echoes so many reactions to Dworkin, she takes the novel's shocking collapse of the metaphorical and the literal, of fantasy and confession, as a sign that its plot is actually a plan. In fact, Dworkin's real plan—always—was simply, unironically, to be as unfettered as Miller was, to beat him at his own game:

> My only chance to be believed is to find a way of writing bolder and stronger than woman hating itself—smarter, deeper, colder. This might mean that I would have to write a prose more terrifying than rape, more abject than torture, more insistent and destabilizing than battery, more desolate than prostitution, more invasive than incest, more filled with threat and aggression than pornography. How would the innocent bystander be able to distinguish it, tell it apart from the tales of rapists themselves if it were so nightmarish and impolite? There are no innocent bystanders.[29]

More than murder, suicide figures in the final stretch of the novel. It is an escape and a protest, a desperate last measure to bestow meaning on a female life. Dworkin retells an ancient legend—the story of nearly a thousand Jews, living in exile in a fortress on the rock of Masada. Under Roman siege, with their extermination or enslavement inevitable, the men decide to kill themselves—everyone—rather than submit. Andrea recalls a past life as an old woman on that rock, who overhears the men and slits her own throat before the massacre begins. Dworkin also depicts Andrea's self-immolation. Like Norman Morrison at the Pentagon decades ago, she burns outside a porn theater in Times Square. "I go to outside *Deep Throat* where my friend Linda is in the screen," she writes, "and I put the gasoline on me. I soak myself in it in broad daylight and many go by and no one looks and I am calm, patient, gray on gray like the Buddhist monks, and I light the fire; free us."

"Revolutionary suicide does not mean that I and my comrades have a death wish; it means just the opposite," wrote Huey Newton, one of Dworkin's militant heroes, speaking of the Black Panther movement in 1973. "We have such a strong desire to live with hope and human dignity that existence without them is impossible." Radical struggle shortens one's life, he writes. "Other so-called revolutionaries cling to an illusion they might have their revolution and die of old age. That cannot be. . ."[30]

Last Days at Hot Slit concludes with an excerpt from the previously unpublished work *My Suicide* (1999),[31] found on Dworkin's hard drive by Stoltenberg after her death in 2005, at age fifty-eight. After years of chronic illness and pain, she died in her sleep; the cause was inflammation of the heart. In its entirety, the piece is a 24,000-word autobiographical essay, dedicated to "J.S." (Stoltenberg) and "E.M." (Elaine Markson, her longtime literary agent and dear friend). Stoltenberg writes of discovering the text, "it was finished; as if for publication. And I understood why she did not show it to me or Elaine. She had to have known it would devastate us. Because she had written it in the form of a suicide note."[32]

It is an account of her drugging and rape in a Paris hotel, where she had gone alone to celebrate the completion of her epic work *Scapegoat*, a book on the Holocaust, which would be published the next year. She tells of reading in a garden, a second cocktail that doesn't taste right, and blacking out in her room. She wakes to find herself bleeding, she finds a bruise, and feels a kind of internal pain that only rape can explain. *My Suicide* is an interrogation of memory and trauma, a searching recitation of the same events again and again, which takes the spiraling form we now recognize from the experimental structures of *Mercy* and *Intercourse*—as well as from her entire body of work, with its vivid, long-running leitmotifs. The drug rape is one more prism through which her life's narrative is refracted, and it's one more aspect of sexual violence she comes to know intimately. "I want to live but I don't know how," she writes, "I can't bear knowing what I know." Her hallmark refrain is delivered in a new register of defeat.

A cruel footnote—which surely felt more like a headline then—is that she was disbelieved during this time of emotional crisis, a period that also marked a sharp decline in her physical health. When she wrote an article for the British magazine *The New Statesman*,[33] chronicling the events and aftermath of her Paris trip, the strange, unverifiable story was met with the raised eyebrows of even sympathetic feminist friends. Stoltenberg, who appears in *My Suicide* as Paul, understandably wished for another explanation, which is the kindest breed of doubt. And then there were the true attacks—her story publicly picked apart to discredit her once and for all, as evidence of a false politics, an entire career rooted in histrionics and paranoid fantasy.

———

Amy and I did not, of course, expect to finish this book under Trump; I didn't expect to write this introduction while witnessing the ascendance of full-throated white supremacist populism, or the consolidation of power under an authoritarian regime in my country—but Dworkin has been my companion through this time. It's hard to argue that she offers comfort, but I will say that just as it was her curse to see the seed of genocide in everything—the calamity waiting in every expression and symbol of inequality, however small or private—it was her gift to see in everything an opportunity to resist.

To read Dworkin at eighteen was to see patriarchy with the skin peeled back. Her work was a bloody revelation that demanded a blood oath in repayment, and who was I at that age—angry, a writer, a punk girl at the dawn of riot grrrl—to deny her? She modeled rage as authority; her imperious voice and dirty mouth represented a feminist literature empty of caveats, equivocation, or the endless positing of one's subjective limits. To me this was a new kind of greatness—I guess it still is. So though I subsequently had a whole career of disagreeing, for the last five years, I've been intermittently immersed in Dworkin, reading everything by and about her—considering her as a person, a symbol, a flashpoint, and an artist—and have become a different kind of loyalist.

There are many ways to be erased. One can be obliterated by caricature—the image of fat, fuck-you Andrea Dworkin in a *Hustler* cartoon or raving in feminism's most uncool margin is one way to pave over her ideas. Then there is the self-perpetuating misrepresentation, the groove made deeper with every unexamined repetition of a rumor; and a sneakier phenomenon—the feminine/feminist race to perfection which renders our movement's dialectics shameful, our human arrogance, floundering, and failures unaccounted for in an honest intellectual history. There's always the blithe forgetfulness of a world where women's writing means less, is worth less, and is swiftly out of print, too. And the irrelevance accidentally initiated by the sycophant: If Dworkin is reduced to source material for a strange dogma, one that extrapolates her singular radical feminism into the present, if her writings exist only as tracts, that's one more kind of death.

Greatness is not synonymous with perfection or popularity. In the long-arc narratives of male genius that reach far beyond a lifetime, greatness is established despite, and in the glaring light of, great flaws. Great men are by definition to be reckoned with and honored for the dilemmas they force us to confront, while the ways to castigate a woman of brilliance and ambition are second-nature and sometimes fatal, whether she's deemed evil or merely, as they say, problematic. My point is, right or wrong—right *and* wrong—Dworkin's oracular voice helped to shape the historic grassroots feminist organizing of the late '70s and '80s; she rallied the forces of the antipornography, antirape and battered women's movements, and she left behind a complex, experimental body of work that will make your blood run cold.

Last Days
at Hot
Slit

April 3, 1973

dear Mom and Dad, received the $30 today, thank you, it
always seems to be saving me from the abyss.   Gringo
is fine, Im ok, let myself get too tired, working too many
hours, so havent been feeling so well these last days. but
sleep will cure that.   I finished revising the chapters that
are finished. the book will be called LAST DAYS AT HOT
SLIT.   I just settled on that title, and you seemed to want
very much to know it. Muriel just read it, just called me to
say she thinks its one of the most important book of our
times--wow!   I must say, Im in a constant state of excitment
about it,   I wonder if Ill forget about it, or if Ill get more
excited every day for a year until it comes out. anyway, the
problem now is to finish it.   be well and love to everyone.

      Andrea

WOMAN HATING

1974

This book is an action, a political action where revolution is the goal. It has no other purpose. It is not cerebral wisdom, or academic horseshit, or ideas carved in granite or destined for immortality. It is part of a process and its context is change. It is part of a planetary movement to restructure community forms and human consciousness so that people have power over their own lives, participate fully in community, live in dignity and freedom.

The commitment to ending male dominance as the fundamental psychological, political, and cultural reality of earth-lived life is the fundamental revolutionary commitment. It is a commitment to transformation of the self and transformation of the social reality on every level. The core of this book is an analysis of sexism (that system of male dominance), what it is, how it operates on us and in us. However, I do want to discuss briefly two problems, tangential to that analysis, but still crucial to the development of revolutionary program and consciousness. The first is the nature of the women's movement as such, and the second has to do with the work of the writer.

Until the appearance of the brilliant anthology *Sisterhood Is Powerful* and Kate Millett's extraordinary book *Sexual Politics*, women did not think of themselves as oppressed people. Most women, it must be admitted, still do not. But the women's movement as a radical liberation movement in Amerika can be dated from the appearance of those two books. We learn as we reclaim our herstory that there was a feminist movement which organized around the attainment of the vote for women. We learn that those feminists were also ardent abolitionists. Women "came out" as abolitionists—out of the closets, kitchens, and bedrooms; into public meetings, newspapers, and the streets. Two activist heroes of the abolitionist movement were Black women, Sojourner Truth and Harriet Tubman, and they stand as prototypal revolutionary models.

Those early Amerikan feminists thought that suffrage was the key to participation in Amerikan democracy and that, free and enfranchised, the former slaves would in fact be free and enfranchised. Those women did not imagine that the vote would be effectively denied Blacks through literacy tests, property qualifications, and vigilante police action by white racists. Nor did they imagine the "separate but equal" doctrine and the uses to which it would be put.

Feminism and the struggle for Black liberation were parts of a compelling whole. That whole was called, ingenuously perhaps, the struggle for human rights. The fact is that consciousness, once experienced, cannot be denied. Once women experienced themselves as *activists* and began to understand the reality and meaning of oppression, they began to articulate a politically conscious feminism. Their focus, their concrete objective, was to attain suffrage for women.

The women's movement formalized itself in 1848 at Seneca Falls when Elizabeth Cady Stanton and Lucretia Mott, both activist abolitionists, called a convention. That convention drafted *The Seneca Falls Declaration of Rights and Sentiments* which is to this day an outstanding feminist declaration.

In struggling for the vote, women developed many of the tactics which were used, almost a century later, in the Civil Rights Movement. In order to change laws, women had to violate them. In order to change convention, women had to violate it. The feminists (suffragettes) were militant political activists who used the tactics of civil disobedience to achieve their goals.

The struggle for the vote began officially with the Seneca Falls Convention in 1848. It was not until August 26, 1920, that women were *given* the vote by the kindly male electorate. Women did not imagine that the vote would scarcely touch on, let alone transform, their own oppressive situations. Nor did they imagine that the "separate but equal" doctrine would develop as a tool of male dominance. Nor did they imagine the uses to which it would be put.

There have also been, always, individual feminists—women who violated the strictures of the female role, who challenged male supremacy, who fought for the right to work, or sexual freedom, or release from the bondage of the marriage contract. Those individuals were often eloquent when they spoke of the oppression they suffered as women in their own lives, but other women, properly trained to their roles, did not listen. Feminists, most often as individuals but sometimes in small militant groups, fought the system which oppressed them, analyzed it, were jailed, were ostracized, but there was no general recognition among women that they were oppressed.

In the last 5 or 6 years, that recognition has become more widespread among women. We have begun to understand the extraordinary violence that has been done to us, that is being done to us: how our minds are aborted in their development by sexist education; how our bodies are violated by oppressive grooming imperatives; how the police function against us in cases of rape and assault; how the media, schools, and churches conspire to deny us dignity and freedom; how the nuclear family and ritualized sexual behavior imprison us in roles and forms which are degrading to us. We developed consciousness-raising sessions to try to fathom the extraordinary extent of our despair, to try to search out the depth and boundaries of our internalized anger, to try to find strategies for freeing ourselves from oppressive relationships, from masochism and passivity, from our own lack of self-respect. There was both pain and ecstasy in this process. Women discovered each other, for truly no oppressed group had ever been so divided and conquered. Women began to deal with concrete oppressions: to become part of the economic process, to erase discriminatory laws, to gain control over our own lives and over our own bodies, to develop the concrete ability to survive on our own terms. Women also began to articulate structural analyses of sexist society—Millett did that with *Sexual Politics*; in *Vaginal Politics* Ellen Frankfort demonstrated the complex and deadly antiwoman biases of the medical establishment; in *Women and Madness* Dr. Phyllis Chesler showed that mental institutions are prisons for women who rebel against society's well-defined female role.

We began to see ourselves clearly, and what we saw was dreadful. We saw that we were, as Yoko Ono wrote, the niggers of the world, slaves to the slave. We saw that we were the ultimate house niggers, ass-licking, bowing, scraping, shuffling fools. We recognized all of our social behavior as learned behavior that functioned for survival in a sexist world: we painted ourselves, smiled, exposed legs and ass, had children, kept house, as our accommodations to the reality of power politics.

Most of the women involved in articulating the oppression of women were white and middle class. We spent, even if we did not earn or control, enormous sums of money. Because of our participation in the middle-class lifestyle we were the oppressors of other people, our poor white sisters, our Black sisters, our Chicana sisters— and the men who in turn oppressed them. This closely interwoven fabric of oppression, which is the racist class structure of Amerika today, assured that wherever one stood, it was with at least one foot heavy on the belly of another human being.

As white, middle-class women, we lived in the house of the oppressor-of-us-all who supported us as he abused us, dressed us as he exploited us, "treasured" us in payment for the many functions we performed. We were the best-fed, best-kept, best-dressed, most willing concubines the world has ever known. We had no dignity and no real freedom, but we did have good health and long lives.

The women's movement has not dealt with this bread-and-butter issue, and that is its most awful failure. There has been little recognition that the *destruction* of the middle-class lifestyle is crucial to the development of decent community forms in which all people can be free and have dignity. There is certainly no program to deal with the realities of the class system in Amerika. On the contrary, most of the women's movement has, with appalling blindness, refused to take that kind of responsibility. Only the day-care movement has in any way reflected, or acted pragmatically on, the concrete needs of all classes of women. The anger at the Nixon administration for cutting day-care funds is naive at best. Given the structure of power politics and capital in Amerika, it is ridiculous to expect the federal government to act in the interests of the people. The money available to middle-class women who identify as feminists must be channeled into the programs we want to develop, and *we* must develop them. In general, middle-class women have absolutely refused to take any action, make any commitment which would interfere with, threaten, or significantly alter a lifestyle, a living standard, which is moneyed and privileged.

The analysis of sexism in this book articulates clearly what the oppression of women is, how it functions, how it is rooted in psyche and culture. But that analysis is useless unless it is tied to a political consciousness and commitment which will totally redefine community. One cannot be free, never, not ever, in an unfree world, and in the course of redefining family, church, power relations, all the institutions which inhabit and order our lives, there is no way to hold onto privilege and comfort. To attempt to do so is destructive, criminal, and intolerable.

The nature of women's oppression is unique: women are oppressed as women, regardless of class or race; some women have access to significant wealth, but that wealth does not signify power; women are to be found everywhere, but own or control no appreciable territory; women live with those who oppress them, sleep with them, have their children—we are tangled, hopelessly it seems, in the gut of the machinery and way of life which is ruinous to us. And perhaps most importantly, most women have little sense of dignity or self-respect or strength, since those qualities are directly related to a sense of manhood. In *Revolutionary Suicide*, Huey P. Newton tells us that the Black Panthers did not use guns because they were symbols of manhood, but found the courage to act as they did because they were men. When we women find the courage to defend our selves, to take a stand against brutality and abuse, we are violating every notion of womanhood we have ever been taught. The way to freedom for women is bound to be torturous for that reason alone.

The analysis in this book applies to the life situations of all women, but all women are not necessarily in a state of primary emergency as women. What I mean by this is simple. As a Jew in Nazi Germany, I would be oppressed as a woman, but hunted, slaughtered, as a Jew. As a Native American, I would be oppressed as a squaw, but hunted, slaughtered, as a Native American. That first identity, the one which brings with it as part of its definition death, is the identity of primary emergency. This is an important recognition because it relieves us of a serious confusion. The fact, for instance, that many Black women (by no means all) experience primary emergency as Blacks in no way lessens the responsibility of the Black community to assimilate this and other analyses of sexism and to apply it in their own revolutionary work.

As a writer with a revolutionary commitment, I am particularly pained by the kinds of books writers are writing, and the reasons why. I want writers to write books because they are committed to the content of those books. I want writers to write books as actions. I want writers to write books that can make a difference in how, and even why, people live. I want writers to write books that are worth being jailed for, worth fighting for, and should it come to that in this country, worth dying for.

Books are for the most part in Amerika commercial ventures. People write them to make money, to become famous, to build or augment other careers. Most Amerikans do not read books—they prefer television. Academics lock books in a tangled web of mindfuck and abstraction. The notion is that there are ideas, then art, then somewhere else, unrelated, life. The notion is that to have a decent or moral idea is to be a decent or moral person. Because of this strange schizophrenia, books and the writing of them have become embroidery on a dying way of life. Because there is contempt for the process of writing, for writing as a way of discovering meaning and truth, and for reading as a piece of that same process, we destroy with regularity the few serious writers we have. We turn them into comic-book figures, bleed them of all privacy and courage and common sense, exorcise their vision from them as sport, demand that they entertain or be ignored into oblivion. And it is a great tragedy, for the work of the writer has never been more important than it is now in Amerika.

Many see that in this nightmared land, language has no meaning and the work of the writer is ruined. Many see that the triumph of authoritarian consciousness is its ability to render the spoken and written word meaningless—so that we cannot talk or hear each other speak. It is the work of the writer to reclaim the language from those who use it to justify murder, plunder, violation. The writer can and must do the revolutionary work of using words to communicate, as community.

Those of us who love reading and writing believe that being a writer is a sacred trust. It means telling the truth. It means being incorruptible. It means not being afraid, and never lying. Those of us who love reading and writing feel great pain because so many people who write books have become cowards, clowns, and liars. Those of us who love reading and writing begin to feel a deadly contempt for books, because we see writers being bought and sold in the market place—we see them vending their tarnished wares on every street corner. Too many writers, in keeping with the Amerikan way of life, would sell their mothers for a dime.

To keep the sacred trust of the writer is simply to respect the people and to love the community. To violate that trust is to abuse oneself and do damage to others. I believe that the writer has a vital function in the community, and an absolute responsibility to the people. I ask that this book be judged in that context.

Specifically *Woman Hating* is about women and men, the roles they play, the violence between them. We begin with fairy tales, the first scenarios of women and men which mold our psyches, taught to us before we can know differently. We go on to pornography, where we find the same scenarios, explicitly sexual and now more recognizable, ourselves, carnal women and heroic men. We go on to herstory—the binding of feet in China, the burning of witches in

Europe and Amerika. There we see the fairy-tale and pornographic definitions of women functioning in reality, the real annihilation of real women—the crushing into nothingness of their freedom, their will, their lives—how they were forced to live, and how they were forced to die. We see the dimensions of the crime, the dimensions of the oppression, the anguish and misery that are a direct consequence of polar role definition, of women defined as carnal, evil, and Other. We recognize that it is the structure of the culture which engineers the deaths, violations, violence, and we look for alternatives, ways of destroying culture as we know it, rebuilding it as we can imagine it.

I write however with a broken tool, a language which is sexist and discriminatory to its core. I try to make the distinctions, not "history" as the whole human story, not "man" as the generic term for the species, not "manhood" as the synonym for courage, dignity, and strength. But I have not been successful in reinventing the language.

Women should be beautiful. All repositories of cultural wisdom from King Solomon to King Hefner agree: women should be beautiful. It is the reverence for female beauty which informs the romantic ethos, gives it its energy and justification. Beauty is transformed into that golden ideal, Beauty—rapturous and abstract. Women must be beautiful and Woman is Beauty.

Notions of beauty always incorporate the whole of a given societal structure, are crystallizations of its values. A society with a well-defined aristocracy will have aristocratic standards of beauty. In Western "democracy" notions of beauty are "democratic": even if a woman is not born beautiful, she can make herself *attractive.*

The argument is not simply that some women are not beautiful, therefore it is not fair to judge women on the basis of physical beauty; or that men are not judged on that basis, therefore women also should not be judged on that basis; or that men should look for character in women; or that our standards of beauty are too parochial in and of themselves; or even that judging women according to their conformity to a standard of beauty serves to make them into products, chattels, differing from the farmer's favorite cow only in terms of literal form. The issue at stake is different, and crucial. Standards of beauty describe in precise terms the relationship that an individual will have to her own body. They prescribe her mobility, spontaneity, posture, gait, the uses to which she can put her body. *They define precisely the dimensions of her physical freedom.* And, of course, the relationship between physical freedom and psychological development, intellectual possibility, and creative potential is an umbilical one.

In our culture, not one part of a woman's body is left untouched, unaltered. No feature or extremity is spared the art, or pain, of improvement. Hair is dyed, lacquered, straightened, permanented; eyebrows are plucked, penciled, dyed; eyes are lined, mascaraed, shadowed; lashes are curled, or false—from head to toe, every feature of a woman's face, every section of her body, is subject to modification, alteration. This alteration is an ongoing, repetitive process. It is vital to the economy, the major substance of male-female role differentiation, the most immediate physical and psychological reality of being a woman. From the age of 11 or 12 until she dies, a woman will spend a large part of her time, money, and energy on binding, plucking, painting, and deodorizing herself. It is commonly and wrongly said that male transvestites through the use of makeup and costuming caricature the women they would become, but any real knowledge of the romantic ethos makes clear that these men have penetrated to the core experience of being a woman, a romanticized construct.

The technology of beauty, and the message it carries, is handed down from mother to daughter. Mother teaches daughter to apply lipstick, to shave under her arms, to bind her breasts, to wear a girdle and highheeled shoes. Mother teaches daughter concomitantly her role, her appropriate behavior, her place. Mother teaches daughter, necessarily, the psychology which defines womanhood: a woman must be beautiful, in order to please the amorphous and amorous Him. What we have called the romantic ethos operates as vividly in 20th-century Amerika and Europe as it did in 10th-century China.

This cultural transfer of technology, role, and psychology virtually affects the emotive relationship between mother and daughter. It contributes substantially to the ambivalent love-hate dynamic of that relationship. What must the Chinese daughter/child have felt toward the mother who bound her feet? What does any daughter/child feel toward the mother who forces her to do painful things to her own body? The mother takes on the role of enforcer: she uses seduction, command, all manner of force to coerce the daughter to conform to the demands of the culture. It is because this role becomes her dominant role in the mother-daughter relationship that tensions and difficulties between mothers and daughters are so often unresolvable. The daughter who rejects the cultural norms enforced by the mother is forced to a basic rejection of her own mother, a recognition of the hatred and resentment she felt toward that mother, an alienation from mother and society so extreme that her own womanhood is denied by both. The daughter who internalizes those values and endorses those same processes is bound to repeat the teaching she was taught—her anger and resentment remain subterranean, channeled against her own female offspring as well as her mother.

Pain is an essential part of the grooming process, and that is not accidental. Plucking the eyebrows, shaving under the arms, wearing a girdle, learning to walk in high-heeled shoes, having one's nose fixed, straightening or curling one's hair—these things *hurt*. The pain, of course, teaches an important lesson: no price is too great, no process too repulsive, no operation too painful for the woman who would be beautiful. *The tolerance of pain and the romanticization of that tolerance begins here*, in preadolescence, in socialization, and serves to prepare women for lives of childbearing, self-abnegation, and husband-pleasing. The adolescent experience of the "pain of being a woman" casts the feminine psyche into a masochistic mold and forces the adolescent to conform to a self-image which bases itself on mutilation of the body, pain happily suffered, and restricted physical mobility. It creates the masochistic personalities generally found in adult women: subservient, materialistic (since all value is placed on the body and its ornamentation), intellectually restricted, creatively impoverished. It forces women to be a sex of lesser accomplishment, weaker, as underdeveloped as any backward nation. Indeed, the effects of that prescribed relationship between women and their bodies are so extreme, so deep, so extensive, that scarcely any area of human possibility is left untouched by it.

Men, of course, like a woman who "takes care of herself." The male response to the woman who is made-up and bound is a learned fetish, societal in its dimensions. One need only refer to the male idealization of the bound foot and say that the same dynamic is operating here. Romance based on role differentiation, superiority based on a culturally determined and rigidly enforced inferiority, shame and guilt and fear of women and sex itself: all necessitate the perpetuation of these oppressive grooming imperatives.

The meaning of this analysis of the romantic ethos surely is clear. A first step in the process of liberation (women from their oppression, men from the unfreedom of their fetishism) is the radical redefining of the relationship between women and their bodies. The body must be freed, liberated, quite literally: from paint and girdles and all varieties of crap. Women must stop mutilating their bodies and start living in them. Perhaps the notion of beauty which will then organically emerge will be truly democratic and demonstrate a respect for human life in its infinite, and most honorable, variety.

ANDROGYNY

We want to destroy sexism, that is, polar role definitions of male and female, man and woman. We want to destroy patriarchal power at its source, the family; in its most hideous form, the nation-state. We want to destroy the structure of culture as we know it, its art, its churches, its laws: all of the images, institutions, and structural mental sets which define women as hot wet fuck tubes, hot slits.

Androgynous mythology provides us with a model which does not use polar role definitions, where the definitions are not, implicitly or explicitly, male = good, female = bad, man = human, woman = other. Androgyny myths are multisexual mythological models. They go well beyond bisexuality as we know it in the scenarios they suggest for building community, for realizing the fullest expression of human sexual possibility and creativity.

Androgyny as a concept has no notion of sexual repression built into it. Where woman is carnality, and carnality is evil, it stands to reason (hail reason!) that woman must be chained, whipped, punished, purged; that fucking is shameful, forbidden, fearful, guilt- ridden. Androgyny as the basis of sexual identity and community life provides no such imperatives. Sexual freedom and freedom for biological women, or all persons "female," are not separable. That they are different, and that sexual freedom has priority, is the worst of sexist hypes. Androgyny can show the way to both. It may be the one road to freedom open to women, men, and that emerging majority, the rest of us.

The *Story of O*, by Pauline Reage, incorporates, along with all literary pornography, principles and characters already isolated in my discussion of children's fairy tales. The female as a figure of innocence and evil enters the adult world—the brutal world of genitalia. The female manifests in her adult form—cunt. She emerges defined by the hole between her legs. In addition, *Story of O* is more than simple pornography. It claims to define epistemologically what a woman is, what she needs, her processes of thinking and feeling, her proper place. It links men and women in an erotic dance of some magnitude: the sado-masochistic complexion of O is not trivial—it is formulated as a cosmic principle which articulates, absolutely, the feminine.

Also, O is particularly compelling for me because I once believed it to be what its defenders claim—the mystical revelation of the true, eternal, and sacral destiny of women. The book was absorbed as a pulsating, erotic, secular Christianity (the joy in pure suffering, woman as Christ figure). I experienced O with the same infantile abandon as the *Newsweek* reviewer who wrote: "What lifts this fascinating book above mere perversity is its movement toward the transcendence of the self through a gift of the self . . . to give the body, to allow it to be ravaged, exploited, and totally possessed can be an act of consequence, if it is done with love for the sake of love."[1] Any clear-headed appraisal of O will show the situation, O's condition, her behavior, and most importantly her attitude toward her oppressor as a logical scenario incorporating Judeo-Christian values of service and self-sacrifice and universal notions of woman-hood, a logical scenario demonstrating the psychology of submission and self-hatred found in all oppressed peoples. *O* is a book of astounding political significance.

This is, then, the story of O: O is taken by her lover Rene to Roissy and cloistered there; she is fucked, sucked, raped, whipped, humiliated, and tortured on a regular and continuing basis—she is programmed to be an erotic slave, Rene's personal whore; after being properly trained she is sent home with her lover; her lover gives her to Sir Stephen, his half-brother; she is fucked, sucked, raped, whipped, humiliated, and tortured on a regular and continuing basis; she is ordered to become the lover of Jacqueline and to recruit her for Roissy, which she does; she is sent to Anne-Marie to be branded with Sir Stephen's mark and to have rings with his insignia inserted in her cunt; she serves as an erotic model for Jacqueline's younger sister Natalie who is infatuated with her; she is taken to a party masked as an owl, led on a leash by Natalie, and there plundered, despoiled, raped, gangbanged; realizing that there is nothing else left for Sir Stephen to do with her or to her, fearing that he will abandon her, she asks his permission to kill herself and receives it. Q. E. D., pornography is never big on plot.

Of course, like most summaries, the above is somewhat sketchy. I have not mentioned the quantities of cock that O sucks, or the anal assaults that she sustains, or the various rapes and tortures perpetrated on her by minor characters in the book, or the varieties of whips used, or described her clothing or the different kinds of nipple rouge, or the many ways in which she is chained, or the shapes and colors of the welts on her body.

From the course of O's story emerges a clear mythological figure: she is woman, and to name her O, zero, emptiness, says it all. Her ideal state is one of complete passivity, nothingness, a submission so absolute that she transcends human form (in becoming an owl). Only the hole between her legs is left to define her, and the symbol of that hole must surely be O. Much, however, even in the rarefied environs of pornography, necessarily interferes with the attainment of utter passivity. Given a body which takes up space, has needs, makes demands, is connected, even symbolically, to a personal history which is a sequence of likes, dislikes, skills, opinions, one is formed, shaped—one exists at the very least as positive space. And since in addition as a woman one is born guilty and carnal, personifying the sins of Eve and Pandora, the wickedness of Jezebel and Lucretia Borgia, O's transcendence of the species is truly phenomenal.

The thesis of O is simple. Woman is cunt, lustful, wanton. She must be punished, tamed, debased. She gives the gift of herself, her body, her well-being, her life, to her lover. This is as it should be—natural and good. It ends necessarily in her annihilation, which is also natural and good, as well as beautiful, because she fulfills her destiny:

> As long as I am beaten and ravished on your behalf, I am naught but the thought of you, the desire of you, the obsession of you. That, I believe, is what you wanted. Well, I love you, and that is what I want too.[2]

> Then let him take her, if only to wound her! O hated herself for her own desire, and loathed Sir Stephen for the self-control he was displaying. She wanted him to love her, there, the truth was out: she wanted him to be chafing under the urge to touch her lips and penetrate her body, to devastate her if need be. . . .[3]

. . . Yet he was certain that she was guilty and, without really wanting to, Rene was punishing her for a sin he knew nothing about (since it remained completely internal), although Sir Stephen had immediately detected it: her wantonness.[4]

. . . no pleasure, no joy, no figment of her imagination could ever compete with the happiness she felt at the way he used her with such utter freedom, at the notion that he could do anything with her, that there was no limit, no restriction in the manner with which, on her body, he might search for pleasure.[5]

O is totally possessed. That means that she is an object, with no control over her own mobility, capable of no assertion of personality. Her body is *a* body, in the same way that a pencil is a pencil, a bucket is a bucket, or, as Gertrude Stein pointedly said, a rose is a rose. It also means that O's energy, or power, as a woman, as Woman, is absorbed. Possession here denotes a biological transference of power which brings with it a commensurate spiritual strength to the possessor. O does more than offer herself; she is herself the offering. To offer herself would be prosaic Christian self-sacrifice, but as the offering she is the vehicle of the miraculous—she incorporates the divine.

Here sacrifice has its ancient, primal meaning: that which was given at the beginning becomes the gift. The first fruits of the harvest were dedicated to and consumed by the vegetation spirit which provided them. The destruction of the victim in human or animal sacrifice or the consumption of the offering was the very definition of the sacrifice—death was necessary because the victim was or represented the life-giving substance, the vital energy source, which had to be liberated, which only death could liberate. An actual death, the sacrifice per se, not only liberated benevolent energy but also ensured a propagation and increase of life energy (concretely expressed as fertility) by a sort of magical ecology, a recycling of basic energy, or raw power. O's victimization is the confirmation of her power, a power which is transcendental and which has as its essence the sacred processes of life, death, and regeneration.

But the full significance of possession, both mystically and mythologically, is not yet clear. In mystic experience communion (wrongly called possession sometimes) has meant the dissolution of the ego, the entry into ecstasy, union with and illumination of the godhead. The experience of communion has been the province of the mystic, prophet, or visionary, those who were able to alchemize their energy into pure spirit and this spirit into a state of grace. Possession, rightly by its very nature demonic because its goal is power, its means are violence and oppression. It spills the blood of its victim and in doing so estranges itself from life-giving union. O's lover thinks that she gives herself freely but if she did not, he would take her anyway. Their relationship is the incarnation of demonic possession:

> Thus he would possess her as a god possesses his creatures, whom he lays hold of in the guise of a monster or bird, of an invisible spirit or a state of ecstasy. He did not wish to leave her. The more he surrendered her, the more he would hold her dear. The fact that he gave her was to him a proof, and ought to be for her as well, that she belonged to him: one can only give what belongs to you. He gave her only to reclaim her immediately, to reclaim her enriched in his eyes, like some common object which had been used for some divine purpose

and has thus been consecrated. For a long time he had wanted to prostitute her, and he was delighted to feel that the pleasure he was deriving was even greater than he had hoped, and that it bound him to her all the more so because, through it, she would be more humiliated and ravished. Since she loved him, she could not help loving whatever derived from him.[6]

A precise corollary of possession is prostitution. The prostitute, the woman as object, is defined by the usage to which the possessor puts her. Her subjugation is the signet of his power. Prostitution means for the woman the carnal annihilation of will and choice, but for the man it once again signifies an increase in power, pure and simple. To call the power of the possessor, which he demonstrates by playing superpimp, divine, or to confuse it with ecstasy or communion, is to grossly misunderstand. "All the mouths that had probed her mouth, all the hands that had seized her breasts and belly, all the members that had been thrust into her had so perfectly provided the living proof that she was worthy of being prostituted and had, so to speak, sanctified her."[7] Of course, it is not O who is sanctified, but Rene, or Sir Stephen, or the others, through her. O's prostitution is a vicious caricature of old-world religious prostitution. The ancient sacral prostitution of the Hebrews, Greeks, Indians, et al., was the ritual expression of respect and veneration for the powers of fertility and generation. The priestesses/prostitutes of the temple were literal personifications of the life energy of the earth goddess, and transferred that energy to those who participated in her rites. The cosmic principles, articulated as divine male and divine female, were ritually united in the temple because clearly only through their continuing and repeated union could the fertility of the earth and the well-being of a people be ensured. Sacred prostitution was "nothing less than an act of communion with god (or godhead) and was as remote from sensuality as the Christian act of communion is remote from gluttony."[8] O and all of the women at Roissy are distinguished by their sterility and bear no resemblance whatsoever to any known goddess. No mention is ever made of conception or menstruation, and procreation is never a consequence of fucking. O's fertility has been rendered O. There is nothing sacred about O's prostitution.

O's degradation is occasioned by the male need for and fear of initiation into manhood. Initiation rites generally include a period of absolute solitude, isolation, followed by tests of physical courage, mental endurance, often through torture and physical mutilation, resulting in a permanent scar or tattoo which marks the successful initiate. The process of initiation is designed to reveal the values, rites, and rules of manhood and confers on the initiate the responsibilities and privileges of manhood. What occurs at Roissy is a clear perversion of real initiation. Rene and the others mutilate O's body, but they are themselves untouched. Her body substitutes for their bodies. O is marked with the scars which they should bear. She undergoes their ordeal for them, endures the solitude and isolation, the torture, the mutilation. In trying to become gods, they have bypassed the necessary rigors of becoming men. The fact that the tortures must be repeated endlessly, not only on O but on large numbers of women who are forced as well as persuaded, demonstrates that the men of Roissy never in fact become men, are never initiates, never achieve the security of realized manhood. What would be the sign of the initiate, the final mark or scar, manifests in the case of O as an ultimate expression of sadism. The rings through O's cunt with Sir Stephen's name and heraldry, and the brand on her ass, are permanent wedding rings rightly placed. They mark her as an owned object and in no way symbolize the passage into maturity and freedom. The same might be said of the conventional wedding ring.

O, in her never-ending role as surrogate everything, also is the direct sexual link between Sir Stephen and Rene. That the two men love each other and fuck each other through O is made clear by the fact that Sir Stephen uses O anally most of the time. The consequences of misdirecting sexual energy are awesome indeed.

But what is most extraordinary about *Story of O* is the mind-boggling literary style of Pauline Reage, its author. O is wanton yet pure, Sir Stephen is cruel yet kind, Rene is brutal yet gentle, a wall is black yet white. Everything is what it is, what it isn't, and its direct opposite. That technique, which is so skillfully executed, might help to account for the compelling irrationality of *Story of O*. For those women who are convinced yet doubtful, attracted yet repelled, there is this schema for self-protection: *the double-double think that the author engages in is very easy to deal with if we just realize that we only have to double-double unthink it.*

To sum up, *Story of O* is a story of psychic cannibalism, demonic possession, a story which posits men and women as being at opposite poles of the universe—the survival of one dependent on the absolute destruction of the other. It asks, like many stories, who is the most powerful, and it answers: men are, literally over women's dead bodies.

this text has been altered in one very serious way. I wanted it to be printed the way it was written—lower case letters, no apostrophes, contractions.

I like my text to be as empty as possible, only necessary punctuation is necessary, when one knows ones purposes one knows what is necessary.

my publisher, in his corporate wisdom, filled the pages with garbage: standard punctuation, he knew his purposes; he knew what was necessary, our purposes differed: mine, to achieve clarity; his, to sell books.

my publisher changed my punctuation because book reviewers (Mammon) do not like lower case letters,

fuck (in the old sense) book reviewers (Mammon).

When I say god and mammon concerning the writer writing, I mean that any one can use words to say something. And in using these words to say what he has to say he may use those words directly or indirectly. If he uses these words indirectly he says what he intends to have heard by somebody who is to hear and in so doing inevitably he has to serve mammon . . . . Now serving god for a writer who is writing is writing anything directly, it makes no difference what it is but it must be direct, the relation between the thing done and the doer must be direct. In this way there is completion and the essence of the completed thing is completion.

—Gertrude Stein

in a letter to me, Grace Paley wrote, "once everyone tells the truth artists will be unnecessary—meanwhile there's work for us."

telling the truth, we know what it is when we do it and when we learn not to do it we forget what it is.

form, shape, structure, spatial relation, how the printed word appears on the page, where to breathe, where to rest, punctuation is marking time, indicating rhythms, even in my original text I used too much of it—I overorchestrated. I forced you to breathe where I do, instead of letting you discover your own natural breath.

I begin by presuming that I am free.

I begin with nothing, no form, no content, and I ask: what do I want to do and how do I want to do it.

I begin by presuming that what I write belongs to me.

I begin by presuming that I determine the form I use—in all its particulars. I work at my craft—in all its particulars.

in fact, everything is already determined,

in fact, all the particulars have been determined and are enforced.

in fact, where I violate what has already been determined I will be stopped.

in fact, the enforcers will enforce.

"Whatever he may seem to us, he is yet a servant of the Law; that is, he belongs to the Law and as such is set beyond human judgment. In that case one dare not believe that the doorkeeper is subordinate to the man. Bound as he is by his service, even at the door of the Law, he is incomparably freer than anyone at large in the world. The man is only seeking the Law, the doorkeeper is already attached to it. It is the Law that has placed him at his post; to doubt his integrity is to doubt the Law itself."

"I don't agree with that point of view," said K., shaking his head, "for if one accepts it, one must accept as true everything the doorkeeper says. But you yourself have sufficiently proved how impossible it is to do that."

"No," said the priest, "it is not necessary to accept everything as true, one must only accept it as necessary."

"A melancholy conclusion," said K. "It turns lying into a universal principle."

—Franz Kafka

I presume that I am free. I act. the enforcers enforce. I discover that I am not free, then: either I lie (it is necessary to lie) or I struggle (if I do not lie, I must struggle), if I struggle, I ask, why am I not free and what can I do to become free? I wrote this book to find out why I am not free and what I can do to become free.

Though the social structure begins by framing the noblest laws and the loftiest ordinances that "the great of the earth" have devised, in the end it comes to this: breach that lofty law and they take you to a prison cell and shut your human body off from human warmth. Ultimately the law is enforced by the unfeeling guard punching his fellow man hard in the belly.

—Judith Malina

without the presumption of freedom, there is no freedom. I am free, how, then, do I want to live my life, do my work, use my body? how, then, do I want to be, in all my particulars?

standard forms are imposed in dress, behavior, sexual relation, punctuation. standard forms are imposed on consciousness and behavior—on knowing and expressing—so that we will not presume freedom, so that freedom will appear—in all its particulars—impossible and unworkable, so that we will not know what telling the truth is, so that we will not feel compelled to tell it, so that we will spend our time and our holy human energy telling the necessary lies.

standard forms are sometimes called conventions, conventions are mightier than armies, police, and prisons. each citizen becomes the enforcer, the doorkeeper, an instrument of the Law, an unfeeling guard punching his fellow man hard in the belly.

> I am an anarchist. I dont sue, I dont get injunctions, I advocate revolution, and when people ask me what can we do that's practical, I say, weakly, weaken the fabric of the system wherever you can, make possible the increase of freedom, all kinds. When I write I try to extend the possibilities of expression.
>
> . . . I had tried to speak to you honestly, in my own way, undisguised, trying to get rid, it's part of my obligation to the muse, of the ancien regime of grammar.
>
> . . . the revisions in typography and punctuation have taken from the voice the difference that distinguishes passion from affection and me speaking to you from me writing an essay.
>
> —Julian Beck, 1965, in a foreword to an edition of *The Brig*

BELIEVE THE PUNCTUATION.

—Muriel Rukeyser

there is a great deal at stake here, many writers fight this battle and most lose it. what is at stake for the writer? freedom of invention, freedom to tell the truth, in all its particulars, freedom to imagine new structures.

(the burden of proof is not on those who presume freedom, the burden of proof is on those who would in any way diminish it.)

what is at stake for the enforcers, the doorkeepers, the guardians of the Law—the publishing corporations, the book reviewers who do not like lower case letters, the librarians who will not stack books without standard punctuation (that was the reason given Muriel Rukeyser when her work was violated)—what is at stake for them? why do they continue to enforce?

while this book may meet much resistance—anger, fear, dislike—law? police? courts?—at this moment I must write: Ive attacked the fundaments of culture, thats ok. Ive attacked male dominance, thats ok. Ive attacked every heterosexual notion of relation, thats ok. Ive in effect advocated the use of drugs, thats ok. Ive in effect advocated fucking animals, thats ok. here and now, New York City, spring 1974, among a handful of people, publisher and editor included, thats ok. lower case letters are not. it does make one wonder.

so Ive wondered and this is what I think right now. there are well-developed, effective mechanisms for dealing with ideas, no matter how powerful the ideas are. very few ideas are more powerful than the mechanisms for defusing them. standard form—punctuation, typography, then on to academic organization, the rigid ritualistic formulation of ideas, etc.—is the actual distance between the individual (certainly the intellectual individual) and the ideas in a book.

standard form is the distance.

one can be excited *about* ideas without changing at all. one can think *about* ideas, talk *about* ideas, without changing at all. people are willing to think about many things. what people refuse to do, or are not permitted to do, or resist doing, is to change the way they think.

reading a text which violates standard form forces one to change mental sets in order to read. there is no distance. the new form, which is in some ways unfamiliar, forces one to read differently— not to read about different things, but to read in different ways.

to permit writers to use forms which violate convention just might permit writers to develop forms which would teach people to think differently: not to think about different things, but to think in different ways. that work is not permitted.

> If it had been possible to build the Tower of Babel without ascending it, the work would have been permitted.
>
> —Franz Kafka

> The Immovable Structure is the villain. Whether that structure calls itself a prison or a school or a factory or a family or a government or The World As It Is. That structure asks each man what he can do for it, not what it can do for him, and for those who do not do for it, there is the pain of death or imprisonment, or social degradation, or the loss of animal rights.
>
> —Judith Malina

this book is about the Immovable Sexual Structure, in the process of having it published, Ive encountered the Immovable Punctuation Typography Structure, and I now testify, as so many have before me, that the Immovable Structure aborts freedom, prohibits invention, and does us verifiable harm: it uses our holy human energy to sustain itself; it turns us into enforcers, or outlaws; to survive, we must learn to lie.

The Revolution, as we live it and as we imagine it, means destroying the Immovable Structure to create a world in which we can use our holy human energy to sustain our holy human lives;

to create a world without enforcers, doorkeepers, guards, and arbitrary Law;

to create a world—a community on this planet—where instead of lying to survive, we can tell the truth and flourish.

OUR BLOOD

1976

In 1970 Kate Millett published *Sexual Politics*. In that book she proved to many of us—who would have staked our lives on denying it—that sexual relations, the literature depicting those relations, the psychology posturing to explain those relations, the economic systems that fix the necessities of those relations, the religious systems that seek to control those relations, are *political*. She showed us that everything that happens to a woman in her life, everything that touches or molds her, is *political*.[1]

Women who are feminists, that is, women who grasped her analysis and saw that it explained much of their real existence in their real lives, have tried to understand, struggle against, and transform the political system called patriarchy which exploits our labor, predetermines the ownership of our bodies, and diminishes our selfhood from the day we are born. This struggle has no dimension to it which is abstract: it has touched us in every part of our lives. But nowhere has it touched us more vividly or painfully than in that part of our human lives which we call "love" and "sex." In the course of our struggle to free ourselves from systematic oppression, a serious argument has developed among us, and I want to bring that argument into this room.

Some of us have committed ourselves in all areas, including those called "love" and "sex," to the goal of *equality*, that is, to the

Delivered at the National Organization for Women Conference on Sexuality, New York City, October 12, 1974.

state of being equal; correspondence in quantity, degree, value, rank, ability; uniform character, as of motion or surface. Others of us, and I stand on this side of the argument, do not see equality as a proper, or sufficient, or moral, or honorable final goal. We believe that to be equal where there is not universal justice, or where there is not universal freedom is, quite simply, to be the same as the oppressor. It is to have achieved "uniform character, as of motion or surface."

Nowhere is this clearer than in the area of sexuality. The male sexual model is based on a polarization of humankind into man/ woman, master/slave, aggressor/victim, active/passive. This male sexual model is now many thousands of years old. The very identity of men, their civil and economic power, the forms of government that they have developed, the wars they wage, are tied *irrevocably* together. All forms of dominance and submission, whether it be man over woman, white over black, boss over worker, rich over poor, are tied *irrevocably* to the sexual identities of men and are derived from the male sexual model. Once we grasp this, it becomes clear that *in fact* men own the sex act, the language which describes sex, the women whom they objectify. Men have written the scenario for any sexual fantasy you have ever had or any sexual act you have ever engaged in.

There is no *freedom* or *justice* in exchanging the female role for the male role. There is, no doubt about it, equality. There is no *freedom* or *justice* in using male language, the language of your oppressor, to describe sexuality. There is no *freedom* or *justice* or even common sense in developing a male sexual sensibility—a sexual sensibility which is aggressive, competitive, objectifying, quantity oriented. There is only equality. To believe that freedom or justice for women, or for any individual woman, can be found in mimicry of male sexuality is to delude oneself and to contribute to the oppression of one's sisters.

Many of us would like to think that in the last four years, or ten years, we have reversed, or at least impeded, those habits and customs of the thousands of years which went before—the habits and customs of male dominance. There is no fact or figure to bear that out. You may feel better, or you may not, but statistics show that women are poorer than ever, that women are raped more and murdered more. I want to suggest to you that a commitment to sexual equality with males, that is, to uniform character as of motion or surface, is a commitment to becoming the rich instead of the poor, the rapist instead of the raped, the murderer instead of the murdered. I want to ask you to make a different commitment—a commitment to the abolition of poverty, rape, and murder; that is, a commitment to ending the system of oppression called patriarchy; to ending the male sexual model itself.

The real core of the feminist vision, its revolutionary kernel if you will, has to do with the abolition of all sex roles—that is, an absolute transformation of human sexuality and the institutions derived from it. In this work, *no part of the male sexual model can possibly apply*. Equality within the framework of the male sexual model, however that model is reformed or modified, can only perpetuate the model itself and the injustice and bondage which are its intrinsic consequences.

I suggest to you that transformation of the male sexual model under which we now all labor and "love" begins where there is a *congruence*, not a separation, a *congruence* of feeling and erotic interest; that it begins in what we do know about female sexuality *as distinct* from male—clitoral touch and sensitivity, multiple orgasms, erotic sensitivity all over the body (which needn't—and shouldn't—be localized or contained genitally), in tenderness, in self-respect and in absolute mutual respect. For men I suspect that this transformation begins in the place they most dread—that is, in a limp penis. I think that men will have to give up their precious erections and begin to make love as women do together. I am saying that men will have to renounce their phallocentric personalities, and the privileges and powers given to them at birth as a consequence of their anatomy, that they will have to excise everything in them that they now value as distinctively "male." No reform, or matching of orgasms, will accomplish this.

I have been reading excerpts from the diary of Sophie Tolstoy, which I found in a beautiful book called *Revelations: Diaries of Women*, edited by Mary Jane Moffat and Charlotte Painter. Sophie Tolstoy wrote:

> And the main thing is not to love. See what I have done by loving him so deeply! It is so painful and humiliating; but he thinks that it is merely silly. "You say one thing and always do another." But what is the good of arguing in this superior manner, when I have nothing in me but this humiliating love and a bad temper; and these two things have been the cause of all my misfortunes, for my temper has always interfered with my love. I want nothing but his love and sympathy, and he won't give it to me; and all my pride is trampled in the mud; I am nothing but a miserable crushed worm, whom no one wants, whom no one loves, a useless creature with morning sickness, and a big belly, two rotten teeth, and a bad temper, a battered sense of dignity, and a love which nobody wants and which nearly drives me insane.[2]

Does anyone really think that things have changed so much since Sophie Tolstoy made that entry in her diary on October 25, 1886? And what would you tell her if she came here today, to her sisters? Would you have handed her a vibrator and taught her how to use it? Would you have given her the techniques of fellatio that might better please Mr. Tolstoy? Would you have suggested to her that her salvation lay in becoming a "sexual athlete"? Learning to cruise? Taking as many lovers as Leo did? Would you tell her to start thinking of herself as a "person" and not as a woman?

Or might you have found the courage, the resolve, the conviction to be her true sisters—to help her to extricate herself from the long darkness of Leo's shadow; to join with her in changing the very organization and texture of this world, still constructed in 1974 to serve him, to force her to serve him?

I suggest to you that Sophie Tolstoy is here today, in the bodies and lives of many sisters. Do not fail her.

THE RAPE ATROCITY AND THE BOY NEXT DOOR

Delivered at State University of New York at Stony Brook, March 1, 1975; University of Pennsylvania, April 25, 1975; State University of New York College at Old Westbury, May 10, 1975; Womanbooks, New York City, July 1, 1975; Woodstock Women's Center, Woodstock, New York, July 3, 1975; Suffolk County Community College, October 9, 1975; Queens College, City University of New York, April 26, 1976.

I want to talk to you about *rape*—rape—what it is, who does it, to whom it is done, how it is done, why it is done, and what to do about it so that it will not be done any more.

First, though, I want to make a few introductory remarks.* From 1964 to 1965 and from 1966 to 1968, I went to Bennington College in Vermont. Bennington at that time was still a women's school, or, as people said then, a girls' school. It was a very insular place—entirely isolated from the Vermont community in which it was situated, exclusive, expensive. There was a small student body highly concentrated in the arts, a low student–faculty ratio, and an apocryphal tradition of intellectual and sexual "freedom." In general, Bennington was a very distressing kind of playpen where wealthy young women were educated to various accomplishments which would insure good marriages for the respectable and good affairs for the bohemians. At that time, there was more actual freedom for

---

* These introductory remarks were delivered only at schools where there was no women's studies program.

women at Bennington than at most schools—in general, we could come and go as we liked, whereas most other schools had rigid curfews and controls; and in general we could wear what we wanted, whereas in most other schools women still had to conform to rigid dress codes. We were encouraged to read and write and make pots, and in general to take ourselves seriously, even though the faculty did not take us seriously at all. Being better educated to reality than we were, they, the faculty, knew what we did not imagine—that most of us would take our highfalutin ideas about James and Joyce and Homer and invest them in marriages and volunteer work. Most of us, as the mostly male faculty knew, would fall by the wayside into silence and all our good intentions and vast enthusiasms had nothing to do with what would happen to us once we left that insulated playpen. At the time I went to Bennington, there was no feminist consciousness there or anywhere else at all. Betty Friedan's *The Feminine Mystique* concerned housewives—we thought that it had nothing to do with us. Kate Millett's *Sexual Politics* was not yet published. Shulamith Firestone's *The Dialectic of Sex* was not yet published. We were in the process of becoming very well-educated women—we were already very privileged women—and yet not many of us had ever heard the story of the movement for women's suffrage in this country or Europe. In the Amerikan history courses I took, women's suffrage was not mentioned. The names of Angelina and Sarah Grimke, or Susan B. Anthony, or Elizabeth Cady Stanton, were never mentioned. Our ignorance was so complete that we did not know that we had been consigned from birth to that living legal and social death called marriage. We imagined, in our ignorance, that we might be novelists and philosophers. A rare few among us even aspired to be mathematicians and biologists. We did not know that our professors had a system of beliefs and convictions that designated us as an *inferior gender class*, and that that system of beliefs and convictions was virtually universal—the cherished assumption of most of the writers, philosophers, and historians we were so ardently studying. We did not know, for instance, to pick an obvious example, that our Freudian psychology professor believed along with Freud that "the effect of penis-envy has a share . . . in the physical vanity of women, since they are bound to value their charms more highly as a late compensation for their original sexual inferiority."[1] In each field of study, such convictions were central, underlying, crucial. And yet we did not know that *they* meant *us*. This was true everywhere where women were being educated.

As a result, women of my age left colleges and universities completely ignorant of what one might call "real life." We did not know that we would meet everywhere a systematic despisal of our intelligence, creativity, and strength. We did not know our herstory as a gender class. We did not know that we were a gender class, inferior by law and custom to men who were defined, by themselves and all the organs of their culture, as supreme. We did not know that we had been trained all our lives to be victims—inferior, submissive, passive objects who could lay no claim to a discrete individual identity. We did not know that because we were women our labor would be exploited wherever we worked—in jobs, in political movements—by men for their own self-aggrandizement. We did not know that all our hard work in whatever jobs or political movements would never advance our responsibilities or our rewards. We did not know that we were there, wherever, to cook, to do menial labor, to be fucked.

I tell you this now because this is what I remembered when I knew I would come here to speak tonight. I imagine that in some ways it is different for you. There is an astounding feminist literature to educate you even if your professors will not. There are feminist philosophers, poets, comedians, herstorians, and politicians who are creating feminist culture. There is your own feminist consciousness, which you must nurture, expand, and deepen at every opportunity.

As of now, however, there is no women's study program here. The development of such a program is essential to you as women. Systematic and rigorous study of woman's place in this culture will make it possible for you to understand the world as it acts on and affects you. Without that study, you will leave here as I left Bennington—ignorant of what it means to be a woman in a patriarchal society—that is, in a society where women are systematically defined as inferior, where women are systematically despised.

I am here tonight to try to tell you as much as I can about what you are up against as women in your efforts to live decent, worthwhile, and productive human lives. And that is why I chose tonight to speak about rape which is, though no contemporary Amerikan male writer will tell you so, the dirtiest four-letter word in the English language. Once you understand what rape is, you will understand the forces that systematically oppress you as women. Once you understand what rape is, you will be able to begin the work of changing the values and institutions of this patriarchal society so that you will not be oppressed anymore. Once you understand what rape is, you will be able to resist all attempts to mystify and mislead you into believing that the crimes committed against you as women are trivial, comic, irrelevant. Once you understand what rape is, you will find the resources to take your lives as women seriously and to organize as women against the persons and institutions which demean and violate you.

———

The word *rape* comes from the Latin word *rapere*, which means "to steal, seize, or carry away."

The first definition of rape in *The Random House Dictionary* is still "the act of seizing and carrying off by force."

The second definition, with which you are probably familiar, defines rape as "the act of physically forcing a woman to have sexual intercourse."

For the moment, I will refer exclusively to the first definition of rape, that is, "the act of seizing and carrying off by force."

Rape precedes marriage, engagement, betrothal, and courtship as sanctioned social behavior. In the bad old days, when a man wanted a woman he simply took her—that is, he abducted and fucked her. The *abduction*, which was always for sexual purposes, was the rape. If the raped woman pleased the rapist, he kept her. If not, he discarded her.

Women, in those bad old days, were chattel. That is, women were property, owned objects, to be bought, sold, used, and stolen—that is, raped. A woman belonged first to her father who was her patriarch, her master, her lord. The very derivation of the word *patriarchy* is instructive. *Pater* means owner, possessor, or master. The basic social unit of patriarchy is the family. The word *family* comes from the Oscan *famel*, which means servant, slave, or possession. *Pater familias* means owner of slaves. The rapist who abducted a woman took the place of her father as her owner, possessor, or master.

The Old Testament is eloquent and precise in delineating the right of a man to rape. Here, for instance, is Old Testament law on the rape of enemy women. Deuteronomy, Chapter 21, verses 10 to 15—

When you go to war against your enemies and Yahweh your God delivers them into your power and you take prisoners, if you see a beautiful woman among the prisoners and find her desirable, you may make her your wife and bring her to your home. She is to shave her head and cut her nails and take off her prisoner's garb; she is to stay inside your house and must mourn her father and mother for a full month. Then you may go to her and be a husband to her, and she shall be your wife. Should she cease to please you, you will let her go where she wishes, not selling her for money; you are not to make any profit out of her, since you have had the use of her.[2]

A discarded woman, of course, was a pariah or a whore.

Rape, then, is the first model for marriage. Marriage laws sanctified rape by reiterating the right of the rapist to ownership of the raped. Marriage laws protected the property rights of the first rapist by designating a second rapist as an adulterer, that is, a thief. Marriage laws also protected the father's ownership of the daughter. Marriage laws guaranteed the father's right to sell a daughter into marriage, to sell her to another man. Any early strictures against rape were strictures against robbery—against the theft of property. It is in this context, and in this context only, that we can understand rape as a capital crime. This is the Old Testament text on the theft of women as a capital offense. Deuteronomy 22:22 to 23:1—

If a man is caught sleeping with another man's wife, both must die, the man who has slept with her and the woman herself. You must banish this evil from Israel.

If a virgin is betrothed and a man meets her in the city and sleeps with her, you shall take them both out to the gate of the town and stone them to death; the girl, because she did not cry for help in the town; the man, because he has violated the wife of his fellow. You must banish this evil from your midst. But if the man has met the betrothed girl in the open country and has taken her by force and lain with her, only the man who lay with her shall die; you must do nothing to the girl, for hers is no capital offence. The case is like that of a man who attacks and kills his fellow; for he came across her in the open country and the betrothed girl could have cried out without anyone coming to her rescue.

If a man meets a virgin who is not betrothed and seizes her and lies with her and is caught in the act, the man who has lain with her must give the girl's father fifty silver shekels; she shall be his wife since he has violated her, and as long as he lives he may not repudiate her.

A man must not take his father's wife, and must not withdraw the skirt of his father's cloak from her.[3]

Women belonged to men; the laws of marriage sanctified that ownership; rape was the theft of a woman from her owner. These biblical laws are the basis of the social order as we know it. They have not to this day been repudiated.

As history advanced, men escalated their acts of aggression against women and invented many myths about us to insure both ownership and easy sexual access. In 500 B. C. Herodotus, the so-called Father of History, wrote: "Abducting young women is not, indeed, a lawful act; but it is stupid after the event to make a fuss about it. The only sensible thing is to take no notice; for it is obvious that no young woman allows herself to be abducted if she does not wish to be."[4] Ovid in the *Ars amatoria* wrote: "Women often wish to give unwillingly what they really like to give."[5] And so, it became official: women want to be raped.

Early English law on rape was a testament to the English class system. A woman who was not married belonged legally to the king. Her rapist had to pay the king fifty shillings as a fine, but if she was a "grinding slave," then the fine was reduced to twenty-five shillings. The rape of a nobleman's serving maid cost twelve shillings. The rape of a commoner's serving maid cost five shillings. But if a slave raped a commoner's serving maid, he was castrated. And if he raped any woman of higher rank, he was killed.[6] Here, too, rape was a crime against the man who owned the woman.

Even though rape is sanctioned in the Bible, even though the Greeks had glorified rape—remember Zeus' interminable adventures—and even though Ovid had waxed euphoric over rape, it was left to Sir Thomas Malory to popularize rape for us English-speaking folk. *Le Morte d'Arthur* is the classic work on courtly love. It is a powerful romanticization of rape. Malory is the direct literary ancestor of those modern male Amerikan writers who postulate rape as mythic lovemaking. A good woman is to be taken, possessed by a gallant knight, sexually forced into a submissive passion which would, by male definition, become her delight. Here rape is transformed, or mystified, into romantic love. Here rape becomes the signet of romantic love. Here we find the first really modern rendering of rape: sometimes a woman is seized and carried off; sometimes she is sexually forced and left, madly, passionately in love with the rapist who is, by virtue of an excellent rape, her owner, her love. (Malory, by the way, was arrested and charged with raping, on two separate occasions, a married woman, Joan Smyth.)[7] In his work, rape is no longer synonymous with abduction—it has now become synonymous with love. At issue, of course, is still male owner-ship—the rapist owns the woman; but now, she loves him as well.

———

This motif of sexual relating—that is, rape—remains our primary model for heterosexual relating. The dictionary defines rape as "the act of physically forcing a woman to have sexual intercourse." But in fact, rape, in our system of masculinist law, remains a right of marriage. A man cannot be convicted of raping his own wife. In all fifty states, rape is defined legally as forced penetration by a man of a woman "not his wife."[8] When a man forcibly penetrates his own wife, he has not committed a crime of theft against another man. Therefore, according to masculinist law, he has not raped. And, of course, a man cannot abduct his own wife since she is required by law to inhabit his domicile and submit to him sexually. Marriage remains, in our time, carnal *ownership* of women. A man cannot be prosecuted for using his own property as he sees fit.

In addition, rape is our primary emblem of romantic love. Our modern writers, from D. H. Lawrence to Henry Miller to Norman Mailer to Ayn Rand, consistently present rape as the means of intro-ducing a woman to her own carnality. A woman is taken, possessed, conquered by brute force—and it is the rape itself that transforms her into a carnal creature. It is the rape itself which defines both her identity and her function: she is a woman, and as a woman she exists to be fucked. In masculinist terms, a woman can never be raped against her will since the notion is that if she does not want to be raped, she does not know her will.

Rape, in our society, is still not viewed as a crime against women. In "Forcible and Statutory Rape: An Exploration of the

Operation and Objectives of the Consent Standard," *The Yale Law Journal*, 1952, an article which is a relentless compendium of misogynistic slander, the intent of modern male jurisprudence in the area of criminal rape is articulated clearly: the laws exist to protect men (1) from the false accusation of rape (which is taken to be the most likely type of accusation) and (2) from the theft of female property, or its defilement, by another man.[9] The notion of consent to sexual intercourse as the inalienable human right of a woman does not exist in male jurisprudence; a woman's withholding of consent is seen only as a socially appropriate form of barter and the notion of consent is honored only insofar as it protects the male's proprietary rights to her body:

> The consent standard in our society does more than protect a significant item of social currency for women; it fosters, and is in turn bolstered by, a masculine pride in the exclusive possession of a sexual object. The consent of a woman to sexual intercourse awards the man a privilege of bodily access, a personal "prize" whose value is enhanced by sole ownership. . . . An additional reason for the man's condemnation of rape may be found in the threat to his status from a decrease in the "value" of his sexual "possession" which would result from forcible violation.[10]

This remains the basic articulation of rape as a social crime: it is a crime against men, a violation of the male right to personal and exclusive possession of a woman as a sexual object.

Is it any wonder, then, that when Andra Medea and Kathleen Thompson, the authors of *Against Rape*, did a study of women and rape, large numbers of women, when asked, "Have you ever been raped?" answered, "I don't know."[11]

———

What is rape?

Rape is the first model for marriage. As such, it is sanctioned by the Bible and by thousands of years of law, custom, and habit.

Rape is an act of theft—a man takes the sexual property of another man.

Rape is, by law and custom, a crime against men, against the particular owner of a particular woman.

Rape is the primary heterosexual model for sexual relating.

Rape is the primary emblem of romantic love.

Rape is the means by which a woman is initiated into her womanhood as it is defined by men.

Rape is the right of any man who desires any woman, as long as she is not explicitly owned by another man. This explains clearly why defense lawyers are allowed to ask rape victims personal and intimate questions about their sexual lives. If a woman is a virgin, then she still belongs to her father and a crime has been committed. If a woman is not married and is not a virgin, then she belongs to no particular man and a crime has not been committed.

———

These are the fundamental cultural, legal, and social assumptions about rape: (1) women want to be raped, in fact, women need to be raped; (2) women provoke rape; (3) no woman can be sexually forced against her will; (4) women love their rapists; (5) in the act of rape, men affirm their own manhood and they also affirm the identity and function of women—that is, women exist to be fucked by men and so, in the act of rape, men actually affirm the very womanhood of women. Is it any wonder, then, that there is an epidemic of forcible rape in this country and that most convicted rapists do not know what it is they have done wrong?

———

In *Beyond God the Father*, Mary Daly says that as women we have been deprived of the power of *naming*.[12] Men, as engineers of this culture, have defined all the words we use. Men, as the makers of law, have defined what is legal and what is not. Men, as the creators of systems of philosophy and morality, have defined what is right and what is wrong. Men, as writers, artists, movie makers, psychologists and psychiatrists, politicians, religious leaders, prophets, and so-called revolutionaries have defined for us who we are, what our values are, how we perceive what happens to us, how we understand what happens to us. At the root of all the definitions they have made is one resolute conviction: that women were put on this earth for the use, pleasure, and sexual gratification of men.

In the case of rape, men have defined for us our function, our value, and the uses to which we may be put.

For women, as Mary Daly says, one fundamental revolutionary act is to reclaim the power of naming, to define for ourselves what our experience is and has been. This is very hard to do. We use a language which is sexist to its core: developed by men in their own interests; formed specifically to exclude us; used specifically to oppress us. The work, then, of naming is crucial to the struggle of women; the work of naming is, in fact, the first revolutionary work we must do. How, then, do *we* define rape?

Rape is a crime against *women*.

Rape is an act of aggression against women.

Rape is a contemptuous and hostile act against women.

Rape is a violation of a woman's right to self-determination.

Rape is a violation of a woman's right to absolute control of her own body.

Rape is an act of sadistic domination.

Rape is a colonializing act.

Rape is a function of male imperialism over and against women.

The crime of rape against one woman is a crime committed against all women.

Generally, we recognize that rape can be divided into two distinct categories: *forcible rape* and *presumptive rape*. In a forcible rape, a man physically assaults a woman and forces her, through physical violence, threat of physical violence, or threat of death, to perform *any* sexual act. *Any* forced sexual act must be considered rape— "contact between the mouth and the anus, the mouth and the penis, the mouth and the vulva, [contact] between the penis and the vulva, [between the] penis and anus, or contact between the anus or vulva" and any phallic substitute like a bottle, stick, or dildo.[13]

In a presumptive rape, we are warranted in presuming that a man has had carnal access to a woman without her consent, because we define *consent* as "meaningful and knowledgeable assent; not mere acquiescence."[14] In a presumptive rape, the constraint on the victim's will is in the circumstance itself; there has been no mutuality of choice and understanding and therefore the basic human rights of the victim have been violated and a crime has been committed against her. This is one instance of presumptive rape, reported by Medea and Thompson in *Against Rape*:

> The woman is seventeen, a high school student. It is about four o'clock in the afternoon. Her boy friend's father has

picked her up in his car after school to take her to meet his son. He stops by his house and says she should wait for him in the car. When he has pulled the car into the garage, this thirty-seven-year-old father of six rapes her.[15]

This sort of rape is common, it is contemptible, and needless to say, it is never reported to the police.

Who, then, commits rape?

The fact is that rape is not committed by psychopaths. Rape is committed by normal men. There is nothing, except a conviction for rape which is very hard to obtain, to distinguish the rapist from the nonrapist.

The Institute for Sex Research did a study of rapists in the 1940's and 1950's. In part, the researchers concluded that ". . . there are no outstandingly ominous signs in [the rapists'] presex-offense histories; indeed, their heterosexual adjustment is quantitatively well above average."[16]

(. . .)

Who are the victims of rape? Women—of all classes, races, from all walks of life, of all ages. Most rapes are intraracial—that is, white men rape white women and black men rape black women. The youngest rape victim on record is a two-week-old female infant.[17] The oldest rape victim on record is a ninety-three-year-old woman.[18]

(. . .)

Now, I could read you testimony after testimony, tell you story after story—after all, in 1974 there were 607, 310 such stories to tell—but I don't think I have to prove to you that rape is a crime of such violence and that it is so rampant that we must view it as an ongoing atrocity against women. All women live in constant jeopardy, in a virtual state of siege. That is, simply, the truth. I do however want to talk to you explicitly about one particularly vicious form of rape which is increasing rapidly in frequency. This is multiple rape—that is, the rape of one woman by two or more men.

In Amir's study of 646 rape cases in Philadelphia in 1958 and 1960, a full 43 percent of all rapes were multiple rapes (16 percent pair rapes, 27 percent group rapes).[19] I want to tell you about two multiple rapes in some detail. The first is reported by Medea and Thompson in *Against Rape*. A twenty-five-year-old woman, mentally retarded, with a mental age of eleven years, lived alone in an apartment in a university town. She was befriended by some men from a campus fraternity. These men took her to the fraternity house, whereupon she was raped by approximately forty men. These men also tried to force intercourse between her and a dog. These men also put bottles and other objects up her vagina. Then, they took her to a police station and charged her with prostitution. Then, they offered to drop the charges against her if she was institutionalized. She was institutionalized; she discovered that she was pregnant; then, she had a complete emotional break down.

One man who had been a participant in the rape bragged about it to another man. That man, who was horrified, told a professor. A campus group confronted the fraternity. At first, the accused men admitted that they had committed all the acts charged, but they denied that it was rape since, they claimed, the woman had consented to all of the sexual acts committed. Subsequently, when the story was made public, these same men denied the story completely.

A woman's group on campus demanded that the fraternity be thrown off campus to demonstrate that the university did not condone gang rape. No action was taken against the fraternity by university officials or by the police.[20]

The second story that I want to tell was reported by Robert Sam Anson in an article called "That Championship Season" in *New Times* magazine.[21] According to Anson, on July 25, 1974, Notre Dame University suspended for at least one year six black football players for what the university called "a serious violation of university regulations." An eighteen-year-old white high school student, it turned out, had charged the football players with gang rape.

The victim's attorney, the county prosecutor, the local reporter assigned to cover the story, a trustee of the local newspaper—all were Notre Dame alumni, and all helped to cover up the rape charge.

Notre Dame University, according to Anson, has insisted that no crime was committed. It was the consensus of university officials that the football players were just sowing their wild oats in an old-fashioned gang bang, and that the victim was a willing participant. The football players were suspended for having sex in their dormitory. The President of Notre Dame, Theodore Hesburgh, a noted liberal and scholar, a Catholic priest, insisted that no rape took place and said that the university would produce, if necessary, "dozens of eyewitnesses." I quote Anson:

> Hesburgh's conclusions are based on an hour-long personal interview with the six football players, along with an investigation conducted by his Dean of Students, John Macheca, a . . . former university public relations man . . . Macheca himself will say nothing about his investigation. . . Various campus sources close to the case say that, throughout his investigation,

no university official spoke either to the girl [*sic*] or her parents. Hesburgh himself professes neither to know or to care. He says testily, "It's irrelevant. . . . I didn't need to talk to the girl. I talked to the boys."[22]

According to Anson, had Dr. Hesburgh talked to "the girl" he would have heard this story: after work late on July 3, she went to Notre Dame to see the football player she had been dating; they made love twice on his dormitory bunk; he left the room; she was alone and undressed, wrapped in a sheet; another football player entered the room; she had a history of hostility and confrontation with this second football player (he had made a friend of hers pregnant, he had refused to pay for an abortion, she had confronted him on this, finally he did pay part of the money); this second football player and the woman began to quarrel and he threatened that, unless she submit to him sexually, he would throw her out the third-story window; then he raped her; four other football players also raped her; during the gang rape, several other football players were in and out of the room; when the woman finally was able to leave the dormitory she drove immediately to a hospital.

Both the police investigator on the case and a source in the prosecutor's office believe the victim's story—that there was a gang rape perpetrated on her by the six Notre Dame football players.

All of the male university authorities who investigated the alleged gang rape determined that the victim was a slut. This they did, all of them, by interviewing the accused rapists. In fact, the prosecutor's character investigation indicated that the woman was a fine person. The coach of the Notre Dame football team placed responsibility for the alleged gang rape on the worsening morals of women who watch soap operas. Hesburgh, moral exemplar that he is, concluded: "I didn't need to talk to the girl. I talked to the boys." The Dean of Students, John Macheca, expelled the students as a result of his secret investigation. Hesburgh overruled the expulsion out of what he called "compassion"—he reduced the expulsion to one year's suspension. The rape victim now attends a university in the Midwest. Her life, according to Anson, has been threatened.

The fact is, as these two stories demonstrate conclusively, that any woman can be raped by any group of men. Her word will not be credible against their collective testimony. A proper investigation will not be done. Remember the good Father Hesburgh's words as long as you live: "I didn't need to talk to the girl. I talked to the boys." Even when a prosecutor is convinced that rape as defined by male law did take place, the rapists will not be prosecuted. Male university officials will protect those sacrosanct male institutions—the football team and the fraternity—no matter what the cost to women.

The reasons for this are terrible and cruel, but you must know them. Men are a privileged gender class over and against women. One of their privileges is the right of rape—that is, the right of carnal access to any woman. Men agree, by law, custom, and habit, that women are sluts and liars. Men will form alliances, or bonds, to protect their gender class interests. Even in a racist society, male bonding takes precedence over racial bonding.

It is very difficult whenever racist and sexist pathologies coincide to delineate in a political way what has actually happened. In 1838, Angelina Grimke, abolitionist and feminist, described Amerikan institutions as "a system of complicated crimes, built up upon the broken hearts and prostrate bodies of my countrymen in chains, and cemented by the blood, sweat, and tears of my sisters in bonds."[23] Racism and sexism are the warp and woof of this

Amerikan society, the very fabric of our institutions, laws, customs, and habits—and we are the inheritors of that complicated system of crimes. In the Notre Dame case, for instance, we can postulate that the prosecutor took the woman's charges of rape seriously at all because her accused rapists were black. That is racism and that is sexism. There is no doubt at all that white male law is more amenable to the prosecution of blacks for the raping of white women than the other way around. We can also postulate that, had the Notre Dame case been taken to court, the rape victim's character would have been impugned irrevocably because her lover was a black. That is racism and that is sexism. We also know that had a black woman been raped, either by blacks or whites, her rape would go unprosecuted, unremarked. That is racism and that is sexism.

In general, we can observe that the lives of rapists are worth more than the lives of women who are raped. Rapists are protected by male law and rape victims are punished by male law. An intricate system of male bonding supports the right of the rapist to rape, while diminishing the worth of the victim's life to absolute zero. In the Notre Dame case, the woman's lover allowed his fellows to rape her. This was a male bond. In the course of the rape, at one point when the woman was left alone—there is no indication that she was even conscious at this point—a white football player entered the room and asked her if she wanted to leave. When she did not answer, he left her there without reporting the incident. This was a male bond. The cover-up and lack of substantive investigation by white authorities was male bonding. All women of all races should recognize that male bonding takes precedence over racial bonding except in one particular kind of rape: that is, where the woman is viewed as the property of one race, class, or nationality, and her rape is viewed as an act of aggression against the males of that race, class, or nationality. Eldridge Cleaver in *Soul on Ice* has described this sort of rape:

> I became a rapist. To refine my technique and modus operandi I started out by practicing on black girls in the ghetto . . . and when I considered myself smooth enough, I crossed the tracks and sought out white prey. I did this consciously, deliberately, willfully, methodically . . .
>
> Rape was an insurrectionary act. It delighted me that I was defying and trampling upon the white man's law, upon his system of values, and that I was defiling his women—and this point, I believe, was the most satisfying to me because I was very resentful over the historical fact of how the white man has used the black woman. I felt I was getting revenge.[24]

In this sort of rape, women are viewed as the property of men who are, by virtue of race or class or nationality, enemies. Women are viewed as the chattel of enemy men. In this situation, and in this situation only, bonds of race or class or nationality will take priority over male bonding. As Cleaver's testimony makes clear, the women of one's own group are also viewed as chattel, property, to be used at will for one's own purposes. When a black man rapes a black woman, no act of aggression against a white male has been committed, and so the man's right to rape will be defended. It is very important to remember that most rape is intraracial—that is, black men rape black women and white men rape white women because rape is a *sexist* crime. Men rape the women they have access to as a function of their masculinity and as a signet of their ownership. Cleaver's outrage "at the historical fact of how the white man has used the black woman" is wrath over the theft of property which is rightly his.

Similarly, classic Southern rage at blacks who sleep with white women is wrath over the theft of property which rightly belongs to the white male. In the Notre Dame case, we can say that the gender class interests of men were served by determining that the value of the black football players to masculine pride—that is, to the championship Notre Dame football team—took priority over the white father's very compromised claim to ownership of his daughter. The issue was *never* whether a crime had been committed against a particular woman.

———

Now, I have laid out the dimensions of the rape atrocity. As women, we live in the midst of a society that regards us as contemptible. We are despised, as a gender class, as sluts and liars. We are the victims of continuous, malevolent, and sanctioned violence against us—against our bodies and our whole lives. Our characters are defamed, as a gender class, so that no individual woman has any credibility before the law or in society at large. Our enemies—rapists and their defenders—not only go unpunished; they remain influential arbiters of morality; they have high and esteemed places in the society; they are priests, lawyers, judges, lawmakers, politicians, doctors, artists, corporation executives, psychiatrists, and teachers.

What can we, who are powerless by definition and in fact, do about it?

First, we must effectively organize to treat the symptoms of this dread and epidemic disease. Rape crisis centers are crucial. Training in self-defense is crucial. Squads of women police formed to handle all rape cases are crucial. Women prosecutors on rape cases are crucial.

New rape laws are needed. These new laws must: (1) eliminate corroboration as a requirement for conviction; (2) eliminate the need for a rape victim to be physically injured to prove rape; (3) eliminate the need to prove lack of consent; (4) redefine *consent* to denote "meaningful and knowledgeable assent, not mere acquiescence"; (5) lower the unrealistic age of consent; (6) eliminate as admissible evidence the victim's prior sexual activity or previous consensual sex with the defendant; (7) assure that marital relationship between parties is no defense or bar to prosecution; (8) define rape in terms of degrees of serious injury.[25] These changes in the rape law were proposed by the New York University Law Clinical Program in Women's Legal Rights, and you can find their whole proposed model rape law in a book called *Rape: The First Sourcebook for Women*, by the New York Radical Feminists. I recommend to you that you investigate this proposal and then work for its implementation.

Also, we must, in order to protect ourselves, refuse to participate in the dating system which sets up every woman as a potential rape victim. In the dating system, women are defined as the passive pleasers of any and every man. The worth of any woman is measured by her ability to attract and please men. The object of the dating game for the man is "to score." In playing this game, as women we put ourselves and our well being in the hands of virtual or actual strangers. As women, we must analyze this dating system to determine its explicit and implicit definitions and values. In analyzing it, we will see how we are coerced into becoming sex-commodities.

Also, we must actively seek to publicize unprosecuted cases of rape, and we must make the identities of rapists known to other women.

There is also work here for men who do not endorse the right of men to rape. In Philadelphia, men have formed a group called

Men Organized Against Rape. They deal with male relatives and friends of rape victims in order to dispel belief in the myth of female culpability. Sometimes rapists who are troubled by their continued aggression against women will call and ask for help. There are vast educative and counseling possibilities here. Also, in Lorton, Virginia, convicted sex offenders have organized a group called Prisoners Against Rape. They work with feminist task forces and individuals to delineate rape as a political crime against women and to find strategies for combating it. It is very important that men who want to work against rape do not, through ignorance, carelessness, or malice, reinforce sexist attitudes. Statements such as "Rape is a crime against men too" or "Men are also victims of rape" do more harm than good. It is a bitter truth that rape becomes a visible crime only when a man is forcibly sodomized. It is a bitter truth that men's sympathy can be roused when rape is viewed as "a crime against men too." These truths are too bitter for us to bear. Men who want to work against rape will have to cultivate a rigorous antisexist consciousness and discipline so that they will not, in fact, make us invisible victims once again.

It is the belief of many men that their sexism is manifested only in relation to women—that is, that if they refrain from blatantly chauvinistic behavior in the presence of women, then they are not implicated in crimes against women. That is not so. It is in male bonding that men most often jeopardize the lives of women. It is among men that men do the most to contribute to crimes against women. For instance, it is the habit and custom of men to discuss with each other their sexual intimacies with particular women in vivid and graphic terms. This kind of bonding sets up a particular woman as the rightful and inevitable sexual conquest of a man's male friends and leads to innumerable cases of rape. Women are raped often by the male friends of their male friends. Men should understand that they jeopardize women's lives by participating in the rituals of privileged boyhood. Rape is also effectively sanctioned by men who harass women on the streets and in other public places; who describe or refer to women in objectifying, demeaning ways; who act aggressively or contemptuously toward women; who tell or laugh at misogynistic jokes; who write stories or make movies where women are raped and love it; who consume or endorse pornography; who insult specific women or women as a group; who impede or ridicule women in our struggle for dignity. Men who do or who endorse these behaviors are the enemies of women and are implicated in the crime of rape. Men who want to support women in our struggle for freedom and justice should understand that it is not terrifically important to us that they learn to cry; it is important to us that they stop the crimes of violence against us.

———

I have been describing, of course, emergency measures, designed to help women survive as atrocity is being waged against us. How can we end the atrocity itself? Clearly, we must determine the root causes of rape and we must work to excise from our social fabric all definitions, values, and behaviors which energize and sanction rape.

What, then, are the root causes of rape?

Rape is the direct consequence of our polar definitions of men and women. Rape is *congruent* with these definitions; rape *inheres* in these definitions. Remember, rape is not committed by psychopaths or deviants from our social norms—rape is committed by *exemplars* of our social norms. In this male-supremacist society, men are defined as one order of being over and against women who are defined as another, opposite, entirely different order of being. Men are defined as aggressive, dominant, powerful. Women are defined as passive, submissive, powerless. Given these polar gender definitions, it is the very nature of men to aggress sexually against women. Rape occurs when a man, who is dominant by definition, takes a woman who, according to men and all the organs of their culture, was put on this earth for his use and gratification. Rape, then, is the logical consequence of a system of definitions of what is normative. Rape is no excess, no aberration, no accident, no mistake—it embodies sexuality as the culture defines it. As long as these definitions remain intact—that is, as long as men are defined as sexual aggressors and women are defined as passive receptors lacking integrity—men who are exemplars of the norm will rape women.

In this society, the norm of masculinity is phallic aggression. Male sexuality is, by definition, intensely and rigidly phallic. A man's identity is located in his conception of himself as the possessor of a phallus; a man's worth is located in his *pride* in phallic identity. The main characteristic of phallic identity is that *worth* is entirely contingent on the possession of a phallus. Since men have no other criteria for worth, no other notion of identity, those who do not have phalluses are not recognized as fully human.

In thinking about this, you must realize that this is not a question of heterosexual or homosexual. Male homosexuality is not a renunciation of phallic identity. Heterosexual and homosexual men are equally invested in phallic identity. They manifest this investment differently in one area—the choice of what men call a "sexual object"—but their common valuation of women consistently reinforces their own sense of phallic worth.

It is this phallocentric identity of men that makes it possible—indeed, necessary—for men to view women as a lower order of creation. Men genuinely do not know that women are individual persons of worth, volition, and sensibility because *masculinity* is the signet of all worth, and masculinity is a function of phallic identity. Women, then, by definition, have no claim to the rights and responsibilities of personhood. Wonderful George Gilder, who can always be counted on to tell us the dismal truth about masculinity, has put it this way: ". . . unlike femininity, relaxed masculinity is at bottom empty, a limp nullity. . . . Manhood at the most basic level can be validated and expressed only in action."[26] And so, what are the actions that validate and express this masculinity: rape, first and foremost rape; murder, war, plunder, fighting, imperializing and colonializing—*aggression* in any and every form, and to any and every degree. All personal, psychological, social, and institutionalized domination on this earth can be traced back to its source: the phallic identities of men.

As women, of course, we do not have phallic identities, and so we are defined as opposite from and inferior to men. Men consider physical strength, for instance, to be implicit in and derived from phallic identity, and so for thousands of years we have been systematically robbed of our physical strength. Men consider intellectual accomplishment to be a function of phallic identity, and so we are intellectually incompetent by their definition. Men consider moral acuity to be a function of phallic identity, and so we are consistently characterized as vain, malicious, and immoral creatures. Even the notion that women need to be fucked—which is the *a priori* assumption of the rapist—is directly derived from the specious conviction that the only worth is phallic worth: men are willing, or able, to recognize us only when we have attached to us a cock in the course of sexual intercourse. Then, and only then, we are for them *real women*.

As nonphallic beings, women are defined as submissive, passive, virtually inert. For all of patriarchal history, we have been defined by law, custom, and habit as inferior because of our nonphallic bodies. Our sexual definition is one of "masochistic passivity": "masochistic" because even men recognize their systematic sadism against us; "passivity" not because we are naturally passive, but because our chains are very heavy and as a result, we cannot move.

The fact is that in order to stop rape, and all of the other systematic abuses against us, we must destroy these very definitions of masculinity and femininity, of men and women. We must destroy completely and for all time the personality structures "dominant-active, or male" and "submissive-passive, or female." We must excise them from our social fabric, destroy any and all institutions based on them, render them vestigial, useless. We must destroy the very structure of culture as we know it, its art, its churches, its laws; we must eradicate from consciousness and memory all of the images, institutions, and structural mental sets that turn men into rapists by definition and women into victims by definition. Until we do, rape will remain our primary sexual model and women will be raped by men.

As women, we must begin this revolutionary work. When we change, those who define themselves over and against us will have to kill us all, change, or die. In order to change, we must renounce every male definition we have ever learned; we must renounce male definitions and descriptions of our lives, our bodies, our needs, our wants, our worth—we must take for ourselves the power of naming. We must refuse to be complicit in a sexual-social system that is built on our labor as an inferior slave class. We must unlearn the passivity we have been trained to over thousands of years. We must unlearn the masochism we have been trained to over thousands of years. And, most importantly, in freeing ourselves, we must refuse to imitate the phallic identities of men. We must not internalize their values and we must not replicate their crimes. In 1870, Susan B. Anthony wrote to a friend:

> So while I do not pray for anybody or any party to commit out rages, still I do pray, and that earnestly and constantly, for some terrific shock to startle the women of this nation into a self-respect which will compel them to see the abject degradation of their present position; which will force them to break their yoke of bondage, and give them faith in themselves; which will make them proclaim their allegiance to woman first; which will enable them to see that man can no more feel, speak, or act for woman than could the old slaveholder for his slave. The fact is, women are in chains, and their servitude is all the more debasing because they do not realize it. O, to compel them to see and feel, and to give them the courage and conscience to speak and act for their own freedom, though they face the scorn and contempt of all the world for doing it.[26]

Isn't rape the outrage that will do this, sisters, and isn't it time?

153 Bridge street
Northampton, Mass 01060
June 15, 1978

Dear Mom and Dad,

I have published articles in the past years that I havent
mentioned, because there is no particular reason to. Or, for
instance, when a piece appeared in Ms. quitexxxxxx awhile ago,
I mentioned it, but there was no particular reason to go into it.

Now I have just published a piece which I want to tell you about.
Since I told you about my "Lesbian pride" lecture before <u>Our
Blood</u> appeared, it has been quite difficult for me to talk about my
work with you. I am sure you can understand that.

In the July issue of <u>Mother Jones</u>, a leftist xxxxx magazine
published in San Francisco but distributed nationally--quite, a
fine magazine--I have an essay of which I am very proud, but
which I am afraid will upset you and cause you pain. They have
titled it "The Bruise That Doesn't Heal," a rather silly title I think.
I called it "A Battered Wife Survives." It is first person, nonfiction,
about the fact that I was a battered wife.

The fact that I managed to write this, after so many years of not
being able to, is something of which I am proud. I wrote it because
I want to help the literally millions of women who are in the
situation I was in. Because I have the talent to write, I also have
a responsibility to write the truth about many things that many
people do not want to x face, or cannot x face.

The piece mentions you in passing, but does not blame you. I
do not go into what happened in Amsterdam, when you came
to visit. It is not a piece about particulars, but about the general
experience.

I wrote the piece around my last birthday, when I turned 31. The
piece should not embarrass you, but I am afraid that it will, since
my work has so often in the past.

There are many kinds of pain one can feel. One kind is empathy
for the sufferings of another. Another kind of pain comes from

feeling embarrassed or humiliated because something bad has happened, and one doesn't want others to know. I am hoping that, if you read this piece, you will feel the first kind of pain, not the second. Once Gloria Steinem and I had a conversation about "Feminism, Art, and My Mother Sylvia," the first essay in Our Blood. She loves that piece very much. In the course of our conversation, she told me that she often feels sorry for the families of writers because they so often feel exposed by the work of the writer in the family, and so often suffer from the prejudices of those around them. She told me that her own mother changed her last name, so as not to be identified with the notorious "Gloria Steinem." (Her father is dead.) Needless to say, this hurt her very much, but she did understand it. It reminded me of when Uncle Leon teases we about why I didnt change my name before I started writing. "It's my name," I told him.

I have always been proud of both of you, even though sometimes you have not thought so. I hope that if you read this piece you will be proud of me--of the strength that I found, of my power as a writer, and of my commitment to helping other women.

Grace Paley told me when I was 18 I think that I should not show you my work. She has found it impossible to show her parents and sisters her work, because it disturbs them profoundly. But I have felt in the past, and feel now, that since others may read this, and it may have an effect on you, you should know about it.

Now that I am really a professional writer of some stature, I dont generally think of sending you my work. I cant keep track of what is published and where. But since this is liable to have a farreaching impact, I feel responsible to tell you about it. Also, because I wrote it and it is true. I cant write to you about the things other people write about me, for instance. I feel that by now you have had ample opportunity to see how things are distorted. Most of what is written about people is rumor at best, often pure fabrication. So if someone writes something dreadful about me, I am not going to (nor have I in the past) bring it to yr attention. Why? For what reason?

But this is different. It strikes the same deep chords as the House of Detention situation, or the Lesbian Pride essay. I hope that you will stand with me in this, because being able to write this essay has been one of the finest achievements of my life.

As far as I know, the magazine is not on the newsstands yet. When it was accepted for publication many months ago, the magazine was not distributed on newsstands, just to subscribers. Publication of the essay was postponed many months, and I was not certain when it would appear. In these months, the circulation of <u>Mother Jones</u> has increased greatly, and it is on newstands, as far as I know, in most places.

So rather than have this come at you from someone else, I am writing to tell you about it. I hope that yr response will he one of support, not of anger.

The essay, read so far on a small scale, has elicited much response, all of it thus far extremely positive. Women extremely grateful to me for writing it. Perhaps knowing that, and that that is likely to be its main reception in the larger world, will mean something to you.

I have told you often, and said in my books, that whatever courage I have, or ability to realize my talent, I owe to the both of you. I am saying that again here. I am hoping that if you encounter pettiness or stupidity on the part of family and friends, you will not see that as more important than what I have done.

You will probably receive this before I call on Sunday to say Happy Fathers Day. I do not know if you will see the essay before then. I could have gone along, leaving to chance whether you would see it or not, but I did not want to risk having you ignorant of the piece if someone brings it up.

I also hope so much that this will not lead to another period of no communication, anger, and hurt. I would like it so much if you could appreciate me for having had the courage to write this piece, and the talent to write it so well.

Please be with me in this, not against me. It is the hardest thing, personally, that I have ever done.

Love,
Andrea

LETTERS FROM A WAR ZONE

1988

A BATTERED WIFE SURVIVES
1978

*This essay is now ten years old. Wife-beating is the most commonly com-
mitted violent crime in the United States, according to the FBI. In New
Hampshire, I meet eighteen-year-old women who work in a battered
women's shelter. One talks about how she feels when women decide to go
home and she has to drive them. In Toronto, I meet two women who
travel through rural Canada in the dead of winter to find and help
battered women. In a project called "Off the Beaten Path," Susan
Faupel is walking 600 miles—from Chicago, Illinois, to Little Rock,
Arkansas—for battered women. In a southern state, I am driven to the
airport by an organizer of the rally I have just spoken at; the car keeps
veering off the road as she says she is being battered now; when? I keep
asking; now, now, she says; she has gone to the organizing meetings for
the antipornography demonstrations with make-up covering the bruises
on her face. In the South especially I meet lesbians, married with children, who are being beaten by their husbands—afraid to leave because
they would lose their children, battered because they are lesbian. In
Seattle, I find safe houses, secret from most feminists, for women being
beaten by their women lovers. In small towns where there are no shelters, especially in the North and Midwest, I find safe houses organized
like an underground railroad for women escaping battery. (1988)*

> I knew not but the next
> Would be my final inch—
> —Emily Dickinson

In a few days, I will turn thirty-one. I am filled with both pride and dread.

The pride comes from accomplishment. I have done what I wanted to do more than any other thing in life. I have become a writer, published two books of integrity and worth. I did not know what those two books would cost me, how very difficult it would be to write them, to survive the opposition to them. I did not imagine that they would demand of me ruthless devotion, spartan discipline, continuing material deprivation, visceral anxiety about the rudiments of survival, and a faith in myself made more of iron than innocence. I have also learned to live alone, developed a rigorous emotional independence, a self-directed creative will, and a passionate commitment to my own sense of right and wrong. This I had to learn not only to do, but to want to do. I have learned not to lie to myself about what I value—in art, in love, in friendship. I have learned to take responsibility for my own intense convictions and my own real limitations. I have learned to resist most of the forms of coercion and flattery that would rob me of access to my own conscience. I believe that, for a woman, I have accomplished a great deal.

The dread comes from memory. Memory of terror and insupportable pain can overpower the present, any present, cast shadows so dark that the mind falters, unable to find light, and the body trembles, unable to find any solid ground. The past literally overtakes one, seizes one, holds one immobile in dread. Each year, near my birthday, I remember, involuntarily, that when I was twenty-five I was still a battered wife, a woman whose whole life was speechless desperation. By the time I was twenty-six I was still a terrorized woman. The husband I had left would come out of nowhere, beat or hit or kick me, disappear. A ghost with a fist, a lightning flash followed by riveting pain. There was no protection or safety. I was ripped up inside.

My mind was still on the edge of its own destruction. Smothering anxiety, waking nightmares, cold sweats, sobs that I choked on were the constants of my daily life. I did not breathe; I gulped in air to try to get enough of it each minute to survive a blow that might come a second, any second, later. But I had taken the first step: he had to find me; I was no longer at home waiting for him. On my twenty-fifth birthday, when I had lived one quarter of a century, I was nearly dead, almost catatonic, without the will to live. By my twenty-sixth birthday, I wanted more than anything to live. I was one year old, an infant born out of a corpse, still with the smell of death on her, but hating death. This year I am six years old, and the anguish of my own long and dreadful dying comes back to haunt me. But this year, for the first time, I do more than tremble from the fear that even memory brings, I do more than grieve. This year, I sit at my desk and write.

———

Rape is very terrible. I have been raped and I have talked with hundreds of women who have been raped. Rape is an experience that pollutes one's life. But it is an experience that is contained within the boundaries of one's own life. In the end, one's life is larger.

Assault by a stranger or within a relationship is very terrible. One is hurt, undermined, degraded, afraid. But one's life is larger.

A battered wife has a life smaller than the terror that destroys her over time.

Marriage circumscribes her life. Law, social convention, and economic necessity encircle her. She is roped in. Her pride depends on projecting her own satisfaction with her lot to family and friends. Her pride depends on believing that her husband is devoted to her and, when that is no longer possible, convincing others anyway.

The husband's violence against her contradicts everything she has been taught about life, marriage, love, and the sanctity of the family. Regardless of the circumstances in which she grew up, she has been taught to believe in romantic love and the essential perfection of married life. Failure is personal. Individuals fail because of what is wrong with them. The troubles of individuals, pervasive as they are, do not reflect on the institution of marriage, nor do they negate her belief in the happy ending, promised everywhere as the final result of male-female conflict. Marriage is intrinsically good. Marriage is a woman's proper goal. Wife-beating is not on a woman's map of the world when she marries. It is, quite literally, beyond her imagination. Because she does not believe that it could have happened, that *he* could have done that to *her*, she cannot believe that it will happen again. He is her *husband*. No, it did not happen. And when it happens again, she still denies it. It was an accident, a mistake. And when it happens again, she blames the hardships of his life outside the home. There he experiences terrible hurts and frustrations. These account for his mistreatment of her. She will find a way to comfort him, to make it up to him. And when it happens again, she blames herself. She will be better, kinder, quieter, more of whatever he likes, less of whatever he dislikes. And when it happens again, and when it happens again, and when it happens again, she learns that she has nowhere to go, no one to turn to, no one who will believe her, no one who will help her, no one who will protect her. If she leaves, she will return. She will leave and return and leave and return. She will find that her parents, doctor, the police, her best friend, the neighbors upstairs and across the hall and next door, all despise the woman who cannot keep her own house in order, her injuries hidden, her despair to herself, her smile amiable and convincing. She will find that society loves its central lie—that marriage means happiness—and hates the woman who stops telling it even to save her own life.

———

The memory of the physical pain is vague. I remember, of course, that I was hit, that I was kicked. I do not remember when or how often. It blurs. I remember him banging my head against the floor until I passed out. I remember being kicked in the stomach. I remember being hit over and over, the blows hitting different parts of my body as I tried to get away from him. I remember a terrible leg injury from a series of kicks. I remember crying and I remember screaming and I remember begging. I remember him punching me in the breasts. One can remember that one had horrible physical pain, but that memory does not bring the pain back to the body. Blessedly, the mind can remember these events without the body reliving them. If one survives without permanent injury, the physical pain dims, recedes, ends. It lets go.

The fear does not let go. The fear is the eternal legacy. At first, the fear infuses every minute of every day. One does not sleep. One cannot bear to be alone. The fear is in the cavity of one's chest. It crawls like lice on one's skin. It makes the legs buckle, the heart race. It locks one's jaw. One's hands tremble. One's throat closes up. The fear makes one entirely desperate. Inside, one is always in upheaval, clinging to anyone who shows any kindness, cowering in the presence of any threat. As years pass, the fear recedes, but it does not let go. It never lets go. And when the mind remembers fear, it also relives it. The victim of encapsulating violence carries both the real fear and the memory of fear with her always. Together, they wash over her like an ocean, and if she does not learn to swim in that terrible sea, she goes under.

And then, there is the fact that, during those weeks that stretch into years when one is a battered wife, one's mind is shattered slowly over time, splintered into a thousand pieces. The mind is slowly submerged in chaos and despair, buried broken and barely alive in an impenetrable tomb of isolation. This isolation is so absolute, so killing, so morbid, so malignant and devouring that there is nothing in one's life but it, it. One is entirely shrouded in a loneliness that no earthquake could move. Men have asked over the centuries a question that, in their hands, ironically becomes abstract: "What is reality?" They have written complicated volumes on this question. The woman who was a battered wife and has escaped knows the answer: reality is when something is happening to you and you know it and can say it and when you say it other people understand what you mean and believe you. That is reality, and the battered wife, imprisoned alone in a nightmare that *is* happening to her, has lost it and cannot find it anywhere.

I remember the isolation as the worst anguish I have ever known. I remember the pure and consuming madness of being invisible and unreal, and every blow making me more invisible and more unreal, as the worst desperation I have ever known. I remember those who turned away, pretending not to see the injuries—my parents, dear god, especially my parents; my closest female friend, next door, herself suffocating in a marriage poisoned by psychic, not physical, violence; the doctor so officious and aloof; the women in the neighborhood who heard every scream; the men in the neighborhood who smiled, yes, lewdly, as they half looked away, half stared, whenever they saw me; my husband's family, especially my mother-in-law, whom I loved, my sisters-in-law, whom I loved. I remember the frozen muscles of my smile as I gave false explanations of injuries that no one wanted to hear anyway. I remember slavishly conforming to every external convention that would demonstrate that I was a "good wife, " that would convince other people that I was happily married. And as the weight of social convention became insupportable, I remember withdrawing further and further into that open grave where so many women hide waiting to die—the house. I went out to shop only when I had to, I walked my dogs, I ran out screaming, looking for help and shelter when I had the strength to escape, with no money, often no coat, nothing but terror and tears. I met only averted eyes, cold stares, and the vulgar sexual aggression of lone, laughing men that sent me running home to a danger that was at least familiar and familial. Home, mine as well as his. Home, the only place I had. Finally, everything inside crumbled. I gave up. I sat, I stared, I waited, passive and paralyzed, speaking to no one, minimally maintaining myself and my animals, as my husband stayed away for longer and longer periods of time, slamming in only to thrash and leave. No one misses the wife who disappears. No one investigates her disappearance. After awhile, people stop asking where she is, especially if they have already refused to face what has been happening to her. Wives, after all, belong in the home. Nothing outside it depends on them. This is a bitter lesson, and the battered wife learns it in the bitterest way.

———

The anger of the survivor is murderous. It is more dangerous to her than to the one who hurt her. She does not believe in murder, even to save herself. She does not believe in murder, even though it would be more merciful punishment than he deserves. She wants him dead but will not kill him. She never gives up wanting him dead. The clarity of the survivor is chilling. Once she breaks out of the prison of terror and violence in which she has been nearly destroyed, a process that takes years, it is very difficult to lie to her or to manipulate her. She sees through the social strategies that have controlled her as a woman, the sexual strategies that have reduced her to a shadow of her own native possibilities. She knows that her life depends on never being taken in by romantic illusion or sexual hallucination.

The emotional severity of the survivor appears to others, even those closest to her, to be cold and unyielding, ruthless in its intensity. She knows too much about suffering to try to measure it when it is real, but she despises self-pity. She is self-protective, not out of arrogance, but because she has been ruined by her own fragility. Like Anya, the survivor of the Nazi concentration camps in Susan Fromberg Schaeffer's beautiful novel of the same name, she might say: "So what have I learned? I have learned not to believe in suffering. It is a form of death. If it is severe enough it is a poison; it kills the emotions." She knows that some of her own emotions have been killed and she distrusts those who are infatuated with suffering, as if it were a source of life, not death.

In her heart she is a mourner for those who have not survived.

In her soul she is a warrior for those who are now as she was then.

In her life she is both celebrant and proof of women's capacity and will to survive, to become, to act, to change self and society. And each year she is stronger and there are more of her.

PORNOGRAPHY:
MEN POSSESSING WOMEN

1979–1989

INTRODUCTION
1989

(. . .)

That same night [July 20, 1944, the attempt by the generals to assassinate Hitler] he [Goebbels] turned his house into "a prison, headquarters and court rolled into one"; Goebbels himself headed a commission of investigation; and he and Himmler cross-examined the arrested generals throughout the night. Those condemned, then or thereafter, were executed with revolting cruelty. They were hanged from meat-hooks and slowly strangled. Goebbels ordered a film to be made of their trial and execution: it was to be shown, *in terrorem* to Wehrmacht audiences. However, the reaction of the first audience was so hostile that it had to be suppressed.

—Hugh Trevor-Roper in his introduction to
Final Entries 1945: The Diaries of Joseph Goebbels

As far as I can determine, Goebbels' film of the generals slowly, horribly dying—their innards caving in from the force of gravity on their hung bodies, the slow strangulation pushing out their tongues and eyes and causing erection (which strangulation invariably does in the male)—was the first snuff film. The master of hate propaganda didn't get it right though—a rare lapse. Audiences became physically sick. These were Nazi audiences watching Nazi generals, men of power, the society's patriarchs, so white they were Aryan; rulers, not slaves. It only works when the torture is done on those who have been dehumanized, made inferior—not just in the eyes of the beholder but in his real world. Goebbels started out with cartoons of Jews before the Nazis came to power; he could have moved on to the films made in Dachau in 1942, for instance, of "the reactions of the men placed in the Luftwaffe's low-pressure chambers"[1]; desensitizing his Nazi audiences to the humiliation, the torture, of Jews, he could have made a film that would have worked—of Jews hanging from meat hooks, slowly strangled. But never of power, never of those who were the same, never of those who had been fully human to the audience the day before, never of those who had been respected. Never.

Des Pres says it is easier to kill if "the victim exhibits self-disgust; if he cannot lift his eyes for humiliation, or if lifted they show only emptiness. . ."[2] There is some pornography in which women are that abject, that easy to kill, that close to being dead already. There is quite a lot of it; and it is highly prized, expensive. There is still more pornography in which the woman wets her lips and pushes out her ass and says hurt me. She is painted so that the man cannot miss the mark: her lips are bright red so that he can find the way into her throat; her vaginal lips are pink or purple so that he can't miss; her anus is darkened while her buttocks are flooded with light. Her eyes glisten. She smiles. Sticking knives up her own vagina, she smiles. She comes. The Jews didn't do it to themselves and they didn't orgasm. In contemporary American pornography, of course, the Jews do do it to themselves—they, usually female, seek out the Nazis, go voluntarily to concentration camps, beg a domineering Nazi to hurt them, cut them, burn them—and they do climax, stupendously, to both sadism and death. But in life, the Jews didn't orgasm. Of course, neither do women; not in life. But no one, not even Goebbels, said the Jews liked it. The society agreed that the Jews deserved it, but not that they wanted it and not that it gave them sexual pleasure. There were no photographs from Ravensbruck concentration camp of the prostitutes who were incarcerated there along with other women gasping for breath in pleasure; the gypsies didn't orgasm either. There were no photographs—real or simulated—of the Jews smiling and waving the Nazis closer, getting on the trains with their hands happily fingering their exposed genitals or using Nazi guns, swastikas, or Iron Crosses for sexual penetration. Such behaviors would not have been credible even in a society that believed the Jews were both subhuman and intensely sexual in the racist sense—the men rapists, the women whores. The questions now really are: why is pornography credible in our society? how can anyone believe it? And then: how subhuman would women have to be for the pornography to be true? To the men who use pornography, how subhuman are women? If men believe the pornography because it makes them come—them, not the women—what is sex to men and how will women survive it?

This book—written from 1977 through 1980, published in 1981 after two separate publishers reneged on contractual agreements to publish it (and a dozen more refused outright), out of print in the United States for the last several years—takes power, sadism, and dehumanization seriously. I am one of those serious women. This book asks how power, sadism, and dehumanization work in pornography—against women, for men—to establish the sexual and social subordination of women to men. This book is distinguished from most other books on pornography by its bedrock conviction that the power is real, the cruelty is real, the sadism is real, the subordination is real: the political crime against women is real. This book says that power used to destroy women is atrocity. *Pornography. Men Possessing Women* is not, and was never intended to be, an effete intellectual exercise. I want real change, an end to the social power of men over women; more starkly, his boot off my neck. In this book, I wanted to dissect male dominance; do an autopsy on it, but it wasn't dead. Instead, there were artifacts—films, photographs, books—an archive of evidence and documentation of crimes against women. This was a living archive, commercially alive, carnivorous in its use of women, saturating the environment of daily life, explosive and expanding, vital because it was synonymous with sex for the men who made it and the men who used it—men so arrogant in their power over us that they published the pictures of what they did to us, how they used us, expecting submission from us, compliance; we were supposed to follow the orders implicit in the pictures. Instead, some of us understood that we could look at those pictures and see them—see the men. Know thyself, if you are lucky enough to have a self that hasn't been destroyed by rape in its many forms; and then, know the bastard on top of you. This book is about him, the collective him: who he is; what he wants; what he needs (the key to both his rage and his political vulnerability); how he's diddling you and why it feels so bad and hurts so much; what's keeping him in place on you; why he won't move off of you; what it's going to take to blow him loose. A different kind of blow job. Is he scared? You bet.

Pornography. Men Possessing Women also puts pornography, finally, into its appropriate context. A system of dominance and submission, pornography has the weight and significance of any other historically real torture or punishment of a group of people because of a condition of birth; it has the weight and significance of any other historically real exile of human beings from human dignity, the purging of them from a shared community of care and rights and respect. Pornography happens. It is not outside the world of material reality because it happens to women, and it is not outside the world of material reality because it makes men come. The man's ejaculation is real. The woman on whom his semen is spread, a typical use in pornography, is real. Men characterize pornography as something mental because their minds, their thoughts, their dreams, their fantasies, are more real to them than women's bodies or lives; in fact, men have used their social power to characterize a $10-billion-a-year trade in women as fantasy. This is a spectacular example of how those in power cannibalize not only people but language. "We do not know," wrote George Steiner, "whether the study of the humanities, of the noblest that has been said and thought, can do very much to humanize. We do not know; and surely there is something rather terrible in our doubt whether the study and delight a man finds in Shakespeare make him any less capable of organizing a concentration camp."[3] As long as language is a weapon of power—used to destroy the expressive abilities of the powerless by destroying their sense of reality—we do know. Beaver knows.

Some have said that pornography is a superficial target; but, truly, this is wrong. Pornography incarnates male supremacy. It is the DNA of male dominance. Every rule of sexual abuse, every nuance of sexual sadism, every highway and byway of sexual exploitation, is encoded in it. It's what men want us to be, think we are, make us into; how men use us; not because biologically they are men but because this is how their social power is organized. From the perspective of the political activist, pornography is the blueprint of male supremacy; it shows how male supremacy is built. The political activist needs to know the blueprint. In cultural terms, pornography is the fundamentalism of male dominance. Its absolutism on women and sexuality, its dogma, is merciless. Women are consigned to rape and prostitution; heretics are disappeared and destroyed. Pornography is the essential sexuality of male power: of hate, of ownership, of hierarchy; of sadism, of dominance. The premises of pornography are controlling in every rape and every rape case, whenever a woman is battered or prostituted, in incest, including in incest that occurs before a child can even speak, and in murder— murders of women by husbands, lovers, and serial killers. If this is superficial, what's deep?

POWER

The major theme of pornography as a genre is male power, its nature, its magnitude, its use, its meaning. Male power, as expressed in and through pornography, is discernible in discrete but interwoven, reinforcing strains: the power of self, physical power over and against others, the power of terror, the power of naming, the power of owning, the power of money, and the power of sex. These strains of male power are intrinsic to both the substance and production of pornography; and the ways and means of pornography are the ways and means of male power. The harmony and coherence of hateful values, perceived by men as normal and neutral values when applied to women, distinguish pornography as message, thing, and experience. The strains of male power are embodied in pornography's form and content, in economic control of and distribution of wealth within the industry, in the picture or story as thing, in the photographer or writer as aggressor, in the critic or intellectual who through naming assigns value, in the actual use of models, in the application of the material in what is called real life (which women are commanded to regard as distinct from fantasy). A saber penetrating a vagina is a weapon; so is the camera or pen that renders it; so is the penis for which it substitutes (*vagina* literally means "sheath"). The persons who produce the image are also weapons as men deployed in war become in their persons weapons. Those who defend or protect the image are, in this same sense, weapons. The values in the pornographic work are also manifest in everything surrounding the work.

The valuation of women in pornography is a secondary theme in that the degradation of women exists in order to postulate, exercise, and celebrate male power. Male power, in degrading women, is first concerned with itself, its perpetuation, expansion, intensification, and elevation. In her essay on the Marquis de Sade, Simone de Beauvoir describes Sade's sexuality as autistic. Her use of the word is figurative, since an autistic child does not require an object of violence outside of himself (most autistic children are male). Male power expressed in pornography is autistic as de Beauvoir uses the word in reference to Sade: it is violent and self-obsessed; no perception of another being ever modifies its behavior or persuades it to abandon violence as a form of self-pleasuring. Male power is the raison d'être of pornography; the degradation of the female is the means of achieving this power.

––––––

The photograph is captioned "BEAVER HUNTERS." Two white men, dressed as hunters, sit in a black Jeep. The Jeep occupies almost the whole frame of the picture. The two men carry rifles. The rifles extend above the frame of the photograph into the white space surrounding it. The men and the Jeep face into the camera. Tied onto the hood of the black Jeep is a white woman. She is tied with thick rope. She is spread-eagle. Her pubic hair and crotch are the dead center of the car hood and the photograph. Her head is turned to one side, tied down by rope that is pulled taut across her neck, extended to and wrapped several times around her wrists, tied around the rearview mirrors of the Jeep, brought back around her arms, crisscrossed under her breasts and over her thighs, drawn down and wrapped around the bumper of the Jeep, tied around her ankles. Between her feet on the car bumper, in orange with black print, is a sticker that reads: I brake for Billy Carter. The text under the photograph reads: "Western sportsmen report beaver hunting was particularly good throughout the Rocky Mountain region during the past season. These two hunters easily bagged their limit in the high country. They told HUSTLER that they stuffed and mounted their trophy as soon as they got her home."

The men in the photograph are self-possessed; that is, they possess the power of self. This power radiates from the photograph. They are armed: first, in the sense that they are fully clothed; second, because they carry rifles, which are made more prominent, suggesting erection, by extending outside the frame of the photograph; third, because they are shielded by being inside the vehicle, framed by the windshield; fourth, because only the top parts of their bodies are shown. The woman is possessed; that is, she has no self. A captured animal, she is naked, bound, exposed on the hood of the car outdoors, her features not distinguishable because of the way her head is twisted and tied down. The men sit, supremely still and confident, displaying the captured prey for the camera. The stillness of the woman is like the stillness of death, underlined by the evocation of taxidermy in the caption. He is, he takes; she is not, she is taken.

The photograph celebrates the physical power of men over women. They are hunters, use guns. They have captured and bound a woman. They will stuff and mount her. She is a trophy. While one could argue that the victory of two armed men over a woman is no evidence of physical superiority, the argument is impossible as one experiences (or remembers) the photograph. The superior strength of men is irrefutably established by the fact of the photograph and the knowledge that one brings to it: that it expresses an authentic and commonplace relationship of the male strong to the female weak, wherein the hunt—the targeting, tracking down, pursuing, the chase, the overpowering of, the immobilizing of, even the wounding of—is common practice, whether called sexual pursuit, seduction, or romance. The photograph exists in an immediate context that supports the assertion of this physical power; and in the society that is the larger context, there is no viable and meaningful reality to contradict the physical power of male over female expressed in the photograph.

In the photograph, the power of terror is basic. The men are hunters with guns. Their prey is women. They have caught a woman and tied her onto the hood of a car. The terror is implicit in the content of the photograph, but beyond that the photograph strikes the female viewer dumb with fear. One perceives that the bound woman must be in pain. The very power to make the photograph (to use the model, to tie her in that way) and the fact of the photograph (the fact that someone did use the model, did tie her in that way, that the photograph is published in a magazine and seen by millions of men who buy it specifically to see such photographs) evoke fear in the female observer unless she entirely dissociates herself from the photograph: refuses to believe or understand that real persons posed for it, refuses to see the bound person as a woman like herself. Terror is finally the content of the photograph, and it is also its effect on the female observer. That men have the power and desire to make, publish, and profit from the photograph engenders fear. That millions more men enjoy the photograph makes the fear palpable. That men who in general champion civil rights defend the photograph without experiencing it as an assault on women intensifies the fear, because if the horror of the photograph does not resonate with these men, that horror is not validated as horror in male culture, and women are left without apparent recourse. Rimbaud's devastating verse comes to mind: "One evening I seated Beauty on my knees. And I found her bitter. And I cursed her. / I armed myself against justice."[1]

The threat in the language accompanying the photograph is also fierce and frightening. She is an animal, think of deer fleeing the hunter, think of seals clubbed to death, think of species nearly extinct. The men will stuff and mount her as a trophy: think of killing displayed proudly as triumph.

Here is the power of naming. Here she is named beaver. In the naming she is diminished to the point of annihilation; her humanity is canceled out. Instead of turning to the American Civil Liberties Union for help, she should perhaps turn to a group that tries to prevent cruelty to animals—beaver, bird, chick, bitch, dog, pussy, and so forth. The words that transform her into an animal have permanence: the male has done the naming. The power of naming includes the freedom to joke. The hunters will brake for Billy Carter. The ridicule is not deadly; they will let him live. The real target of the ridicule is the fool who brakes for animals, here equated with women. The language on the bumper sticker suggests the idea of the car in motion, which would otherwise be lacking. The car becomes a weapon, a source of death, its actual character as males use it. One is reminded of the animal run over on the road, a haunting image of blood and death. One visualizes the car, with the woman tied onto its hood, in motion crashing into something or someone.

Owning is expressed in every aspect of the photograph. These hunters are sportsmen, wealth suggested in hunting as a leisure-time pursuit of pleasure. They are equipped and outfitted. Their car shines. They have weapons: guns, a car. They have a woman, bound and powerless, to do with as they like. They will stuff and mount her. Their possession of her extends over time, even into (her) death. She is owned as a thing, a trophy, or as something dead, a dead bird, a dead deer; she is dead beaver. The camera and the photographer behind it also own the woman. The camera uses and keeps her. The photographer uses her and keeps the image of her. The publisher of the photograph can also claim her as a trophy. He has already mounted her and put her on display. Hunting as a sport suggests that these hunters have hunted before and will hunt again, that each captured woman will be used and owned, stuffed and mounted, that this right to own inheres in man's relationship to nature, that this right to own is so natural and basic that it can be taken entirely for granted, that is, expressed as play or sport.

Wealth is implicit in owning. The woman is likened to food (a dead animal), the hunter's most immediate form of wealth. As a trophy, she is wealth displayed. She is a commodity, part of the measure of male wealth. Man as hunter owns the earth, the things of it, its natural resources. She is part of the wildlife to be plundered for profit and pleasure, collected, used. That they "bagged their limit," then used what they had caught, is congruent with the idea of economy as a sign of mature masculinity.

The fact of the photograph signifies the wealth of men as a class. One class simply does not so use another class unless that usage is maintained in the distribution of wealth. The female model's job is the job of one who is economically imperiled, a sign of economic degradation. The relationship of the men to the woman in the photograph is not fantasy; it is symbol, meaningful because it is rooted in reality. The photograph shows a relationship of rich to poor that is actual in the larger society. The fact of the photograph in relation to its context—an industry that generates wealth by producing images of women abjectly used, a society in which women cannot adequately earn money because women are valued precisely as the woman in the photograph is valued—both proves and perpetuates the real connection between masculinity and wealth. The sexual-economic significance of the photograph is so simple that it is easily overlooked: the photograph could not exist as a type of photograph that produces wealth without the wealth of men to produce and consume it.

Sex as power is the most explicit meaning of the photograph. The power of sex unambiguously resides in the male, though the characterization of the female as a wild animal suggests that the sexuality of the untamed female is dangerous to men. But the triumph of the hunters is the nearly universal triumph of men over women, a triumph ultimately expressed in the stuffing and mounting. The hunters are figures of virility. Their penises are hidden but their guns are emphasized. The car, beloved ally of men in the larger culture, also indicates virility, especially when a woman is tied to it naked instead of draped over it wearing an evening gown. The pornographic image explicates the advertising image, and the advertising image echoes the pornographic image.

The power of sex is ultimately defined as the power of conquest. They hunted her down, captured, tied, stuffed, and mounted her. The excitement is precisely in the nonconsensual character of the event. The hunt, the ropes, the guns, show that anything done to her was or will be done against her will. Here again, the valuation of conquest as being natural—of nature, of man in nature, of natural man—is implicit in the visual and linguistic imagery. The power of sex, in male terms, is also funereal. Death permeates it. The male erotic trinity—sex, violence, and death—reigns supreme. She will be or is dead. They did or will kill her. Everything that they do to or with her is violence. Especially evocative is the phrase "stuffed and mounted her," suggesting as it does both sexual violation and embalming.

Everything in life is part of it. Nothing is off in its own corner, isolated from the rest. While on the surface this may seem self-evident, the favorite conceit of male culture is that experience can be fractured, literally its bones split, and that one can examine the splinters as if they were not part of the bone, or the bone as if it were not part of the body. This conceit replicates in its values and methodology the sexual reductionism of the male and is derived from it. Everything is split apart: intellect from feeling and/or imagination; act from consequence; symbol from reality; mind from body. Some part substitutes for the whole and the whole is sacrificed to the part. So the scientist can work on bomb or virus, the artist on poem, the photographer on picture, with no appreciation of its meaning outside itself; and even reduce each of these things to an abstract element that is part of its composition and focus on that abstract element and nothing else—literally attribute meaning to or discover meaning in nothing else. In the mid-twentieth century, the post-Holocaust world, it is common for men to find meaning in nothing: nothing has meaning; Nothing is meaning. In prerevolu-tionary Russia, men strained to be nihilists; it took enormous effort. In this world, here and now, after Auschwitz, after Hiroshima, after Vietnam, after Jonestown, men need not strain. Nihilism, like gravity, is a law of nature, male nature. The men, of course, are tired. It has been an exhausting period of extermination and devastation, on a scale genuinely new, with new methods, new possibilities. Even when faced with the probable extinction of themselves at their own hand, men refuse to look at the whole, take all the causes and all the effects into account, perceive the intricate connections between the world they make and themselves. They are alienated, they say, from this world of pain and torment; they make romance out of this alienation so as to avoid taking responsibility for what they do and what they are. Male dissociation from life is not new or particularly modern, but the scale and intensity of this disaffection are new. And in the midst of this Brave New World, how comforting and familiar it is to exercise passionate cruelty on women. The old-fashioned values still obtain. The world may end tomorrow, but tonight there is rape—a kiss, a fuck, a pat on the ass, a fist in the face. In the intimate world of men and women, there is no mid-twentieth century distinct from any other century. There are only the old values, women there for the taking, the means of taking determined by the male. It is ancient and it is modern; it is feudal, capitalist, socialist; it is caveman and astronaut, agricultural and industrial, urban and rural. For men, the right to abuse women is elemental, the first principle, with no beginning unless one is willing to trace origins back to God and with no end plausibly in sight. For men, their right to control and abuse the bodies of women is the one comforting constant in a world rigged to blow up but they do not know when.

In pornography, men express the tenets of their unchanging faith, what they must believe is true of women and of themselves to sustain themselves as they are, to ward off recognition that a commitment to masculinity is a double-edged commitment to both suicide and genocide. In life, the objects are fighting back, rebelling, demanding that every breath be reckoned with as the breath of a living person, not a viper trapped under a rock, but an authentic, willful, living being. In pornography, the object is slut, sticking daggers up her vagina and smiling. A bible piling up its code for centuries, a secret corpus gone public, a private corpus gone political, pornography is the male's sacred stronghold, a monastic retreat for manhood on the verge of its own destruction. As one goes through the pictures of the tortured and maimed, reads the stories of gang rape and bondage, what emerges most clearly is a portrait of men who need to believe in their own absolute, unchangeable, omnipresent, eternal, limitless power over others. Every image reveals not the so-called object in it but the man who needs it: to keep his prick big when every bomb dwarfs it; to keep his sense of masculine self intact when the world of his own creation has made that masculine self a useless and rather silly anachronism; to keep women the enemy even though men will destroy him and he by being faithful to them will be responsible for that destruction; to sustain his belief in the righteousness of his real abuses of women when, in fact, they would be insupportable and unbearable if he dared to experience them as what they are—the bullying brutalities of a coward too afraid of other men to betray or abandon them. Pornography is the holy corpus of men who would rather die than change. Dachau brought into the bedroom and celebrated, every vile prison or dungeon brought into the bedroom and celebrated, police torture and thug mentality brought into the bedroom and celebrated—men reveal themselves and all that matters to them in these depictions of real history, plasticized and rarefied, represented as the common erotic stuff of male desire. And the pictures and stories lead right back to history—to peoples enslaved, maimed, murdered—because they show that, for men, the history of atrocity they pretend to mourn is coherent and utterly intentional if one views it as rooted in male sexual obsession. Pornography reveals that slavery, bondage, murder, and maiming have been acts suffused with pleasure for those who committed them or who vicariously experienced the power expressed in them. Pornography reveals that male pleasure is inextricably tied to victimizing, hurting, exploiting; that sexual fun and sexual passion in the privacy of the male imagination are inseparable from the brutality of male history. The private world of sexual dominance that men demand as their right and their freedom is the mirror image of the public world of sadism and atrocity that men consistently and self-righteously deplore. It is in the male experience of pleasure that one finds the meaning of male history.

The word *pornography*, derived from the ancient Greek *pórnē* and *graphos*, means "writing about whores." *Pórnē* means "whore," specifically and exclusively the lowest class of whore, which in ancient Greece was the brothel slut available to all male citizens. The *pórnē* was the cheapest (in the literal sense), least regarded, least protected of all women, including slaves. She was, simply and clearly and absolutely, a sexual slave. *Graphos* means "writing, etching, or drawing."

The word *pornography* does not mean "writing about sex" or "depictions of the erotic" or "depictions of sexual acts" or "depictions of nude bodies" or "sexual representations" or any other such euphemism. It means the graphic depiction of women as vile whores. In ancient Greece, not all prostitutes were considered vile: only the *porneia*.

Contemporary pornography strictly and literally conforms to the word's root meaning: the graphic depiction of vile whores, or, in our language, sluts, cows (as in: sexual cattle, sexual chattel), cunts. The word has not changed its meaning and the genre is not misnamed. The only change in the meaning of the word is with respect to its second part, *graphos*: now there are cameras—there is still photography, film, video. The methods of graphic depiction have increased in number and in kind: the content is the same; the meaning is the same; the purpose is the same; the status of the women depicted is the same; the sexuality of the women depicted is the same; the value of the women depicted is the same. With the technologically advanced methods of graphic depiction, real women are required for the depiction as such to exist.

The word *pornography* does not have any other meaning than the one cited here, the graphic depiction of the lowest whores. Whores exist to serve men sexually. Whores exist only within a framework of male sexual domination. Indeed, outside that framework the notion of whores would be absurd and the usage of women as whores would be impossible. The word *whore* is incomprehensible unless one is immersed in the lexicon of male domination. Men have created the group, the type, the concept, the epithet, the insult, the industry, the trade, the commodity, the reality of woman as whore. Woman as whore exists within the objective and real system of male sexual domination. The pornography itself is objective and real and central to the male sexual system. The valuation of women's sexuality in pornography is objective and real because women are so regarded and so valued. The force depicted in pornography is objective and real because force is so used against women. The debasing of women depicted in pornography and intrinsic to it is objective and real in that women are so debased. The uses of women depicted in pornography are objective and real because women are so used. The women used in pornography are used in pornography. The definition of women articulated systematically and consistently in pornography is objective and real in that real women exist within and must live with constant reference to the boundaries of this definition. The fact that pornography is widely believed to be "sexual representations" or "depictions of sex" emphasizes only that the valuation of women as low whores is widespread and that the sexuality of women is perceived as low and whorish in and of itself. The fact that pornography is widely believed to be "depictions of the erotic" means only that the debasing of women is held to be the real pleasure of sex. As Kate Millett wrote, women's sexuality is reduced to the one essential: "cunt. . . our essence, our offense."[1] The idea that pornography is "dirty" originates in the conviction that the sexuality of women is dirty and is actually portrayed in pornography; that women's bodies (especially women's genitals) are dirty and lewd in themselves. Pornography does not, as some claim, refute the idea that female sexuality is dirty: instead, pornography embodies and exploits this idea; pornography sells and promotes it.

In the United States, the pornography industry is larger than the record and film industries combined. In a time of widespread economic impoverishment, it is growing: more and more male consumers are eager to spend more and more money on pornography— on depictions of women as vile whores. Pornography is now carried by cable television; it is now being marketed for home use in video machines. The technology itself demands the creation of more and more *porneia* to meet the market opened up by the technology. Real women are tied up, stretched, hanged, fucked, gang-banged, whipped, beaten, and begging for more. In the photographs and films, real women are used as *porneia* and real women are depicted as *porneia*. To profit, the pimps must supply the *porneia* as the technology widens the market for the visual consumption of women being brutalized and loving it. One picture is worth a thousand words. The number of pictures required to meet the demands of the marketplace determines the number of *porneia* required to meet the demands of graphic depiction. The numbers grow as the technology and its accessibility grow. The technology by its very nature encourages more and more passive acquiescence to the graphic depictions. Passivity makes the already credulous consumer more credulous. He comes to the pornography a believer; he goes away from it a missionary. The technology itself legitimizes the uses of women conveyed by it.

In the male system, women are sex; sex is the whore. The whore is *pórnē*, the lowest whore, the whore who belongs to *all* male citizens: the slut, the cunt. Buying her is buying pornography. Having her is having pornography. Seeing her is seeing pornography. Seeing her sex, especially her genitals, is seeing pornography. Seeing her in sex is seeing the whore in sex. Using her is using pornography. Wanting her means wanting pornography. Being her means being pornography.

The best houses do not exhibit the women in cages.
—*The Nightless City or the History of the Yoshiwara Yukwaku*, 1899 report on a red-light district in Japan

Male sexual domination is a material system with an ideology and a metaphysics. The sexual colonialization of women's bodies is a material reality: men control the sexual and reproductive uses of women's bodies. The institutions of control include law, marriage, prostitution, pornography, health care, the economy, organized religion, and systematized physical aggression against women (for instance, in rape and battery). Male domination of the female body is the basic material reality of women's lives; and all struggle for dignity and self-determination is rooted in the struggle for actual control of one's own body, especially control over physical access to one's own body. The ideology of male sexual domination posits that men are superior to women by virtue of their penises; that physical possession of the female is a natural right of the male; that sex is, in fact, conquest and possession of the female, especially but not exclusively phallic conquest and phallic possession; that the use of the female body for sexual or reproductive purposes is a natural right of men; that the sexual will of men properly and naturally defines the parameters of a woman's sexual being, which is her whole identity. The metaphysics of male sexual domination is that women are whores. This basic truth transcends all lesser truths in the male system. One does not violate something by using it for what it is: neither rape nor prostitution is an abuse of the female because in both the female is fulfilling her natural function; that is why rape is absurd and incomprehensible as an abusive phenomenon in the male system, and so is prostitution, which is held to be voluntary even when the prostitute is hit, threatened, drugged, or locked in. The woman's effort to stay innocent, her effort to prove innocence, her effort to prove in any instance of sexual use that she was used against her will, is always and unequivocably an effort to prove that she is not a whore. The presumption that she is a whore is a metaphysical presumption: a presumption that underlies the system of reality in which she lives. A whore cannot be raped, only used. A whore by nature cannot be forced to whore—only revealed through circumstance to be the whore she is. The point is her nature, which is a whore's nature. The word *whore* can be construed to mean that she is a cunt with enough gross intelligence to manipulate, barter, or sell. The cunt wants it; the whore knows enough to use it. *Cunt* is the most reductive word; *whore* adds the dimension of character—greedy, manipulative, not nice. The word whore reveals her sensual nature (cunt) and her natural character.

"No prostitute of anything resembling intelligence," writes Mencken, "is under the slightest duress. . ."[1] "What is a prostitute?" asks William Acton in his classic work on prostitution. "She is a woman who gives for money that which she ought to give only for love. . ."[2] Jane Addams, who worked against the so-called white slave trade, noted that "[t]he one impression which the trial [of procurers] left upon our minds was that all the men concerned in the prosecution felt a keen sense of outrage against the method employed to secure the girl [kidnapping], but took for granted that the life she was about to lead was in the established order of things, if she had chosen it voluntarily."[3] Only the maternal can mitigate the whorish, an opposition more conceptual than real, based on the assumption that the maternal or older woman is no longer desired. Freud writes Jung that a son approaching adulthood naturally loses his incestuous desires for the mother "with her sagging belly and varicose veins."[4] René Guyon, who argued for male-defined sexual liberation, writes that "[w]oman ages much sooner. Much earlier in life she loses her freshness, her charm, and begins to look withered or over-ripe. She ceases to be an object of desire."[5] The mother is not the whore only when men have stopped desiring her.

Guyon, in whose name societies for sexual freedom exist today, held that women were defined exclusively by their sexuality, which was essentially, and intrinsically the sexuality of the prostitute. "Women's sexual parasitism," writes Guyon, "is innate. She has a congenital tendency to rely on man for support, availing herself of her sexual arts, offering in return for maintenance (and more, if she can get it) the partial or complete possession of her person."[6] This propensity for exchanging her body for material goods is her sexuality, her purpose, her passion, and consequently "[s]ale or contract, monogamy or harem—these words mean little to her in comparison with the goal."[7] For this reason, Guyon contends that even the so-called white slave trade—the organized abduction of lone or young or destitute women for the purposes of prostitution—cannot be construed as forcible prostitution:

> How hypocritical it is to speak of the White [sic] Slave Trade only as a means for recruiting the ranks of prostitution. The White [sic] Slave Trade is universal, being carried on with the consent of the "slaves," since every woman has a specific sexual

value. She must sell herself to the highest bidder, even though she cheat as to the quality of the goods.[8]

Like most male advocates of sexual freedom (the unrestrained expression of male sexuality), Guyon theoretically and repeatedly deplores the use of force; he simply never recognizes its existence in the sexual use of women.

Typically, every charge by women that force is used to violate women—in rape, battery, or prostitution—is dismissed by positing a female nature that is essentially fulfilled by the act of violation, which in turn transforms violation into merely using a thing for what it is and blames the thing if it is not womanly enough to enjoy what is done to it.

Sometimes "consent" is construed to exist. More often, the woman is perceived to have an active desire to be used by the male on his terms. Great Britain's Wolfenden Report, renowned for its recommendation that legal persecution of consenting male homosexuals cease, was also a report on female prostitution. The Wolfenden Report stressed that "there are women who, even when there is no economic need to do so, choose this form of livelihood."[9] The Wolfenden Report recommended increasing legal penalties against prostitutes and argued for more stringent enforcement of laws aimed at prostitutes. Male sexual privilege was affirmed both in the vindication of consensual male homosexuality and in the advocacy of greater persecution of female prostitutes. At the same time, women's degraded status was affirmed. The whore has a nature that chooses prostitution. She should be punished for her nature, which determines her choice and which exists independent of any social or economic necessity. The male homosexual also has a nature, for which he should not be punished.

This desire of the woman to prostitute herself is often portrayed as greed for money or pleasure or both. The natural woman is a whore, but the professional prostitute is a greedy whore: greedy for sensation, pleasure, money, men. Novelist Alberto Moravia, like many leftist writers seemingly obsessed with the prostituted woman, writes in an assumed first-person-female voice to convey the woman's pleasure in prostitution:

> The feeling I experienced at that moment bewildered me and, no matter how or when I have received money from men since, I have never again experienced it so clearly and so intensely. It was a feeling of complicity and sensual conspiracy . . . It was a feeling of inevitable subjection which showed me in a flash an aspect of my own nature I had ignored until then. I knew, of course, that I ought to refuse the money, but at the same time I wanted to accept. And not so much from greed, as from a new kind of pleasure which this offering had afforded me.[10]

The pleasure of the prostitute is the pleasure of any woman used in sex—but heightened. The specific—the professional whore—exists in the context of the general—women who are whores by nature. There is additional pleasure in being bought because money fixes her status as one who is for sex, not just woman but essence of woman or double-woman. The professional prostitute is distinguished from other women not in kind but by degree. "There are certainly no women absolutely devoid of the prostitute instinct to covet being sexually excited by any stranger,"[11] writes Weininger, emphasizing both pleasure and vanity. "If a woman hasn't got a tiny streak of a harlot in her," writes D. H. Lawrence, "she's a dry stick as a rule."[12] The tininess of Lawrence's "streak" should not be misunderstood: "really, most wives sold themselves, in the past, and plenty of harlots gave themselves, when they felt like it, for nothing."[13] The "tiny streak" is her sexual nature: without a streak of whore, "she's a dry stick as a rule."

There is a right-wing ideology and a left-wing ideology. The right-wing ideology claims that the division of mother and whore is phenomenologically real. The virgin is the potential mother. The left-wing ideology claims that sexual freedom is in the unrestrained use of women, the use of women as a collective natural resource, not privatized, not owned by one man but instead used by many. The metaphysics is the same on the Left and on the Right: the sexuality of the woman actualized is the sexuality of the whore; desire on her part is the slut's lust; once sexually available, it does not matter how she is used, why, by whom, by how many, or how often. Her sexual will can exist only as a will to be used. Whatever happens to her, it is all the same. If she loathes it, it is not wrong, she is.

Within this system, the only choice for the woman has been to embrace herself as whore, as sexual wanton or sexual commodity within phallic boundaries, or to disavow desire, disavow her body. The most cynical use of women has been on the Left—cynical because the word *freedom* is used to capture the loyalties of women who want, more than anything, to be free and who are then valued and used as left-wing whores: collectivized cunts. The most cynical use of women has been on the Right—cynical because the word *good* is used to capture the loyalties of women who want, more than anything, to be good and who are then valued and used as rightwing whores: wives, the whores who breed. As Kate Millett writes: ". . . the great mass of women throughout history have been confined to the cultural level of animal life in providing the male with sexual outlet and exercising the animal functions of reproduction and care of the young."[14]

Men of the Right and men of the Left have an undying allegiance to prostitution as such, regardless of their theoretical relationship to marriage. The Left sees the prostitute as the free, public woman of sex, exciting because she flaunts it, because of her brazen availability. The Right sees in the prostitute the power of the bad woman of sex, the male's use of her being his dirty little secret. The old pornography industry was a right-wing industry: secret money, secret sin, secret sex, secret promiscuity, secret buying and selling of women, secret profit, secret pleasure not only from sex but also from the buying and selling. The new pornography industry is a left-wing industry: promoted especially by the boys of the sixties as simple pleasure, lusty fun, public sex, the whore brought out of the bourgeois (*sic*) home into the streets for the democratic consumption of all men; her freedom, her free sexuality, is as his whore—and she likes it. It is her political will as well as her sexual will; it is liberation. The dirty little secret of the left-wing pornography industry is not sex but commerce.

The new pornography industry is held, by leftist males, to be inherently radical. Sex is claimed by the Left as a leftist phenomenon; the trade in women is most of sex. The politics of liberation are claimed as indigenous to the Left by the Left; central to the politics of liberation is the mass-marketing of material that depicts women being used as whores. The pimps of pornography are hailed by leftists as saviors and savants. Larry Flynt has been proclaimed a savior of the counterculture, a working-class hero, and even, in a full-page advertisement in *The New York Times* signed by distinguished leftist literati, an "American Dissident" persecuted as Soviet dissidents are. Hugh Hefner is viewed as a pioneer of sexual freedom who showed, in the words of columnist Max Lerner, "how the legislating of sexuality could be fought, how the absurd antiplay and anti-pleasure ethic could be turned into a stylish hedonism and a lifeway which includes play and playfulness along with work." [15] Lerner also credits Hefner with being a precursor of the women's movement.

On the Left, the sexually liberated woman is the woman of pornography. Free male sexuality wants, has a right to, produces, and consumes pornography because pornography is pleasure. Leftist sensibility promotes and protects pornography because pornography is freedom. The pornography glut is bread and roses for the masses. Freedom is the mass-marketing of woman as whore. Free sexuality for the woman is in being massively consumed, denied an individual nature, denied any sexual sensibility other than that which serves the male. Capitalism is not wicked or cruel when the commodity is the whore; profit is not wicked or cruel when the alienated worker is a female piece of meat; corporate bloodsucking is not wicked or cruel when the corporations in question, organized crime syndicates, sell cunt; racism is not wicked or cruel when the black cunt or yellow cunt or red cunt or Hispanic cunt or Jewish cunt has her legs splayed for any man's pleasure; poverty is not wicked or cruel when it is the poverty of dispossessed women who have only themselves to sell; violence by the powerful against the powerless is not wicked or cruel when it is called sex; slavery is not wicked or cruel when it is sexual slavery; torture is not wicked or cruel when the tormented are women, whores, cunts. The new pornography is left-wing; and the new pornography is a vast graveyard where the Left has gone to die. The Left cannot have its whores and its politics too.

———

But the example of Bluebeard should give us pause. For years he has been, for one reason or another, killing off his wives. Now, finding his life disgusting, devoid of sense, he searches his experience for pattern, sees that he has regularly murdered his wives, and asserts that next time he will do it on purpose. *Voila!*

—John Gardner, *On Moral Fiction*

In the introduction to *Black Fashion Model*, a book, the reader is warned that this story "was tempered by the fire of experience, molded in the cauldron of intense, adult desire. . ." Those who are shy or those who want to see the world through rose-colored glasses are advised not to read the book. Watergate has shaken public confidence in the president and elected officials. *Black Fashion Model* will scrutinize "the possibilities for tragedy when public power becomes a tool for private use." Another major theme in the story is "the simple unalterable fact of [the main character's] color—she is a Negress, a young, beautiful black woman." The abuse of power and the fact of prejudice are in the center of her life. Her name is Kelly Morris. She moves like a bird or snake. When she was five, she won a dance contest in the ghetto. She started studying dance when she was eight. Kelly's mother wanted her to be a professional dancer but she had ideas of her own since she was "one of the most physically charming black women ever to leave the streets of the ghetto." Her body is long, her breasts are big. Her features show "a perfect, savage beauty." She has dark, thick lips, a wide and slightly squashed nose. She is beautiful and innocent. Her skin is "dark mellow cocoa" and deep brown. Kelly walks down the street in high heels and her tightest skirt. Men talk about how they want a piece of her, but how she will be famous one day. Kelly tires of dance. When she was seventeen, she allowed someone to take photographs of her. The savage beauty of her face became important in front of the camera. Men respected her for her innocence but the camera made Kelly "into a wanton, lusty *woman*!" Kelly became one of the most famous models in the country and the most famous black model. She remained innocent, a savage beauty, a black diamond. Robert Grey watches Kelly posing. Robert Grey imagines her on her knees between his white thighs. Robert Grey imagines her touching his cock. Robert Grey imagines her pink tongue sucking his cock. Robert Grey imagines her two hot red nipples. Robert Grey imagines her two black naked breasts and his pink hardening cock. Robert Grey imagines her saying: "I like a big stiff cock like that, Mr. Robert Grey. I really do . . . Kelly stops posing. Kelly has a weakness for men like Robert Grey who look so helpless. Kelly thinks of her love, Doug, who is white. Robert Grey tells Kelly that Doug has been arrested on a morals charge. Robert Grey watches her breasts shimmer. Doug did something to a little girl. Robert Grey wonders what it would be like to be a photographer and take pictures of naked girls all day long. Robert Grey asks the photographer if he ever got the chance to—ah, ah—Eric, the photographer, blushes. Kelly returns wearing a fur coat and a bikini. Kelly thinks Robert Grey is a policeman. She follows him to his car to go to Doug in jail. Robert Grey abducts Kelly. Robert Grey pushes Kelly into a run-down house. A white woman is in the room. She is holding wet, glossy photographs in her hands. She calls Kelly a bitch. Kelly demands an explanation. The white girl winks at Robert Grey. The white girl tells Kelly she will explain. She shows Kelly pictures of Doug with a child, then another child, then another child. Kelly is sick. Robert Grey closes the blinds and double-locks the door. Robert Grey calls Kelly "little black girl." Her black breasts shimmer. The white woman is going to take photographs of Kelly. Kelly's breasts are exposed. The white female fingers are on her big black breasts. She gets upset. She struggles free. Robert Grey hits her. He hits her again. She cries and feels "pain and humiliating submissiveness." She falls into a heap of "half-naked black flesh," her thighs undulate. Robert Grey undoes his pants. Robert Grey says: we know you want it. Angela, the white girl, is naked too. Angela mimics black slang. Kelly says that she always tried to be nice to white people. Angela tells her that this has nothing to do with race. Angela wants to use the photographs she is going to take of Kelly to make a career for herself, but she gets pleasure too from having Kelly there naked. Robert Grey's prick is getting even harder. Robert Grey takes off Kelly's bikini bottom. He sees the young black girl's black hips. He wants to get his mouth around her black nipples. His hand touches her black breast. She squirms like a black snake. She is like an animal in a zoo. Angela takes photographs. Robert Grey's fingers are on her black ankles and his soft white lips are on her thick black mouth. His cock rubs against her black thigh. Angela tells him to get Kelly in the cunt. Robert Grey fingerfucks her between her black loins. She screams. Robert Grey lets her go and watches her anus, which is in the middle of her black buttocks. He calls her "my little brown butterfly." He grabs her and pulls her humiliatingly downward. Kelly tells them that what they are doing is not right. The white girl says: "you'd think this was a convention for the promotion of black-white relations the way she talks." The white girl wants Kelly tied up. The white man ties up "the young pretty Negress." She is tied spread-eagle. "Her naked black flesh shimmered . . ." Angela kisses her and touches her all over. Robert Grey takes photographs. A chill goes up Kelly's "small, black spine." Angela kisses the black girl's dark flesh. She arrives at "the Negress's black nipple." Angela sucks the black girl's vagina. Kelly moans: do it, do it. Angela's hand slides down the black girl's belly and her dark hip. Angela's hand holds her black breast. Angela takes her tongue away from "Kelly's black cuntal lips" and calls Kelly her little black princess. Robert Grey gets excited. Kelly is "beginning to go out of her mind with the powerful affects [*sic*] of cunt-licking lust!" Angela continues to kiss the environs of Kelly's cunt as Kelly wonders how she could have been a fashion model for a national magazine only a few hours ago and now she is in the middle of a nightmare with an ambitious lesbian photographer. Robert Grey now wants his. Angela tells him to give our little black friend a rest. Robert Grey demands that Angela suck him. Kelly looks on, despite herself. Angela sucks his cock. Angela wonders if our little black bitch can suck cock as well as she can. Angela keeps sucking. Kelly is disgusted to have to watch a white couple performing oral sex while she is tied like an animal. But an inner voice with masochistic urges is telling her that she loves being forced. Angela keeps sucking. Robert Grey begins to play with her vagina with his fingers. Robert Grey can see the black girl with her black thighs. Angela keeps sucking. Angela keeps sucking. Robert Grey looks at Angela's vicious face. Angela sucks "with wanton frenzy." Kelly is disgusted. Kelly feels an erotic thrill. Kelly keeps watching. Angela keeps sucking. Angela's cheeks bloat. Angela has become a wild animal in heat, a bitch. Angela keeps sucking. Robert Grey jams his fingers into her cunt. Angela sucks harder. The cum pours out of Robert Grey's prick. Kelly tries to turn away but it is too late. Angela keeps sucking. Robert Grey rams his cock deep into her throat. Robert Grey says that he should have saved all that for our little black girl. Kelly tries not to think. Robert Grey decides to fuck the black girl. He licks her black breasts and her black lips. Robert Grey gloats that she is the wealthiest, most famous black fashion girl in the world. She struggles as he violates her black flesh. He climbs between her legs. He has never really looked at the vagina of a black girl before. It is just like his wife's cunt except that his wife is an old hag. He sucks her. She has chills in her black loins. His penis touches her young black leg. She prays. His lips clamp down on her clitoris. She experiences erotic excitement and moral frustration. She prays. Robert Grey sucks. He looks at her cunt. Her skin and hair are deeply black. Her pubic hair is black fleece. He likes the deep crimson of "the inner cuntal area." He sucks. Robert Grey extracts his tongue to say that "times like this I wish I was a black man." He chomps on his lips. His lips and tongue are wanton and lewd. He sucks. She begs him to stop. She is hot. Robert Grey tells her to "grin and bear it like a good little nigger girl." Kelly is hurt. She is being defiled physically and her self-respect is also being defiled. She is being made to enjoy it. She cries. He keeps calling her "little nigger girl." He starts putting his fingers in her cunt. He calls her a dumb bitch. She is feeling the hot passions of arousal. Robert Grey is hurting her with his fingers. Kelly prays. Kelly thinks she will be torn. Kelly thinks she will faint. Robert Grey is sadistic and blushing. He makes her smell his fingers. She licks his fingers. She begs him to stop. He asks her what she would rather he do. He asks if he should ram her pussy with his fist or use a big rhino dildo or get the Great Dane that fucks women to come fuck her. She asks where Doug is. Robert Grey has a plan. Kelly looks up. She sees her smooth black belly. Robert Grey fingerfucks her. He keeps withdrawing. He spreads the fluid from her cunt on his cock with his fingers. He tells her it excites her. His monstrous white shaft is between her black thighs. His fingers pinch her clitoris. He puts his finger in her. Robert Grey's "blood-filled cock would soon be ramming into her body." Robert Grey does not want to hurt her by forcing his cock in too fast. He wants her to like it too. But Kelly is so excited she can't wait. When his cock is buried in her belly she feels as though she is being stretched apart. She loves it. Robert Grey keeps fucking her. Kelly tries to resist wanting it but she can't. Robert Grey is twice as excited because she is black and he is white! Robert Grey thrusts harder. She is hopelessly impaled. Angela comes from the darkroom with new photos. She laughs as she sees Kelly's "writhing body welcoming the forceful thrusts of Robert Grey's driving cock. The young black girl's hot little gash seemed to gape in greedy desire." Angela gets excited. Kelly feels ashamed and excited. Kelly starts screaming: Fuck me, fuck me, fuck me. Robert Grey sadistically stops. Robert Grey sadistically begins again. He keeps fucking her until she finally goes limp. "Her body was beaten and bruised and satiated from the ravishment, but she slowly but surely remembered who she was and who the man was she was with." The camera is clicking. Angela shows her the photographs of her being fucked by Robert Grey. Kelly asks for Doug. They call Bart, Kelly's former boyfriend. Bart is going to be the third person. Bart Kurtis stands above her. He undresses. He is a policeman with a detective's 38. He has had Doug arrested. He wants revenge on Kelly. They untie her. Her breasts hang like wild black fruits. Angela sucks Bart. He wants Kelly to suck him. She is lustwracked. He makes her suck. Her black lips suck. His prick is too big for any natural orifice. His cock keeps sticking at the bottom of her throat. She feels lust. She considers herself "the worst little nigger girl in the entire city." Bart lunges viciously in her throat but she is sucking with a wild abandon. Her pain is horrible but her lust is overwhelming. She pulls away and manages to stop Bart from coming in her mouth. The white lavalike cum erupts. He tries to get it on her black cheek. She wonders how it is that a black man's cum and a white man's cum are the same color. Robert Grey gets her on top of him. Bart's long, thick cock is getting ripe again. It is too big to fit in her cunt. Angela puts Robert Grey's cock in Kelly's cunt. Bart says: "Okay now, you little black whore, what about some brown-eye. . . just to let you feel how good it is to be home again, eh? I bet you'd really like to have my cock up your tail, hey?" She screams. Bart has a huge, meaty erection. Bart pushes and pushes and pushes in. She realizes with terror that Bart's cock is not even nearly in her yet. He keeps going in farther and farther. It is like a crucifixion, "the nail pounding into her. . . defiling her asshole." Then she starts to get excited and like it. She screams, fuck me, fuck me, fuck me, hurt me, fuck my ass my lover. Robert Grey fucks harder. Angela makes Kelly eat her cunt while the two men are fucking Kelly. Bart cums. Kelly cums and cums and cums. Her cumming makes the two men hard again. The four continue their lusty, wild abandonment. Kelly returns to work the next day. She tries to keep the secret of her "molestation and the horrible agony of her ultimate defilement and humiliation." A national newspaper prints one of the lascivious photos and Kelly is ruined forever. The once most famous black fashion model retires to anonymity with Doug, the white lover she tried to protect.

The relationship of all this to Watergate is not entirely clear.

At the heart of the story, however, is indeed "the simple unalterable fact of her color."

All the sex in *Black Fashion Model* is the standard stuff of pornography: rape, bondage, humiliation, pain, fucking, ass-fucking, fingerfucking, cocksucking, cuntsucking, kidnapping, hitting, the sexual cruelty of one woman toward another, pair sex, gang sex.

All the values are the standard values of pornography: the excitement of humiliation, the joy of pain, the pleasure of abuse, the magnificence of cock, the woman who resists only to discover that she loves it and wants more.

The valuation of the woman is the standard valuation ("a wanton, lusty *woman!*"), except that her main sexual part is her skin, its color. Her skin with its color is her sex with its nature. She is punished in sex by sex and she is punished as a consequence of sex: she loses her status. All this punishment is deserved, owing to her sex, which is her skin. The genital shame of any woman is transferred to the black woman's skin. The shame of sex is the shame of her skin. The stigma of sex is the stigma of her skin. The use of her sex is the use of her skin. The violence against her sex is violence against her skin. The excitement of torturing her sex is the excitement of torturing her skin. The hatred of her sex is the hatred of her skin. Her sex is stretched over her like a glove and when he touches her skin he puts on that glove. She models her skin, her sex. Her sex is as close, as available, as her skin. Her sex is as dark as her skin. The black model need not model naked to be sex; any display of her skin is sex. Her sex is right on the surface—her essence, her offense.

Bart, the black male policeman with a gun, punishes her for leaving him, leaving home, leaving by moving up and out. His race is first made clear in a description of the size of his cock. Later the text reveals that he is a black man; but the reader, having encountered the size of his cock ("His prick is too big for any natural orifice"), is presumed to know already. He is the boss. The white folks are under his orders and doing what he wants. He is on top; he is the meanest; he fucks the black woman in the ass to hurt her the worst. These are all reasons to fear him, especially to fear his sex. He avenges his masculinity and his race on her—by using his huge cock. She ends up calling him her lover and begging him to hurt her: with each other, race is neutralized—they are just male and female after all.

Kelly is a good girl *(sic)*. Only in front of the camera is she wanton, lewd, lusty—a woman! Her sexual nature is in what the camera captures—her skin. Once actually used—revealed in sex to be what she is in skin—she loses everything. The camera captures her skin in sexual action, her skin actualized, being used for what it is. The huge cock reveals the black man. The black female's skin reveals her: her skin is cunt; it has that sexual value in and of itself. Her face is savage beauty, savage cunt. She has no part that is not cunt. One wants her; one wants her skin. One has her; one has her skin. One rapes her; one rapes her skin. One humiliates her; one humiliates her skin. As long as her skin shows, her cunt shows. This is the specific sexual value of the black woman in pornography in the United States, a race-bound society fanatically committed to the sexual devaluing of black skin perceived as a sex organ and a sexual nature. No woman of any other race bears this specific burden in this country. In no other woman is skin sex, cunt in and of itself—her essence, her offense. This meaning of the black woman's skin is revealed in the historical usage of her, even as it developed from the historical usage of her. This valuation of the black woman is real, especially vivid in urban areas where she is used as a street whore extravagantly and without conscience. Poverty forces her; but it is the sexual valuation of her skin that predetermines her poverty and permits the simple, righteous use of her as a whore.

How, then, does one fight racism and jerk off to it at the same time? The Left cannot have its whores and its politics too. The imperial United States cannot maintain its racist system without its black whores, its bottom, the carnal underclass. The sexualization of race within a racist system is a prime purpose and consequence of pornography. In using the black woman, pornography depicts the whore by depicting her skin; in using the pornography, men spit on her sex and her skin. Here the relationship of sex and death could not be clearer: this sexual use of the black woman is the death of freedom, the death of justice, the death of equality.

RIGHT-WING WOMEN

1983

There is a rumor, circulated for centuries by scientists, artists, and philosophers both secular and religious, a piece of gossip as it were, to the effect that women are "biologically conservative." While gossip among women is universally ridiculed as low and trivial, gossip among men, especially if it is about women, is called theory, or idea, or fact. This particular rumor became dignified as high thought because it was Whispered-Down-The-Lane in formidable academies, libraries, and meeting halls from which women, until very recently, have been formally and forcibly excluded.

The whispers, however multisyllabic and footnoted they sometimes are, reduced to a simple enough set of assertions. Women have children because women by definition have children. This "fact of life," which is not subject to qualification, carries with it the instinctual obligation to nurture and protect those children. Therefore, women can be expected to be socially, politically, economically, and sexually conservative because the status quo, whatever it is, is safer than change, whatever the change. Noxious male philosophers from all disciplines have, for centuries, maintained that women follow a biological imperative derived directly from their reproductive capacities that translates necessarily into narrow lives, small minds, and a rather meanspirited puritanism.

This theory, or slander, is both specious and cruel in that, in fact, women are forced to bear children and have been throughout history in all economic systems, with but teeny-weeny time-outs while the men were momentarily disoriented, as, for instance, in the immediate postcoital aftermath of certain revolutions. It is entirely irrational in that, in fact, women of all ideological persuasions, with the single exception of absolute pacifists, of whom there have not been very many, have throughout history supported wars in which the very children they are biologically ordained to protect are maimed, raped, tortured, and killed. Clearly, the biological explanation of the so-called conservative nature of women obscures the realities of women's lives, buries them in dark shadows of distortion and dismissal.

The disinterested or hostile male observer can categorize women as "conservative" in some metaphysical sense because it is true that women as a class adhere rather strictly to the traditions and values of their social context, whatever the character of that context. In societies of whatever description, however narrowly or broadly defined, women as a class are the dulled conformists, the orthodox believers, the obedient followers, the disciples of unwavering faith. To waver, whatever the creed of the men around them, is tantamount to rebellion; it is dangerous. Most women, holding on for dear life, do not dare abandon blind faith. From father's house to husband's house to a grave that still might not be her own, a woman acquiesces to male authority in order to gain some protection from male violence. She conforms, in order to be as safe as she can be. Sometimes it is a lethargic conformity, in which case male demands slowly close in on her, as if she were a character buried alive in an Edgar Allan Poe story. Sometimes it is a militant conformity. She will save herself by proving that she is loyal, obedient, useful, even fanatic in the service of the men around her. She is the happy hooker, the happy homemaker, the exemplary Christian, the pure academic, the perfect comrade, the terrorist par excellence.

Whatever the values, she will embody them with a perfect fidelity. The males rarely keep their part of the bargain as she understands it: protection from male violence against her person. But the militant conformist has given so much of herself—her labor, heart, soul, often her body, often children—that this betrayal is akin to nailing the coffin shut; the corpse is beyond caring.

Women know, but must not acknowledge, that resisting male control or confronting male betrayal will lead to rape, battery, destitution, ostracization or exile, confinement in a mental institution or jail, or death. As Phyllis Chesler and Emily Jane Goodman make clear in *Women, Money, and Power*, women struggle, in the manner of Sisyphus, to avoid the "something worse" that can and will always happen to them if they transgress the rigid boundaries of appropriate female behavior. Most women cannot afford, either materially or psychologically, to recognize that whatever burnt offerings of obedience they bring to beg protection will not appease the angry little gods around them.

It is not surprising, then, that most girls do not want to become like their mothers, those tired, preoccupied domestic sergeants beset by incomprehensible troubles. Mothers raise daughters to conform to the strictures of the conventional female life as defined by men, whatever the ideological values of the men. Mothers are the immediate enforcers of male will, the guards at the cell door, the flunkies who administer the electric shocks to punish rebellion.

Most girls, however much they resent their mothers, do become very much like them. Rebellion can rarely survive the aversion therapy that passes for being brought up female. Male violence acts directly on the girl through her father or brother or uncle or any number of male professionals or strangers, as it did and does on her mother, and she too is forced to learn to conform in order to survive. A girl may, as she enters adulthood, repudiate the particular set of males with whom her mother is allied, run with a different pack as it were, but she will replicate her mother's patterns in acquiescing to male authority within her own chosen set. Using both force and threat, men in all camps demand that women accept abuse in silence and shame, tie themselves to hearth and home with rope made of self-blame, unspoken rage, grief, and resentment.

It is the fashion among men to despise the smallness of women's lives. The so-called bourgeois woman with her shallow vanity, for instance, is a joke to the brave intellectuals, truck drivers, and revolutionaries who have wider horizons on which to project and indulge deeper vanities that women dare not mock and to which women dare not aspire. The fishwife is a vicious caricature of the small-mindedness and material greed of the working-class wife who harasses her humble, hardworking, ever patient husband with petty tirades of insult that no gentle rebuke can mellow. The Lady, the Aristocrat, is a polished, empty shell, good only for spitting at, because spit shows up on her clean exterior, which gives immediate gratification to the spitter, whatever his technique. The Jewish mother is a monster who wants to cut the phallus of her precious son into a million pieces and put it in the chicken soup. The black woman, also a castrator, is a grotesque matriarch whose sheer endurance desolates men. The lesbian is half monster, half moron: having no man to nag, she imagines herself Napoleon.

And the derision of female lives does not stop with these toxic, ugly, insidious slanders because there is always, in every circumstance, the derision in its skeletal form, all bone, the meat stripped clean: she is pussy, cunt. Every other part of the body is cut away, severed, and there is left a thing, not human, and it, which is the funniest joke of all, an unending source of raucous humor to those who have done the cutting. The very butchers who cut up the meat and throw away the useless parts are the comedians. The paring down of a whole person to vagina and womb and then to a dismembered obscenity is their best and favorite joke.

Every woman, no matter what her social, economic, or sexual situation, fights this paring down with every resource at her command. Because her resources are so astonishingly meager and because she has been deprived of the means to organize and expand them, these attempts are simultaneously heroic and pathetic. The whore, in defending the pimp, finds her own worth in the light reflected from his gaudy baubles. The wife, in defending the husband, screams or stammers that her life is not a wasteland of murdered possibilities. The woman, in defending the ideologies of men who rise by climbing over her prone body in military formation, will not publicly mourn the loss of what those men have taken from her: she will not scream out as their heels dig into her flesh because to do so would mean the end of meaning itself; all the ideals that motivated her to deny herself would be indelibly stained with blood that she would have to acknowledge, at last, as her own.

So the woman hangs on, not with the delicacy of a clinging vine, but with a tenacity incredible in its intensity, to the very persons, institutions, and values that demean her, degrade her, glorify her powerlessness, insist upon constraining and paralyzing the most honest expressions of her will and being. She becomes a lackey, serving those who ruthlessly and effectively aggress against her and her kind. This singularly self-hating loyalty to those committed to her own destruction is the very essence of womanhood as men of all ideological persuasions define it.

———

Marilyn Monroe, shortly before she died, wrote in her notebook on the set of *Let's Make Love*: "What am I afraid of? Why am I so afraid? Do I think I can't act? I know I can act but I am afraid. I am afraid and I should not be and I must not be."[1]

The actress is the only female culturally empowered to act. When she acts well, that is, when she convinces the male controllers of images and wealth that she is reducible to current sexual fashion, available to the male on his own terms, she is paid and honored. Her acting must be imitative, not creative; rigidly conforming, not self-generated and self-renewing. The actress is the puppet of flesh, blood, and paint who acts as if she is the female acting. Monroe, the consummate sexual doll, is empowered to act but afraid to act, perhaps because no amount of acting, however inspired, can convince the actor herself that her ideal female life is not a dreadful form of dying. She grinned, she posed, she pretended, she had affairs with famous and powerful men. A friend of hers claimed that she had so many illegal abortions wrongly performed that her reproductive organs were severely injured. She died alone, possibly acting on her own behalf for the first time. Death, one imagines, numbs pain that barbiturates and alcohol cannot touch.

Monroe's premature death raised one haunting question for the men who were, in their own fantasy, her lovers, for the men who had masturbated over those pictures of exquisite female compliance: was it possible, could it be, that she hadn't liked It all along—It— the It they had been doing to her, how many millions of times? Had those smiles been masks covering despair or rage? If so, how endangered they had been to be deceived, so fragile and exposed in their masturbatory delight, as if she could leap out from those photos of what was now a corpse and take the revenge they knew she deserved. There arose the male imperative that Monroe must not be a suicide.

Norman Mailer, savior of masculine privilege and pride on many fronts, took up the challenge by theorizing that Monroe may have been killed by the FBI, or CIA, or whoever killed the Kennedys, because she had been mistress to one or both. Conspiracy was a cheerful and comforting thought to those who had wanted to slam into her until she expired, female death and female ecstasy being synonymous in the world of male metaphor. But they did not want her dead yet, not really dead, not while the illusion of her open invitation was so absolutely compelling. In fact, her lovers in both flesh and fantasy had fucked her to death, and her apparent suicide stood at once as accusation and answer: no, Marilyn Monroe, the ideal sexual female, had not liked it.

People—as we are always reminded by counterfeit egalitarians— have always died too young, too soon, too isolated, too full of insupportable anguish. But only women die one by one, whether famous or obscure, rich or poor, isolated, choked to death by the lies tangled in their throats. Only women die one by one, attempting until the last minute to embody an ideal imposed upon them by men who want to use them up. Only women die one by one, smiling up to the last minute, smile of the siren, smile of the coy girl, smile of the madwoman. Only women die one by one, polished to perfection or unkempt behind locked doors too desperately ashamed to cry out. Only women die one by one, still believing that if only they had been perfect—perfect wife, mother, or whore— they would not have come to hate life so much, to find it so strangely difficult and empty, themselves so hopelessly confused and despairing. Women die, mourning not the loss of their own lives, but their own inexcusable inability to achieve perfection as men define it for them. Women desperately try to embody a male-defined feminine ideal because survival depends on it. The ideal, by definition, turns a woman into a function, deprives her of any individuality that is self-serving or self-created, not useful to the male in his scheme of things. This monstrous female quest for male-defined perfection, so intrinsically hostile to freedom and integrity, leads inevitably to bitterness, paralysis, or death, but like the mirage in the desert, the life-giving oasis that is not there, survival is promised in this conformity and nowhere else.

Like the chameleon, the woman must blend into her environment, never calling attention to the qualities that distinguish her, because to do so would be to attract the predator's deadly attention. She is, in fact, hunted meat—all the male *auteurs*, scientists, and homespun philosophers on street corners will say so proudly. Attempting to strike a bargain, the woman says: I come to you on your own terms. Her hope is that his murderous attention will focus on a female who conforms less artfully, less willingly. In effect, she ransoms the remains of a life—what is left over after she has renounced willful individuality—by promising indifference to the fate of other women. This sexual, sociological, and spiritual adaptation, which is, in fact, the maiming of all moral capacity, is the primary imperative of survival for women who live under male-supremacist rule.

———

. . . I gradually came to see that I would have to stay within the survivor's own perspective. This will perhaps bother the historian, with his distrust of personal evidence; but radical suffering transcends relativity, and when one survivor's account of an event or circumstance is repeated in exactly the same way by dozens of other survivors, men and women in

different camps, from different nations and cultures, then one comes to trust the validity of such reports and even to question rare departures from the general view.[2]
—Terrence Des Pres, *The Survivor: An Anatomy of Life in the Death Camps*

The accounts of rape, wife beating, forced childbearing, medical butchering, sex-motivated murder, forced prostitution, physical mutilation, sadistic psychological abuse, and the other common places of female experience that are excavated from the past or given by contemporary survivors should leave the heart seared, the mind in anguish, the conscience in upheaval. But they do not. No matter how often these stories are told, with whatever clarity or eloquence, bitterness or sorrow, they might as well have been whispered in wind or written in sand: they disappear, as if they were nothing. The tellers and the stories are ignored or ridiculed, threatened back into silence or destroyed, and the experience of female suffering is buried in cultural invisibility and contempt. Because women's testimony is not and cannot be validated by the witness of men who have experienced the same events and given them the same value, the very reality of abuse sustained by women, despite its overwhelming pervasiveness and constancy, is negated. It is negated in the transactions of everyday life, and it is negated in the history books, left out, and it is negated by those who claim to care about suffering but are blind to this suffering.

The problem, simply stated, is that one must believe in the existence of the person in order to recognize the authenticity of her suffering. Neither men nor women believe in the existence of women as significant beings. It is impossible to remember as real the suffering of someone who by definition has no legitimate claim to dignity or freedom, someone who is in fact viewed as something, an object or an absence. And if a woman, an individual woman multiplied by billions, does not believe in her own discrete existence and therefore cannot credit the authenticity of her own suffering, she is erased, canceled out, and the meaning of her life, whatever it is, whatever it might have been, is lost. This loss cannot be calculated or comprehended. It is vast and awful, and nothing will ever make up for it.

No one can bear to live a meaningless life. Women fight for meaning just as women fight for survival: by attaching themselves to men and the values honored by men. By committing themselves to male values, women seek to acquire value. By advocating male meaning, women seek to acquire meaning. Subservient to male will, women believe that subservience itself is the meaning of a female life. In this way, women, whatever they suffer, do not suffer the anguish of a conscious recognition that, because they are women, they have been robbed of volition and choice, without which no life can have meaning.

———

The political Right in the United States today makes certain metaphysical and material promises to women that both exploit and quiet some of women's deepest fears. These fears originate in the perception that male violence against women is uncontrollable and unpredictable. Dependent on and subservient to men, women are always subject to this violence. The Right promises to put enforceable restraints on male aggression, thus simplifying survival for women—to make the world slightly more habitable, in other words—by offering the following:

Form. Women experience the world as mystery. Kept ignorant of technology, economics, most of the practical skills required to function autonomously, kept ignorant of the real social and sexual demands made on women, deprived of physical strength, excluded from forums for the development of intellectual acuity and public self-confidence, women are lost and mystified by the savage momentum of an ordinary life. Sounds, signs, promises, threats, wildly crisscross, but what do they mean? The Right offers women a simple, fixed, predetermined social, biological, and sexual order. Form conquers chaos. Form banishes confusion. Form gives ignorance a shape, makes it look like something instead of nothing.

Shelter. Women are brought up to maintain a husband's home and to believe that women without men are homeless. Women have a deep fear of being homeless—at the mercy of the elements and of strange men. The Right claims to protect the home and the woman's place in it.

Safety. For women, the world is a very dangerous place. One wrong move, even an unintentional smile, can bring disaster—assault, shame, disgrace. The Right acknowledges the reality of danger, the validity of fear. The Right then manipulates the fear. The promise is that if a woman is obedient, harm will not befall her.

Rules. Living in a world she has not made and does not understand, a woman needs rules to know what to do next. If she knows what she is supposed to do, she can find a way to do it. If she learns the rules by rote, she can perform with apparent effortlessness, which will considerably enhance her chances for survival. The Right, very considerately, tells women the rules of the game on which their lives depend. The Right also promises that, despite their absolute sovereignty, men too will follow specified rules.

Love. Love is always crucial in effecting the allegiance of women. The Right offers women a concept of love based on order and stability, with formal areas of mutual accountability. A woman is loved for fulfilling her female functions: obedience is an expression of love and so are sexual submission and childbearing. In return, the man is supposed to be responsible for the material and emotional well-being of the woman. And, increasingly, to redeem the cruel inadequacies of mortal men, the Right offers women the love of Jesus, beautiful brother, tender lover, compassionate friend, perfect healer of sorrow and resentment, the one male to whom one can submit absolutely—be Woman as it were—without being sexually violated or psychologically abused.

It is important and fascinating, of course, to note that women never, no matter how deluded or needy or desperate, worship Jesus as the perfect son. No faith is that blind. There is no religious or cultural palliative to deaden the raw pain of the son's betrayal of the mother: only her own obedience to the same father, the sacrifice of her own life on the same cross, her own body nailed and bleeding, can enable her to accept that her son, like Jesus, has come to do his Father's work. Feminist Leah Fritz, in *Thinking Like a Woman*, described the excruciating predicament of women who try to find worth in Christian submission: "Unloved, unrespected, unnoticed by the Heavenly Father, condescended to by the Son, and fucked by the Holy Ghost, western woman spends her entire life trying to please."[3]

But no matter how hard she tries to please, it is harder still for her to be pleased. In *Bless This House*, Anita Bryant describes how each day she must ask Jesus to "help me love my husband and children."[4] In The Total Woman, Marabel Morgan explains that it is only through God's power that "we can love and accept others, including our husbands."[5] In *The Gift of Inner Healing*, Ruth Carter Stapleton counsels a young woman who is in a desperately unhappy marriage: "Try to spend a little time each day visualizing Jesus coming in the door from work. Then see yourself walking up to him, embracing him. Say to Jesus, it's good to have you home Nick.'"[6]

Ruth Carter Stapleton married at nineteen. Describing the early years of her marriage, she wrote:

> After moving four hundred fifty miles from my first family in order to save my marriage, I found myself in a cold, threatening, unprotected world, or so it seemed to my confused heart. In an effort to avoid total destruction, I indulged in escapes of every kind. . .
>
> A major crisis arose when I discovered I was pregnant with my first child. I knew that this was supposed to be one of the crowning moments of womanhood, but not for me. . . . When my baby was born, I wanted to be a good mother, but I felt even more trapped. . . . Then three more babies were born in rapid succession, and each one, so beautiful, terrified me. I did love them, but by the fourth child I was at the point of total desperation.[7]

Apparently the birth of her fourth child occasioned her surrender to Jesus. For a time, life seemed worthwhile. Then, a rupture in a cherished friendship plummeted her into an intolerable depression. During this period, she jumped out of a moving car in what she regards as a suicide attempt.

A male religious mentor picked up the pieces. Stapleton took her own experience of breakdown and recovery and from it shaped a kind of faith psychotherapy. Nick's transformation into Jesus has already been mentioned. A male homosexual, traumatized by an absent father who never played with him as a child, played baseball with Jesus under Stapleton's tutelage—a whole nine innings. In finding Jesus as father and chum, he was healed of the hurt of an absent father and "cured" of his homosexuality. A woman who was forcibly raped by her father as a child was encouraged to remember the event, only this time Jesus had his hand on the father's shoulder and was forgiving him. This enabled the woman to forgive her father too and to be reconciled with men. A woman who as a child was rejected by her father on the occasion of her first date—the father did not notice her pretty dress—was encouraged to imagine the presence of Jesus on that fateful night. Jesus loved her dress and found her very desirable. Stapleton claims that this devotional therapy, through the power of the Holy Spirit, enables Jesus to erase damaging memories.

A secular analysis of Stapleton's own newfound well-being seems, by contrast, pedestrian. A brilliant woman has found a socially acceptable way to use her intellect and compassion in the public domain—the dream of many women. Though fundamentalist male ministers have called her a witch, in typical female fashion Stapleton disclaims responsibility for her own inventiveness and credits the Holy Spirit, clearly male, thus soothing the savage misogyny of those who cannot bear for any woman to be both seen and heard. Also, having founded an evangelical ministry that demands constant travel, Stapleton is rarely at home. She has not given birth again.

Marabel Morgan's description of her own miserable marriage in the years preceding her discovery of God's will is best summarized in this one sentence: "I was helpless and unhappy."[8] She describes years of tension, conflict, boredom, and gloom. She took her fate into her own hands by asking the not-yet-classic question, What do men want? Her answer is stunningly accurate: "It is only when a woman surrenders her life to her husband, reveres and worships him, and is willing to serve him, that she becomes really beautiful to him."[9] Or, more aphoristically, "A Total Woman caters to her man's special quirks, whether it be in salads, sex, or sports."[10] Citing God as the authority and submission to Jesus as the model, Morgan defines love as "unconditional acceptance of [a man] and his feelings."[11]

Morgan's achievement in *The Total Woman* was to isolate the basic sexual scenarios of male dominance and female submission and to formulate a simple set of lessons, a pedagogy, that teaches women how to act out those scenarios within the context of a Christian value system: in other words, how to cater to male pornographic fantasies in the name of Jesus Christ. As Morgan explains in her own extraordinary prose style: "That great source book, the Bible, states, 'Marriage is honourable in all, and the bed undefiled. . .' In other words, sex is for the marriage relationship only, but within those bounds, anything goes. Sex is as clean and pure as eating cottage cheese."[12] Morgan's detailed instructions on how to eat cottage cheese, the most famous of which involves Saran Wrap, make clear that female submission is a delicately balanced commingling of resourcefulness and lack of self-respect. Too little resourcefulness or too much self-respect will doom a woman to failure as a Total Woman. A submissive nature is the miracle for which religious women pray.

No one has prayed harder, longer, and with less apparent success than Anita Bryant. She has spent a good part of her life on her knees begging Jesus to forgive her for the sin of existing. In *Mine Eyes Have Seen the Glory*, an autobiography first published in 1970, Bryant described herself as an aggressive, stubborn, bad-tempered child. Her early childhood was spent in brutal poverty. Through singing she began earning money when still a child. When she was very young, her parents divorced, then later remarried. When she was thirteen, her father abandoned her mother, younger sister, and herself, her parents were again divorced, and shortly thereafter her father remarried. At thirteen, "[w]hat stands out most of all in my memory are my feelings of intense ambition and a relentless drive to succeed at doing well the thing I loved [singing]."[13] She blamed herself, especially her driving ambition, for the loss of her father.

She did not want to marry. In particular, she did not want to marry Bob Green. He "won" her through a war of attrition. Every "No" on her part was taken as a "Yes" by him. When, on several occasions, she told him that she did not want to see him again, he simply ignored what she said. Once, when she was making a trip to see a close male friend whom she described to Green as her fiance, he booked passage on the same plane and went along. He hounded her.

Having got his hooks into her, especially knowing how to hit on her rawest nerve—guilt over the abnormality of her ambition, by definition unwomanly and potentially satanic—Green manipulated Bryant with a cruelty nearly unmatched in modern love stories. From both of Bryant's early books, a picture emerges. One sees a woman hemmed in, desperately trying to please a husband who manipulates and harasses her and whose control of her life on every level is virtually absolute. Bryant described the degree of Green's control in *Mine Eyes*: "That's how good a manager my husband is. He willingly handles all the business in my life—even to including the Lord's business. Despite our sometimes violent scraps, I love him for it."[14] Bryant never specifies how violent the violent scraps were, though Green insists they were not violent. Green himself, in *Bless This House*, is very proud of spanking the children, especially the oldest son, who is adopted: "I'm a father to my children, not a pal. I assert my authority. I spank them at times, and they respect me for it. Sometimes I take Bobby into the music room, and it's not so I can play him a piece on the piano. We play a piece on the seat of his pants!"[15] Some degree of physical violence, then, was admittedly an accepted part of domestic life. Bryant's unselfconscious narrative makes clear that over a period of years, long before her antihomosexual crusade was a glint in Bob Green's eye, she was badgered into giving public religious testimonies that deeply distressed her:

> Bob has a way of getting my dander up and backing me up against a wall. He gets me so terrifically mad at him that I hate him for pushing me into a corner. He did that now.
>
> "You're a hypocrite," Bob said. "You profess to have Christ in your life, but you won't profess Him in public, which Christ tells you to do."
>
> Because I know he's right, and hate him for making me feel so bad about it, I end up doing what I'm so scared to do.[16]

Conforming to the will of her husband was clearly a difficult struggle for Bryant. She writes candidly of her near constant rebellion. Green's demands—from increasing her public presence as religious witness to doing all the child care for four children without help while pursuing the career she genuinely loves—were endurable only because Bryant, like Stapleton and Morgan, took Jesus as her real husband:

> Only as I practice yielding to Jesus can I learn to submit, as the Bible instructs me, to the loving leadership of my husband. Only the power of Christ can enable a woman like me to become submissive in the Lord.[17]

In Bryant's case, the "loving leadership" of her husband, this time in league with her pastor, enshrined her as the token spokeswoman of antihomosexual bigotry. Once again Bryant was reluctant to testify, this time before Dade County's Metropolitan Commission in hearings on a homosexual-rights ordinance. Bryant spent several nights in tears and prayer, presumably because, as she told *Newsweek*, "I was scared and I didn't want to do it."[18] Once again, a desire to do Christ's will brought her into conformity with the expressed will of her husband. One could speculate that some of the compensation in this conformity came from having the burdens of domestic work and child care lessened in the interest of serving the greater cause. Conformity to the will of Christ and Green, synonymous in this instance as so often before, also offered an answer to the haunting question of her life: how to be a public leader of significance—in her terminology, a "star"—and at the same time an obedient wife acting to protect her children. A singing career, especially a secular one, could never resolve this raging conflict.

Bryant, like all the rest of us, is trying to be a "good" woman. Bryant, like all the rest of us, is desperate and dangerous, to herself and to others, because "good" women live and die in silent selflessness and real women cannot. Bryant, like all the rest of us, is having one hell of a hard time.*

---

*This analysis of Bryant's situation was written in 1978 and published in *Ms.* in June 1979. In May 1980, Bryant filed for divorce. In a statement issued separately from the divorce petition, she contended that Green had "violated my most precious asset—my conscience" (*The New York Times*, May 24, 1980). Within three weeks after the divorce decree (August 1980), the state citrus agency of Florida, which Bryant had represented for eleven years, decided she was no longer a suitable representative because of her divorce: "The contract had to expire, because of the divorce and so forth," one agency executive said (*The New York Times*, September 2, 1980). Feminist lawyer and former National Organization for Women president Karen

Phyllis Schlafly, the Right's not-born-again philosopher of the absurd, is apparently not having a hard time. She seems possessed by Machiavelli, not Jesus. It appears that she wants to be The Prince. She might be viewed as that rare woman of any ideological persuasion who really does see herself as one of the boys, even as she claims to be one of the girls. Unlike most other right-wing women, Schlafly, in her written and spoken work, does not acknowledge experiencing any of the difficulties that tear women apart. In the opinion of many, her ruthlessness as an organizer is best demonstrated by her demagogic propaganda against the Equal Rights Amendment, though she also waxes eloquent against reproductive freedom, the women's movement, big government, and the Panama Canal Treaty. Her roots, and perhaps her heart such as it is, are in the Old Right, but she remained unknown to any significant public until she mounted her crusade against the Equal Rights Amendment. It is likely that her ambition is to use women as a constituency to effect entry into the upper echelon of rightwing male leadership. She may yet discover that she is a woman (as feminists understand the meaning of the word) as her male colleagues refuse to let her escape the ghetto of female issues

DeCrow urged Bryant to bring suit under the 1977 Florida Human Rights Act, which prohibits job discrimination on the basis of marital status. Even before DeCrow's sisterly act, however, Bryant had reevaluated her position on the women's movement, to which, under Green's tutelage, she had been bitterly opposed. "What has happened to me," Bryant told the *National Enquirer* in June 1980, "makes me understand why there are angry women who want to pass ERA [Equal Rights Amendment]. That still is not the answer. But the church doesn't deal with the problems of women as it should. There's been some really bad teachings, and I think that's why I'm really concerned for my own children—particularly the girls. You have to recognize that there has been discrimination against women, that women have not had the teaching of the fullness and uniqueness of their abilities." *Pace*, sister.

and enter the big time.* At any rate, she seems to be able to manipulate the fears of women without experiencing them. If this is indeed the case, this talent would give her an invaluable, cold-blooded detachment as a strategist determined to convert women into antifeminist activists. It is precisely because women have been trained to respect and follow those who use them that Schlafly inspires awe and devotion in women who are afraid that they will be deprived of the form, shelter, safety, rules, and love that the Right promises and on which they believe survival depends.

------

* According to many newspaper reports, Phyllis Schlafly wanted Reagan to appoint her to a position in the Pentagon. This he did not do. In a debate with Schlafly (Stanford University, January 26, 1982) lawyer Catharine A. MacKinnon tried to make Schlafly understand that she had been discriminated against as a woman: "Mrs. Schlafly tells us that being a woman has not gotten in her way. I propose that any man who had a law degree and graduate work in political science; had given testimony on a wide range of important subjects for decades; had done effective and brilliant political, policy and organizational work within the party [the Republican Party]; had published widely, including nine books; and stopped a major social initiative to amend the constitution just short of victory dead in its tracks [the Equal Rights Amendment]; and had a beautiful accomplished family—any man like that would have a place in the current administration. . . . I would accept correction if this is wrong; and she may yet be appointed. She was widely reported to have wanted such a post, but I don't believe everything I read, especially about women. I do think she should have wanted one and they should have found her a place she wanted. She certainly deserved a place in the Defense Department. Phyllis Schlafly is a qualified woman." Answered Schlafly: "This has been an interesting debate. More interesting than I thought it was going to be. . . . I think my opponent did have one good point—[audience laughter] Well, she had a couple of good points. . . . She did have a good point about the Reagan administration, but it is the Reagan administration's loss that they didn't ask me to [drowned out by audience applause] but it isn't my loss."

At the National Women's Conference (Houston, Texas, November 1977), I spoke with many women on the Right. The conversations were ludicrous, terrifying, bizarre, instructive, and, as other feminists have reported, sometimes strangely moving.

Right-wing women fear lesbians. A liberal black delegate from Texas told me that local white women had tried to convince her that lesbians at the conference would assault her, call her dirty names, and were personally filthy. She told me that she would vote against the sexual-preference resolution* because otherwise she would not be able to return home. But she also said that she would tell the white women that the lesbians had been polite and clean. She said that she knew it was wrong to deprive anyone of a job and had had no idea before coming to Houston that lesbian mothers lost their children. This, she felt, was genuinely terrible. I asked her if she thought a time would come when she would have to stand up for lesbian rights in her hometown. She nodded yes gravely, then explained with careful, evocative emphasis that the next-closest town to where she lived was 160 miles away. The history of blacks in the South was palpable.

Right-wing women consistently spoke to me about lesbians as if lesbians were rapists, certified committers of sexual assault

---

* "Congress, State, and local legislatures should enact legislation to eliminate discrimination on the basis of sexual and affectional preference in areas including, but not limited to, employment, housing, public accommodations, credit, public facilities, government funding, and the military.

"State legislatures should reform their penal codes or repeal State laws that restrict private sexual behavior between consenting adults.

"State legislatures should enact legislation that would prohibit consideration of sexual or affectional orientation as a factor in any judicial determination of child custody or visitation rights. Rather, child custody cases should be evaluated solely on the merits of which party is the better parent, without regard to that person's sexual and affectional orientation."

against women and girls. No facts could intrude on this psychosexual fantasy. No facts or figures on male sexual violence against women and children could change the focus of their fear. They admitted that they knew of many cases of male assault against females, including within families, and did not know of any assaults by lesbians against females. The men, they acknowledged when pressed, were sinners, and they hated sin, but there was clearly something comforting in the normalcy of heterosexual rape. To them, the lesbian was inherently monstrous, experienced almost as a demonic sexual force hovering closer and closer. She was the dangerous intruder, encroaching, threatening by her very presence a sexual order that cannot bear scrutiny or withstand challenge.

Right-wing women regard abortion as the callous murder of infants. Female selflessness expresses itself in the conviction that a fertilized egg surpasses an adult female in the authenticity of its existence. The grief of these women for fetuses is real, and their contempt for women who become pregnant out of wedlock is awesome to behold. The fact that most illegal abortions in the bad old days were performed on married women with children, and that thousands of those women died each year, is utterly meaningless to them. They see abortion as a criminal act committed by godless whores, women absolutely unlike themselves.

Right-wing women argue that passage of the Equal Rights Amendment will legalize abortion irrevocably. No matter how often I heard this argument (and I heard it constantly), I simply could not understand it. Fool that I was, I had thought that the Equal Rights Amendment was abhorrent because of toilets. Since toilets figured prominently in the resistance to civil rights legislation that would protect blacks, the argument that centered on toilets—while irrational—was as Amerikan as apple pie. No one mentioned toilets. I brought them up, but no one cared to discuss them. The passionate, repeated cause-and-effect arguments linking the Equal Rights Amendment and abortion presented a new mystery. I resigned myself to hopeless confusion. Happily, after the conference, I read *The Power of the Positive Woman*, in which Schlafly explains: "Since the mandate of ERA is for sex equality, abortion is essential to relieve women of their unequal burden of being forced to bear an unwanted baby."[19] Forcing women to bear unwanted babies is crucial to the social program of women who have been forced to bear unwanted babies and who cannot bear the grief and bitterness of such a recognition. The Equal Rights Amendment has now become the symbol of this devastating recognition. This largely accounts for the new wave of intransigent opposition to it.

Right-wing women, as represented in Houston, especially from the South, white and black, also do not like Jews. They live in a Christian country. A fragile but growing coalition between white and black women in the New South is based on a shared Christian fundamentalism, which translates into a shared anti-Semitism. The stubborn refusal of Jews to embrace Christ and the barely masked fundamentalist perception of Jews as Christ killers, communists and usurers both, queers, and, worst of all, urban intellectuals, mark Jews as foreign, sinister, and an obvious source of the many satanic conspiracies sweeping the nation.

The most insidious expression of this rife anti-Semitism was conveyed by a fixed stare, a self-conscious smile and the delightful words "Ah just love tha Jewish people." The slime variety of anti-Semite, very much in evidence, was typified by a Right to Life leader who called doctors who perform abortions "Jewish baby killers." I was asked a hundred times: "Am Ah speakin with a Jewish girl?" Despite my clear presence as a lesbian-feminist with press credentials plastered all over me from the notorious *Ms.* magazine, it was as a Jew that I was consistently challenged and, on several occasions, implicitly threatened. Conversation after conversation stopped abruptly when I answered that yes, I was a Jew.

———

The Right in the United States today is a social and political movement controlled almost totally by men but built largely on the fear and ignorance of women. The quality of this fear and the pervasiveness of this ignorance are consequences of male sexual domination over women. Every accommodation that women make to this domination, however apparently stupid, self-defeating, or dangerous, is rooted in the urgent need to survive somehow on male terms. Inevitably this causes women to take the rage and contempt they feel for the men who actually abuse them, those close to them, and project it onto others, those far away, foreign, or different. Some women do this by becoming right-wing patriots, nationalists determined to triumph over populations thousands of miles removed. Some women become ardent racists, anti-Semites, or homophobes. Some women develop a hatred of loose or destitute women, pregnant teenage girls, all persons unemployed or on welfare. Some hate individuals who violate social conventions, no matter how superficial the violations. Some become antagonistic to ethnic groups other than their own or to religious groups other than their own, or they develop a hatred of those political convictions that contradict their own. Women cling to irrational hatreds, focused particularly on the unfamiliar, so that they will not murder their fathers, husbands, sons, brothers, lovers, the men with whom they are intimate, those who do hurt them and cause them grief. Fear of a greater evil and a need to be protected from it intensify the loyalty of women to men who are, even when dangerous, at least known quantities. Because women so displace their rage, they are easily controlled and manipulated haters. Having good reason to hate, but not the courage to rebel, women require symbols of danger that justify their fear. The Right provides these symbols of danger by designating clearly defined groups of outsiders as sources of danger. The identities of the dangerous outsiders can change over time to meet changing social circumstances—for example, racism can be encouraged or contained; anti-Semitism can be provoked or kept dormant; homophobia can be aggravated or kept under the surface—but the existence of the dangerous outsider always functions for women simultaneously as deception, diversion, pain-killer, and threat.

The tragedy is that women so committed to survival cannot recognize that they are committing suicide. The danger is that self-sacrificing women are perfect foot soldiers who obey orders, no matter how criminal those orders are. The hope is that these women, upset by internal conflicts that cannot be stilled by manipulation, challenged by the clarifying drama of public confrontation and dialogue, will be forced to articulate the realities of their own experiences as women subject to the will of men. In doing so, the anger that necessarily arises from a true perception of how they have been debased may move them beyond the fear that transfixes them to a meaningful rebellion against the men who in fact diminish, despise, and terrorize them. This is the common struggle of all women, whatever their male-defined ideological origins; and this struggle alone has the power to transform women who are enemies against one another into allies fighting for individual and collective survival that is not based on self-loathing, fear, and humiliation, but instead on self-determination, dignity, and authentic integrity.

LETTERS FROM A WAR ZONE

1988

I WANT A TWENTY-FOUR-HOUR TRUCE
DURING WHICH THERE IS NO RAPE
1983

This was a speech given at the Midwest Regional Conference of the National Organization for Changing Men in the fall of 1983 in St Paul, Minnesota. One of the organizers kindly sent me a tape and a transcript of my speech. The magazine of the men's movement, M., published it. I was teaching in Minneapolis. This was before Catharine MacKinnon and I had proposed or developed the civil rights approach to pornography as a legislative strategy. Lots of people were in the audience who later became key players in the fight for the civil rights bill. I didn't know them then. It was an audience of about 500 men, with scattered women. I spoke from notes and was actually on my way to Idaho—an eight-hour trip each way (because of bad air connections) to give a one-hour speech on Art—fly out Saturday, come back Sunday, can't talk more than one hour or you'll miss the only plane leaving that day, you have to run from the podium to the car for the two-hour drive to the plane. Why would a militant feminist under this kind of pressure stop off on her way to the airport to say hi to 500 men? In a sense, this was a feminist dream-come-true. What would you say to 500 men if you could? This is what I said, how I used my chance. The men reacted with considerable love and support and also with considerable anger. Both. I hurried out to get my plane, the first hurdle for getting to Idaho. Only one man in the 500 threatened me physically. He was stopped by a woman bodyguard (and friend) who had accompanied me.

I have thought a great deal about how a feminist, like myself, addresses an audience primarily of political men who say that they are antisexist. And I thought a lot about whether there should be a qualitative difference in the kind of speech I address to you. And then I found myself incapable of pretending that I really believe that that qualitative difference exists. I have watched the men's movement for many years. I am close with some of the people who participate in it. I can't come here as a friend even though I might very much want to. What I would like to do is to scream: and in that scream I would have the screams of the raped, and the sobs of the battered; and even worse, in the center of that scream I would have the deafening sound of women's silence, that silence into which we are born because we are women and in which most of us die.

And if there would be a plea or a question or a human address in that scream, it would be this: why are you so slow? Why are you so slow to understand the simplest things; not the complicated ideological things. You understand those. *The simple things.* The clichés. Simply that women are human to precisely the degree and quality that you are.

And also: that we do not have time. We women. We don't have forever. Some of us don't have another week or another day to take time for you to discuss whatever it is that will enable you to go out into those streets and do something. We are very close to death. All women are. And we are very close to rape and we are very close to beating. And we are inside a system of humiliation from which there is no escape for us. We use statistics not to try to quantify the injuries, but to convince the world that those injuries even exist. Those statistics are not abstractions. It is easy to say, "Ah, the statistics, somebody writes them up one way and somebody writes them up another way." That's true. But I hear about the rapes one by one by one by one by one, which is also how they happen. Those statistics are not abstract to me. Every three minutes a woman is being raped. Every eighteen seconds a woman is being beaten. There is nothing abstract about it. It is happening right now as I am speaking.

And it is happening for a simple reason. There is nothing complex and difficult about the reason. Men are doing it, because of the kind of power that men have over women. That power is real, concrete, exercised from one body to another body, exercised by someone who feels he has a right to exercise it, exercised in public and exercised in private. It is the sum and substance of women's oppression.

It is not done 5000 miles away or 3000 miles away. It is done here and it is done now and it is done by the people in this room as well as by other contemporaries: our friends, our neighbors, people that we know. Women don't have to go to school to learn about power. We just have to be women, walking down the street or trying to get the housework done after having given one's body in marriage and then having no rights over it.

The power exercised by men day to day in life is power that is institutionalized. It is protected by law. It is protected by religion and religious practice. It is protected by universities, which are strongholds of male supremacy. It is protected by a police force. It is protected by those whom Shelley called "the unacknowledged legislators of the world": the poets, the artists. Against that power, we have silence.

It is an extraordinary thing to try to understand and confront why it is that men believe—and men do believe—that they have the right to rape. Men may not believe it when asked. Everybody raise your hand who believes you have the right to rape. Not too many hands will go up. It's in life that men believe they have the right to force sex, which they don't call rape. And it is an extraordinary thing to try to understand that men really believe that they have the right to hit and to hurt. And it is an equally extraordinary thing to try to understand that men really believe that they have the right to buy a woman's body for the purpose of having sex: that that is a right. And it is very amazing to try to understand that men believe that the seven-billion-dollar-a-year industry that provides men with cunts is something that men have a right to.

That is the way the power of men is manifest in real life. That is what theory about male supremacy means. It means you can rape. It means you can hit. It means you can hurt. It means you can buy and sell women. It means that there is a class of people there to provide you with what you need. You stay richer than they are, so that they have to sell you sex. Not just on street corners, but in the workplace. That's another right that you can presume to have: sexual access to any woman in your environment, when you want.

Now, the men's movement suggests that men don't want the kind of power I have just described. I've actually heard explicit whole sentences to that effect. And yet, everything is a reason not to do something about changing the fact that you do have that power.

Hiding behind guilt, that's my favorite. I love that one. Oh, it's horrible, yes, and I'm so sorry. You have the time to feel guilty. We don't have the time for you to feel guilty. Your guilt is a form of acquiescence in what continues to occur. Your guilt helps keep things the way they are.

I have heard in the last several years a great deal about the suffering of men over sexism. Of course, I have heard a great deal about the suffering of men all my life. Needless to say, I have read *Hamlet*. I have read *King Lear*. I am an educated woman. I know that men suffer. This is a new wrinkle. Implicit in the idea that this is a different kind of suffering is the claim, I think, that in part you are actually suffering because of something that you know happens to someone else. That would indeed be new.

But mostly your guilt, your suffering, reduces to: gee, we really feel so bad. Everything makes men feel so bad: what you do, what you don't do, what you want to do, what you don't want to want to do but are going to do anyway. I think most of your distress is: gee, we really feel so bad. And I'm sorry that you feel so bad—so uselessly and stupidly bad—because there is a way in which this really is your tragedy. And I don't mean because you can't cry. And I don't mean because there is no real intimacy in your lives. And I don't mean because the armor that you have to live with as men is stultifying: and I don't doubt that it is. But I don't mean any of that.

I mean that there is a relationship between the way that women are raped and your socialization to rape and the war machine that grinds you up and spits you out: the war machine that you go through just like that woman went through Larry Flynt's meat grinder on the cover of *Hustler*. You damn well better believe that you're involved in this tragedy and that it's your tragedy too. Because you're turned into little soldier boys from the day that you are born and everything that you learn about how to avoid the humanity of women becomes part of the militarism of the country in which you live and the world in which you live. It is also part of the economy that you frequently claim to protest.

And the problem is that you think it's out there: and it's not out there. It's in you. The pimps and the warmongers speak for you. Rape and war are not so different. And what the pimps and the warmongers do is that they make you so proud of being men who can get it up and give it hard. And they take that acculturated sexuality and they put you in little uniforms and they send you out to kill and to die. Now, I am not going to suggest to you that I think that's more important than what you do to women, because I don't.

But I think that if you want to look at what this system does to you, then that is where you should start looking: the sexual politics of aggression; the sexual politics of militarism. I think that men are very afraid of other men. That is something that you sometimes try to address in your small groups, as if you changed your attitudes towards each other, you wouldn't be afraid of each other.

But as long as your sexuality has to do with aggression and your sense of entitlement to humanity has to do with being superior to other people, and there is so much contempt and hostility in your attitudes towards women and children, how could you not be afraid of each other? I think that you rightly perceive—without being willing to face it politically—that men are very dangerous: because you are.

The solution of the men's movement to make men less dangerous to each other by changing the way you touch and feel each other is not a solution. It's a recreational break.

These conferences are also concerned with homophobia. Homophobia is very important: it is very important to the way male supremacy works. In my opinion, the prohibitions against male homosexuality exist in order to protect male power. *Do it to her.* That is to say: as long as men rape, it is very important that men be directed to rape women. As long as sex is full of hostility and expresses both power over and contempt for the other person, it is very important that men not be declassed, stigmatized as female, used similarly. The power of men as a class depends on keeping men sexually inviolate and women sexually used by men. Homophobia helps maintain that class power: it also helps keep you as individuals safe from each other, safe from rape. If you want to do something about homophobia, you are going to have to do something about the fact that men rape, and that forced sex is not incidental to male sexuality but is in practice paradigmatic.

Some of you are very concerned about the rise of the Right in this country, as if that is something separate from the issues of feminism or the men's movement. There is a cartoon I saw that brought it all together nicely. It was a big picture of Ronald Reagan as a cowboy with a big hat and a gun. And it said: "A gun in every holster; a pregnant woman in every home. Make America a man again." Those are the politics of the Right.

If you are afraid of the ascendancy of fascism in this country—and you would be very foolish not to be right now—then you had better understand that the root issue here has to do with male supremacy and the control of women; sexual access to women; women as reproductive slaves; private ownership of women. That is the program of the Right. That is the morality they talk about. That is what they mean. That is what they want. And the only opposition to them that matters is an opposition to men owning women.

What's involved in doing something about all of this? The men's movement seems to stay stuck on two points. The first is that men don't really feel very good about themselves. How could you? The second is that men come to me or to other feminists and say: "What you're saying about men isn't true. It isn't true of me. I don't feel that way. I'm opposed to all of this."

And I say: don't tell me. Tell the pornographers. Tell the pimps. Tell the warmakers. Tell the rape apologists and the rape celebrationists and the pro-rape ideologues. Tell the novelists who think that rape is wonderful. Tell Larry Flynt. Tell Hugh Hefner. There's no point in telling me. I'm only a woman. There's nothing I can do about it. These men presume to speak for you. They are in the public arena saying that they represent you. If they don't, then you had better let them know.

Then there is the private world of misogyny: what you know about each other; what you say in private life; the exploitation that you see in the private sphere; the relationships called love, based on exploitation. It's not enough to find some traveling feminist on the road and go up to her and say: "Gee, I hate it. "

Say it to your friends who are doing it. And there are streets out there on which you can say these things loud and clear, so as to affect the actual institutions that maintain these abuses. You don't like pornography? I wish I could believe it's true. I will believe it when I see you on the streets. I will believe it when I see an organized political opposition. I will believe it when pimps go out of business because there are no more male consumers.

You want to organize men. You don't have to search for issues.

The issues are part of the fabric of your everyday lives.

I want to talk to you about equality, what equality is and what it means. It isn't just an idea. It's not some insipid word that ends up being bullshit. It doesn't have anything at all to do with all those statements like: "Oh, that happens to men too." I name an abuse and I hear: "Oh, it happens to men too." That is not the equality we are struggling for. We could change our strategy and say: well, okay, we want equality; well stick something up the ass of a man every three minutes.

You've never heard that from the feminist movement, because for us equality has real dignity and importance—it's not some dumb word that can be twisted and made to look stupid as if it had no real meaning.

As a way of practicing equality, some vague idea about giving up power is useless. Some men have vague thoughts about a future in which men are going to give up power or an individual man is going to give up some kind of privilege that he has. That is not what equality means either.

Equality is a practice. It is an action. It is a way of life. It is a social practice. It is an economic practice. It is a sexual practice.

It can't exist in a vacuum. You can't have it in your home if, when the people leave the home, he is in a world of his supremacy based on the existence of his cock and she is in a world of humiliation and degradation because she is perceived to be inferior and because her sexuality is a curse.

This is not to say that the attempt to practice equality in the home doesn't matter. It matters, but it is not enough. If you love equality, if you believe in it, if it is the way you want to live—not just men and women together in a home, but men and men together in a home and women and women together in a home—if equality is what you want and what you care about, then you have to fight for the institutions that will make it socially real.

It is not just a matter of your attitude. You can't think it and make it exist. You can't try sometimes, when it works to your advantage, and throw it out the rest of the time. Equality is a discipline. It is a way of life. It is a political necessity to create equality in institutions. And another thing about equality is that it cannot coexist with rape. It cannot. And it cannot coexist with pornography or with prostitution or with the economic degradation of women on any level, in any way. It cannot coexist, because implicit in all those things is the inferiority of women.

I want to see this men's movement make a commitment to ending rape because that is the only meaningful commitment to equality. It is astonishing that in all our worlds of feminism and antisexism we never talk seriously about ending rape. Ending it. Stopping it. No more. No more rape. In the back of our minds, are we holding on to its inevitability as the last preserve of the biological? Do we think that it is always going to exist no matter what we do? All of our political actions are lies if we don't make a commitment to ending the practice of rape. This commitment has to be political. It has to be serious. It has to be systematic. It has to be public. It can't be self-indulgent.

The things the men's movement has wanted are things worth having. Intimacy is worth having. Tenderness is worth having. Cooperation is worth having. A real emotional life is worth having. But you can't have them in a world with rape. Ending homophobia is worth doing. But you can't do it in a world with rape. Rape stands in the way of each and every one of those things you say you want. And by rape you know what I mean. A judge does not have to walk into this room and say that according to statute such and such these are the elements of proof. We're talking about any kind of coerced sex, including sex coerced by poverty.

You can't have equality or tenderness or intimacy as long as there is rape, because rape means terror. It means that part of the population lives in a state of terror and pretends—to please and pacify you—that it doesn't. So there is no honesty. How can there be? Can you imagine what it is like to live as a woman day in and day out with the threat of rape? Or what it is like to live with the reality? I want to see you use those legendary bodies and that legendary strength and that legendary courage and the tenderness that you say you have in behalf of women; and that means against the rapists, against the pimps, and against the pornographers. It means something more than a personal renunciation. It means a systematic, political, active, public attack. And there has been very little of that.

I came here today because I don't believe that rape is inevitable or natural. If I did, I would have no reason to be here. If I did, my political practice would be different than it is. Have you ever wondered why we are not just in armed combat against you? It's not because there's a shortage of kitchen knives in this country. It is because we believe in your humanity, against all the evidence.

We do not want to do the work of helping you to believe in your humanity. We cannot do it anymore. We have always tried. We have been repaid with systematic exploitation and systematic abuse. You are going to have to do this yourselves from now on and you know it.

The shame of men in front of women is, I think, an appropriate response both to what men do do and to what men do not do. I think you should be ashamed. But what you do with that shame is to use it as an excuse to keep doing what you want and to keep not doing anything else; and you've got to stop. You've got to stop. Your psychology doesn't matter. How much you hurt doesn't matter in the end any more than how much we hurt matters. If we sat around and only talked about how much rape hurt us, do you think there would have been one of the changes that you have seen in this country in the last fifteen years? There wouldn't have been.

It is true that we had to talk to each other. How else, after all, were we supposed to find out that each of us was not the only woman in the world not asking for it to whom rape or battery had ever happened? We couldn't read it in the newspapers, not then. We couldn't find a book about it. But you do know and now the question is what you are going to do; and so your shame and your guilt are very much beside the point. They don't matter to us at all, in any way. They're not good enough. They don't do anything.

As a feminist, I carry the rape of all the women I've talked to over the past ten years personally with me. As a woman, I carry my own rape with me. Do you remember pictures that you've seen of European cities during the plague, when there were wheelbarrows that would go along and people would just pick up corpses and throw them in? Well, that is what it is like knowing about rape. Piles and piles and piles of bodies that have whole lives and human names and human faces.

I speak for many feminists, not only myself, when I tell you that I am tired of what I know and sad beyond any words I have about what has already been done to women up to this point, now, up to 2:24 p.m. on this day, here in this place.

And I want one day of respite, one day off, one day in which no new bodies are piled up, one day in which no new agony is added to the old, and I am asking you to give it to me. And how could I ask you for less—it is so little. And how could you offer me less: it is so little. Even in wars, there are days of truce. Go and organize a truce. Stop your side for one day. I want a twenty-four-hour truce during which there is no rape.

I dare you to try it. I demand that you try it. I don't mind begging you to try it. What else could you possibly be here to do? What else could this movement possibly mean? What else could matter so much?

And on that day, that day of truce, that day when not one woman is raped, we will begin the real practice of equality, because we can't begin it before that day. Before that day it means nothing because it is nothing: it is not real; it is not true. But on that day it becomes real. And then, instead of rape we will for the first time in our lives—both men and women—begin to experience freedom.

If you have a conception of freedom that includes the existence of rape, you are wrong. You cannot change what you say you want to change. For myself, I want to experience just one day of real freedom before I die. I leave you here to do that for me and for the women whom you say you love.

RUINS

1978–1983

GOODBYE TO ALL THIS

(WITH APOLOGIES—ON MANY LEVELS—TO R. MORGAN)

1983

Goodbye, sisters, I've had it.

Goodbye, Pat, cow, cunt, silly bitch, whatever obscenity you are organizing for the right to call other women this week, fare thee well. Enjoy. Keep writing articles for Bob Guiccione on how to tie women up. Bet the money is fun too.

Goodbye, Ellen, baaad baaad Ellen, naughty girl, cheeky thing, sexy little devil. Goodbye to the Contradictions: good girl, bad girl, good Jew, bad Jew—how do you do it? It was all too deep, too radical, *too taboo* for conventional, conforming, ladylike, virginal me anyway. Have a good time lacerating Freud and Marx and enjoy the fantasy (use the perfume too, go all the way).

Goodbye, Amber, hot stuff, outlaw, Jesse James but oh so femme fatale, daring to be blond, daring to wear make-up (it takes the breath away, Amber, really it does, so Brave), keep fighting for the right to be femme, honey, take it all the way to the Pentagon, bring the military industrial complex to its knees.

Goodbye, Gayle. As you are already on your knees, just keep shuffling along. Reading Foucault really is kinky—chained or not, it brings a whole new dimension to masochism. Bow and scrape *except* when standing up for your lover's right to dress like a Nazi and then hang tough, kike. Being a woman and a Jew means double-your-pleasure (chew the gum too, go all the way).

Goodbye all you swastika-wielding dykettes, all you tough dangerous feminist leatherettes, all you sexy, nonmonogamous (it does take the breath away), pierced, whipped, bitten, fist-fucked and fist-fucking, wild wonderful heretofore unimaginable feminist Girls. Keep the Jews in line and the cows dying. (Oh for the good old days of Lesbian-Feminist-Vegetarians for Jesus.)

Goodbye all you proud, pro-sex, liberated *Cosmo* intellectuals (*Village Voice* girls? *Mother Jones* eroticists?), fighting those oh so repressed (in fact dead) Victorians for the right to get laid, braving the scorn and censure of the nineteenth century, being nearly delinquent, letting boys do more than feel you up (is it true? do you really?). Keep organizing against repression—keep those men pumping away for freedom now (how many fucks does it take to screw in a lightbulb?). *And not being married.* Gosh.

Goodbye to all you cunts, my sisters, fighting for the right to be humiliated, for the right to walk the streets, for the right to be tied up and proud, for the right to be hurt, for the right to masturbate with rubber duckies, for the right to kiss ass, for the right to call blacks "niggers" and Jews "kikes," for the right to use the swastika as a sex toy and the plantation as a game, for the right to be called "nigger" and "kike," for the right to be what this society already says women, Jews, and blacks are. Brave. Smart. *Radical.* Goodbye to all this. Stay militant. Tie those knots *tight.* Watch the patriarchy crumble when confronted with your demands. That's it! You want it to collapse laughing! Goodbye, winners, enjoy the victory. It's nice to see girls get what they want. It's astonishing to see girls want what they get. Goodbye comedians. Give the rapists, pornographers, and pimps a good laugh. An army of baaad girls cannot fail.

Goodbye to stupid feminist academics who romanticize prostitution and to stupid feminist magazine editors who romanticize pornography and fetishism and sadomasochism. And especially goodbye to stupid feminist writers who romanticize rituals of degradation and symbols of inferiority. Oh, and incidentally, goodbye to all you feminists who go to bars and concerts but won't buy books. Goodbye to all this, all them, all you.

Goodbye Women's movement, hello girls. Goodbye to the great women who have done really brave things but are quiet now. Goodbye to the great women who are not quiet now. Goodbye to the organizers—blessed be. Goodbye to poor Women Against Pornography, which committed the crime of trying to fight the pornography industry, misogyny, the buying and selling of women, the use of women as objects—tried to stop all those good things— I mean all those baaad things—I mean all those *erotic* things. Goodbye Dorchen—you really are the *worst*: skinny, pretty, smart, employed, well-dressed, and still wanting what?—freedom? justice? equality? Still identifying with whom? Women? Still what? A feminist? Sister, it's a girls' movement now. Goodbye, Kathy the Incorrigible—come on, why shouldn't women be locked up in brothels and fucked and beaten until they die? *Moralist*. Goodbye, Robin. You had a dream. *Dummy*. You were supposed to have a fantasy. Goodbye Adrienne. The poems were supposed to be baaad, not good. Bye bye, Florence. Don't you know by now that children eat candy so as to be fucked by grown men? Goodbye all you born-again virgins, all you timid fragile creatures, all you conforming, ladylike Victorians with your puritanical aversions to suffering. Goodbye women. Goodbye to all this.

Goodbye to the silly women who went to jail fighting *Snuff* and goodbye to the fools who fought *Playboy* and *Hustler* and all the rest of it. Goodbye to all you Gidget-types breaking laws, risking beatings, organizing against criminal misogynists, picketing, demonstrating, marching, so you can stay chaste for and faithful to the beach-bum-who-is-really-going-to-be-a-doctor of your choice. There are easier ways, but goodbye to you naive rightwing humorless fanatics who won't use them. Goodbye, Linda, held captive, repeatedly beaten and raped, forced to make *Deep Throat*, forced to be fucked by a dog. The girls say it's just fantasy not violence. Goodbye to all them.

Goodbye to the dummies who thought sex could express reciprocity and equality and still be sexy. Goodbye to the dummies who thought this movement could change the world. Goodbye to those precious Madonna-types who shouted "Free Our Sisters Free Ourselves" in the streets and at rallies, at pimps and at police. Free Pat Free Ellen Free Gayle Free Amber Free Me. Goodbye to all this. Free the women. Give the girls what they want.

ICE AND FIRE

1986

The apartment is a storefront. You walk down a few steps to get to the door. Anyone can hide down where you have to walk. The whole front of the apartment is a store window. There is no way to open it. It is level with the street. It has nothing to keep anyone out, no bars, no grating. It is just a solid sheet of glass. The front room is right there, on the street. We keep it empty except for some clothes in our one closet. The middle room is right behind the front room, no door, just a half wall dividing the two rooms. No window. We have one single mattress, old, a sheet or two, a pillow or two, N's record player and her great jazz and blues and classical records, her clarinet, her saxophone, my typewriter, an Olivetti portable, a telephone. Behind the middle room is a large kitchen, no door between the rooms. There is a big wooden table with chairs. There are old, dirty appliances: old refrigerator, old stove. We don't cook much or eat much. We make buckets of iced tea. We have vodka in the refrigerator, sometimes whiskey too. Sometimes we buy orange juice. There are cigarettes on the table, butts piled up in muddy ashtrays or dirty, wet cups. There are some books and some paper and some pencils. There is a door and a window leading out back. The door has heavy metal grating over it, iron, weaved, so that no one can break in. The window is covered in the same heavy metal. The door is bolted with a heavy metal bolt and locked with a heavy metal police lock.

The floors are wooden and painted. The apartment is painted garish red and garish blue. It is insufferably dark, except for the front room on the street. We have to cover the window. It is insufferably hot with virtually no ventilation. It is a palace for us, a wealth of space. Off the kitchen is a thin wooden door, no lock, just a wooden latch. Through it is a toilet, shared with the next door apartment, also a storefront but vacant.

Before Juan comes, we are in the kitchen talking about our movie. We are going to make a movie, a tough, unsentimental avant-garde little number about women in a New York City prison. I have written it. It strangely resembles my own story: jailed over Vietnam the woman is endlessly strip-searched and then mangled inside by jail doctors. N will make it—direct it, shoot it, edit it. It is her film. R is the star. She is N's lover for years, plans on forever, it is on the skids but she hangs on, pretending not to know. She is movingly loyal and underneath pathetically desperate. N and I are not allowed to be lovers so we never are, alone. We evade the spirit of the law. N refuses to make a political film. Politics, she argues, is boring and temporary. Vietnam will be over and forgotten. A work of art must outlast politics. She uses words sparingly. Her language is almost austere, never ornate. We are artists, she says. I am liberal with her. She always brings out my generosity. I take no hard line on politics. I too want art. We need money. Most of ours goes for cigarettes, after which there isn't any left. We fuck for drugs. Speed is cheaper than food. We fuck for pills. We fuck for prescriptions. We fuck for meals when we have to. We fuck for drinks in bars. We fuck for tabs of acid. We fuck for capsules of mescaline. We fuck for loose change. We fuck for fun. We fuck for adventure. We fuck when we are hot from the weather. We fuck for big bucks to pro-duce our movie. In between, we discuss art and politics. We listen to music and read books. She plays sax and clarinet and I write short stories. We are poor but educated.

The day we moved in the men, our neighbors, paid us a visit. We will get you, they said. We will come when we are ready. We will fuck you when we are ready. We will come one night when we decide. Maybe we will sell you. N is worth a lot of money in Puerto Rico, they say. I am worth not so much but still a little something. They are relaxed, sober. Some have knives. They take their time. How will you keep us out, one man asks logically. What can you do to keep us out. One night we will come. There are six or seven of them there. Two speak, alternating promises. One night we will come.

Our friend M shows up then, cool cool pacifist hippie type, white, long hair in a ponytail. Hey man, he says, hey man, hey man, let's talk peace not war, let's be friends man, let's have some smoke. He invites them into our storefront. The men sit in a circle in the front room, the front door wide open. Hey, man, come on, these chicks are cool. Hey, man, come on, these chicks are cool. Hey, man, come on, I got some good smoke, let's just cool this out man smoke some smoke man together man these are cool chicks man. He passes a pipe, passes joints: it is a solemn ceremony. We gonna come in and get these chicks when we want them man. Hey man, come on, man, these chicks are real cool, man, you don't wanna mess with these chicks man they are cool man. The pipe goes round and round. The neighbors become quiet. The threats cease. M gloats with his hip, his cool, his ponytail accomplishment as peacemaker. Hey man any time you want some smoke you just come to me man just leave these chicks alone man smoke and peace man, you know, man.

They file out, quiet and stoned. M is elated. He has forged a treaty, man. M is piss-proud, man. We get stoned. Smoke, man. The front door stays wide open as we sit in the front room and smoke. Night comes, the dark. M points to the open door. Just stay cool with those guys, man. Those guys come back you just invite them in for a little smoke. It's cool, man.

———

I have a habit, not nice. I am two years into it this time. I have had it before. Black beauties. I take a lot of pills. The pills cost a lot of money. N takes them too. I don't know if it is addiction or pleasure for her or how long she has been taking them or if she can do without them. I never ask. These are privacies I respect. I have my own dignity too. I pretend it is cheaper than food.

One night N brings home a fuck, a Leo named Leo. He steals our speed and all our cash. The speed is gone. I go into emergency gear. I pretend it is a joke. How the fuck, I ask her repeatedly, can anyone be stupid enough to fuck someone who says he is a Leo named Leo? I ask this question, tell this joke, many times. I am scared. We find a trick. She fucks him because she lost the pills. It is our code and her own personal sense of courtesy. We get the pills. A Leo named Leo, I say. How can anyone be so stupid? We pop the pills. A Leo named Leo. We sit in our middle room, she is drinking scotch and I am drinking vodka, we are momentarily flush: and the pills hit. A Leo named Leo. We laugh until we start to cry. We hold our guts and shake. A Leo named Leo. She grins from ear to ear. She has done something incredibly witty: fucked a Leo named Leo. We are incredibly delighted with her.

———

Walking down St Mark's Place I run into an old lover, Nikko. He is Greek. I love Greece. We say hello, how are you in Greek. It is hot. I take him back with me. N is not there. We have a fight. I am insulted because he wants to wear a condom. But women are dirty, he says as a point of fact. I am offended. I won't allow the condom. We fight. He hits me hard in the face several times. He hits me until I fall. He fucks me. He leaves. It is two weeks before I remember that this is what happened last time. Last winter. Women carry diseases, he said. No condoms, I said. He hit me several times, hard in the face, holding me up so he could keep hitting. He fucked me and left. I had another lover coming, a woman I had been waiting for weeks to see, married, hard to see. I picked myself up and forgot about him. She was shameless: she liked the bruises, the fresh semen. He didn't use the condom. Either time.

———

We proceed with our film project. We are intensely committed to it, for the sake of art. The politics of it is mine, a hidden smile behind my eyes. We call a famous avant-garde film critic. He says he will come to see us at midnight. At midnight he comes. We sit in the front room, huddled on the floor. He is delicate, soft-spoken, a saintly smile: he likes formal, empty filmic statements not burdened by content: our film is some baroque monster in his presence, overgrown with values and story and plot and drama. It will never have this appearance again. Despite his differences with us—aesthetic, formal, ethereal—he will publish an interview with us to help us raise money. We feel lifted up, overwhelmed with recognition: what he must see in us to do this for us, a pure fire. We wait for the other shoe to drop.

But he sits there, beatific. We can interview each other and send it to him along with photographs of us. He drinks our pathetic iced tea. He smiles. No shoe drops. He leaves. The next days we spend in a frenzy of aesthetic busywork. We take pencils in hand and plot out long, interesting conversations about art. We try to document an interesting, convoluted discussion of film. We discuss Godard at some length and write down for posterity our important criticisms of him. We are brassy, hip, radical, cool. We haunt the photo machines at Woolworth's, taking artistic pictures of ourselves, four poses for four quarters. We use up all our change. We hustle more. Excuse me, sir, but someone just stole my money and I don't have a subway token to get home with. Excuse me, sir, I am very hungry and can't you spare a quarter so I can get some food. Excuse me, sir, I just lost my wallet and I don't have bus fare home.

Then we go back to the machine and pose and look intense and avant-garde. We mess up our hair and sulk, or we try grinning, we stare into the hidden camera, looking intense, looking deep, looking sulky and sultry and on drugs. We write down some more thoughts on art. We pick the photos we want. We hustle for money for stamps. Excuse me, sir, my child is sick and I don't have any money to buy her medicine.

The critic prints our interview. He doesn't print our photographs. We are famous. Our thoughts on film and art are in the newspaper. We wait for people to send us money.

INTERCOURSE

1987–1995

PREFACE TO THE SECOND EDITION
1995

When I finished writing *Intercourse* one colleague advised me to add an introduction to explain what the book said. That way, readers would not be shocked, afraid, or angry, because the ideas would be familiar—prechewed, easier to digest; I would be protected from bad or malicious readings and purposeful distortions; and my eagerness to explain myself would show that I wanted people to like me and my book, the quintessential feminine pose. At least one knee would be visibly bent.

Other colleagues—probably more to the point—told me straight-out to publish it under a pseudonym. I would not; and *Intercourse* became—socially speaking—a Rorschach inkblot in which people saw their fantasy caricatures of me and what they presumed to know about me. First published in the United States in 1987—simultaneously with my novel *Ice and Fire*—*Intercourse* is still being reviled in print by people who have not read it, reduced to slogans by journalists posing as critics or sages or deep thinkers, treated as if it were odious and hateful by every asshole who thinks that what will heal this violent world is more respect for dead white men.

My colleagues, of course, had been right; but their advice offended me. I have never written for a cowardly or passive or stupid reader, the precise characteristics of most reviewers—overeducated but functionally illiterate, members of a gang, a pack, who do their drive-by shootings in print and experience what they call "the street" at cocktail parties. "I heard it on the street," they say, meaning a penthouse closer to heaven. It is no accident that most of the books published in the last few years about the decline and fall of Anglo-European culture because of the polluting effect of women of all races and some men of color—and there are a slew of such books—have been written by white-boy journalists. Abandoning the J-school ethic of "who, what, where, when, how" and the discipline of Hemingway's lean, masculine prose, they now try to answer "why." That decline and fall, they say, is because talentless, uppity women infest literature; or because militant feminists are an obstacle to the prorape, prodominance art of talented living or dead men; or because the multicultural reader—likely to be female and/or not white—values Alice Walker and Toni Morrison above Aristotle and the Marquis de Sade. Hallelujah, I say.

Intercourse is a book that moves through the sexed world of dominance and submission. It moves in descending circles, not in a straight line, and as in a vortex each spiral goes down deeper. Its formal model is Dante's *Inferno*; its lyrical debt is to Rimbaud; the equality it envisions is rooted in the dreams of women, silent generations, pioneer voices, lone rebels, and masses who agitated, demanded, cried out, broke laws, and even begged. The begging was a substitute for retaliatory violence: doing bodily harm back to those who use or injure you. I want women to be done with begging.

The public censure of women as if we are rabid because we speak without apology about the world in which we live is a strategy of threat that usually works. Men often react to women's words—speaking and writing—as if they were acts of violence; sometimes men react to women's words with violence. So we lower our voices. Women whisper. Women apologize. Women shut up. Women trivialize what we know. Women shrink. Women pull back. Most women have experienced enough dominance from men—control, violence, insult, contempt—that no threat seems empty.

Intercourse does not say, forgive me and love me. It does not say, I forgive you, I love you. For a woman writer to thrive (or, arguably, to survive) in these current hard times, forgiveness and love must be subtext. No. I say no.

Can a man read *Intercourse*? Can a man read a book written by a woman in which she uses language without its ever becoming decorative or pretty? Can a man read a book written by a woman in which she, the author, has a direct relationship to experience, ideas, literature, life, including fucking, without mediation—such that what she says and how she says it are not determined by boundaries men have set for her? Can a man read a woman's work if it does not say what he already knows? Can a man let in a challenge not just to his dominance but to his cognition? And, specifically, am I saying that I know more than men about fucking? Yes, I am. Not just different: more and better, deeper and wider, the way anyone used knows the user.

Intercourse does not narrate my experience to measure it against Norman Mailer's or D. H. Lawrence's. The first-person is embedded in the way the book is built. I use Tolstoy, Kobo Abe, James Baldwin, Tennessee Williams, Isaac Bashevis Singer, Flaubert not as authorities but as examples: I use them; I cut and slice into them in order to exhibit them ; but the authority behind the book—behind each and every choice—is mine. In formal terms, then, *Intercourse* is arrogant, cold, and remorseless. You, the reader, will not be looking at me, the girl; you will be looking at them. In *Intercourse* I created an intellectual and imaginative environment in which you can see them. The very fact that I usurp their place—make them my characters—lessens the unexamined authority that goes not with their art but with their gender. I love the literature these men created; but I will not live my life as if they are real and I am not. Nor will I tolerate the continuing assumption that they know more about women than we know about ourselves. And I do not believe that they know more about intercourse. Habits of deference can be broken, and it is up to writers to break them. Submission can be refused; and I refuse it.

Of course, men have read and do read *Intercourse*. Many like it and understand it. Some few have been thrilled by it—it suggests to them a new possibility of freedom, a new sexual ethic: and they do not want to be users. Some men respond to the radicalism of *Intercourse*: the ideas, the prose, the structure, the questions that both underlie and intentionally subvert meaning. But if one's sexual experience has always and without exception been based on dominance—not only overt acts but also metaphysical and ontological assumptions—how can one read this book? The end of male dominance would mean—in the understanding of such a man—the end of sex. If one has eroticized a differential in power that allows for force as a natural and inevitable part of intercourse, how could one understand that this book does not say that all men are rapists or that all intercourse is rape? Equality in the realm of sex is an antisexual idea if sex requires dominance in order to register as sensation. As sad as I am to say it, the limits of the old Adam—and the material power he still has, especially in publishing and media—have set limits on the public discourse (by both men and women) about this book.

In general women get to say yea or nay to intercourse, which is taken to be a synonym for sex, *echt* sex. In this reductive brave new world, women like sex or we do not. We are loyal to sex or we are not. The range of emotions and ideas expressed by Tolstoy et al. is literally forbidden to contemporary women. Remorse, sadness, despair, alienation, obsession, fear, greed, hate—all of which men, especially male artists, express—are simple no votes for women. Compliance means yes; a simplistic rah-rah means yes; affirming the implicit right of men to get laid regardless of the consequences to women is a yes. Reacting against force or exploitation means no; affirming pornography and prostitution means yes. "I like it" is the standard for citizenship, and "I want it" pretty much exhausts the First Amendment's meaning for women. Critical thought or deep feeling puts one into the Puritan camp, that hallucinated place of exile where women with complaints are dumped, after which we can be abandoned. Why—socially speaking—feed a woman you can't fuck? Why fuck a woman who might ask a question let alone have a complex emotional life or a political idea? I refuse to tolerate this loyalty-oath approach to women and intercourse or women and sexuality or, more to the point, women and men. The pressure on women to say yes now extends to thirteen-year-old girls, who face a social gulag if they are not hot, accommodating, and loyal; increasingly they face violence from teenage boys who think that intercourse is ownership. The refusal to let women feel a whole range of feelings, express a whole range of ideas, address our own experience with an honesty that is not pleasing to men, ask questions that discomfit and antagonize men in their dominance, has simply created a new generation of users and victims—children, boys and girls respectively. The girls are getting fucked but they are not getting free or equal. It is time to notice. They get fucked; they get hit; they get raped—by boyfriends in high school. *Intercourse* wants to change what is happening to those girls. *Intercourse* asks at least some of the right questions. *Intercourse* conveys the density, complexity, and political significance of the act of intercourse: what it means that men—and now boys—feel entitled to come into the privacy of a woman's body in a context of inequality. *Intercourse* does this outside the boundaries set by men for women. It crosses both substantive and formal boundaries in what it says and how it says it.

For me, the search for truth and change using words is the meaning of writing; the prose, the thinking, the journey is sensuous and demanding. I have always loved the writing that takes one down deep, no matter how strange or bitter or dirty the descent. As a writer, I love the experience of caring, of remembering, of learning more, of asking, of wanting to know and to see and to say. *Intercourse* is search and assertion, passion and fury; and its form—no less than its content—deserves critical scrutiny and respect.

This is nihilism; or this is truth. He has to push in past boundaries. There is the outline of a body, distinct, separate, its integrity an illusion, a tragic deception, because unseen there is a slit between the legs, and he has to push into it. There is never a real privacy of the body that can coexist with intercourse: with being entered. The vagina itself is muscled and the muscles have to be pushed apart. The thrusting is persistent invasion. She is opened up, split down the center. She is occupied—physically, internally, in her privacy.

A human being has a body that is inviolate; and when it is violated, it is abused. A woman has a body that is penetrated in intercourse: permeable, its corporeal solidness a lie. The discourse of male truth—literature, science, philosophy, pornography—calls that penetration *violation*. This it does with some consistency and some confidence. *Violation* is a synonym for intercourse. At the same time, the penetration is taken to be a use, not an abuse; a normal use; it is appropriate to enter her, to push into ("violate") the boundaries of her body. She is human, of course, but by a standard that does not include physical privacy. She is, in fact, human by a standard that precludes physical privacy, since to keep a man out altogether and for a lifetime is deviant in the extreme, a psychopathology, a repudiation of the way in which she is expected to manifest her humanity.

There is a deep recognition in culture and in experience that intercourse is both the normal use of a woman, her human potentiality affirmed by it, and a violative abuse, her privacy irredeemably compromised, her selfhood changed in a way that is irrevocable, unrecoverable. And it is recognized that the use and abuse are not distinct phenomena but somehow a synthesized reality: both are true at the same time as if they were one harmonious truth instead of mutually exclusive contradictions.

Intercourse in reality is a use and an abuse simultaneously, experienced and described as such, the act parlayed into the illuminated heights of religious duty and the dark recesses of morbid and dirty brutality. She, a human being, is supposed to have a privacy that is absolute; except that she, a woman, has a hole between her legs that men can, must, do enter. This hole, her hole, is synonymous with entry. A man has an anus that can be entered, but his anus is not synonymous with entry. A woman has an anus that can be entered, but her anus is not synonymous with entry. The slit between her legs, so simple, so hidden—frankly, so innocent—for instance, to the child who looks with a mirror to see if it *could* be true—is there an entrance to her body down there? and something big comes into it? (how?) and something as big as a baby comes out of it? (how?) and doesn't that hurt?—that slit that means entry into her—intercourse—appears to be the key to women's lower human status. By definition, as the God who does not exist made her, she is intended to have a lesser privacy, a lesser integrity of the body, a lesser sense of self, since her body can be physically occupied and in the occupation taken over. By definition, as the God who does not exist made her, this lesser privacy, this lesser integrity, this lesser self, establishes her lesser significance: not just in the world of social policy but in the world of bare, true, real existence. She is defined by how she is made, that hole, which is synonymous with entry; and intercourse, the act fundamental to existence, has consequences to her being that may be intrinsic, not socially imposed. There is no analogue anywhere among subordinated groups of people to this experience of being made for intercourse: for penetration, entry, occupation.

There is no analogue in occupied countries or in dominated races or in imprisoned dissidents or in colonialized cultures or in the submission of children to adults or in the atrocities that have marked the twentieth century ranging from Auschwitz to the Gulag. There is nothing exactly the same, and this is not because the political invasion and significance of intercourse is banal up against these other hierarchies and brutalities. Intercourse is a particular reality for women as an inferior class; and it has in it, as part of it, violation of boundaries, taking over, occupation, destruction of privacy, all of which are construed to be normal and also fundamental to continuing human existence. There is nothing that happens to any other civilly inferior people that is the same in its meaning and in its effect even when those people are forced into sexual availability, heterosexual or homosexual; while subject people, for instance, may be forced to have intercourse with those who dominate them, the God who does not exist did not make human existence, broadly speaking, dependent on their compliance. The political meaning of intercourse for women is the fundamental question of feminism and freedom: can an occupied people—physically occupied inside, internally invaded—be free; can those with a metaphysically compromised privacy have self-determination; can those without a biologically based physical integrity have self-respect?

There are many explanations, of course, that try to be kind. Women are different but equal. Social policy is different from private sexual behavior. The staggering civil inequalities between men and women are simple, clear injustices unrelated to the natural, healthy act of intercourse. There is nothing implicit in intercourse that mandates male dominance in society. Each individual must be free to choose—and so we expand tolerance for those women who do not want to be fucked by men. Sex is between individuals, and social relations are between classes, and so we preserve the privacy of the former while insisting on the equality of the latter. Women flourish as distinct, brilliant individuals of worth in the feminine condition, including in intercourse, and have distinct, valuable qualities. For men and women, fucking is freedom; and for men and women, fucking is the same, especially if the woman chooses both the man and the act. Intercourse is a private act engaged in by individuals and has no implicit social significance. Repression, as opposed to having intercourse, leads to authoritarian social policies, including those of male dominance. Intercourse does not have a metaphysical impact on women, although, of course, particular experiences with individual men might well have a psychological impact. Intercourse is not a political condition or event or circumstance because it is natural. Intercourse is not occupation or invasion or loss of privacy because it is natural. Intercourse does not violate the integrity of the body because it is natural. Intercourse is fun, not oppression. Intercourse is pleasure, not an expression or confirmation of a state of being that is either ontological or social. Intercourse is because the God who does not exist made it; he did it right, not wrong; and he does not hate women even if women hate him. Liberals refuse categorically to inquire into even a possibility that there is a relationship between intercourse per se and the low status of women. Conservatives use what appears to be God's work to justify a social and moral hierarchy in which women are lesser than men. Radicalism on the meaning of intercourse—its political meaning to women, its impact on our very being itself—

is tragedy or suicide. "The revolutionary," writes Octavio Paz paraphrasing Ortega y Gasset, "is always a radical, that is, he [*sic*] is trying to correct the uses themselves rather than the mere abuses. . ."[1] With intercourse, the use is already imbued with the excitement, the derangement, of the abuse; and abuse is only recognized as such socially if the intercourse is performed so recklessly or so violently or so stupidly that the man himself has actually signed a confession through the manner in which he has committed the act. What intercourse *is* for women and what it *does* to women's identity, privacy, self-respect, self-determination, and integrity are forbidden questions; and yet how can a radical or any woman who wants freedom not ask precisely these questions? The quality of the sensation or the need for a man or the desire for love: these are not answers to questions of freedom; they are diversions into complicity and ignorance.

Some facts are known.

Most women do not experience orgasm from intercourse itself. When Shere Hite, in her groundbreaking study, asked women to report their own sexual experiences in detail and depth, she discovered that only three in ten women regularly experience orgasm from intercourse. The women's self-reports are not ideological. They want men, love, sex, intercourse; they want orgasm; but for most women, seven out of ten, intercourse does not *cause* orgasm. The women want, even strive for, orgasm from intercourse but are unable to achieve it. Hite, the strongest feminist and most honorable philosopher among sex researchers, emphasizes that women can and must take responsibility for authentic sexual pleasure: "the ability to orgasm when we want, to be in charge of our stimulation, represents owning our own bodies, being strong, free, and autonomous human beings."[2]

Intercourse occurs in a context of a power relation that is pervasive and incontrovertible. The context in which the act takes place, whatever the meaning of the act in and of itself, is one in which men have social, economic, political, and physical power over women. Some men do not have all those kinds of power over all women; but all men have some kinds of power over all women; and most men have controlling power over what they call *their* women—the women they fuck. The power is predetermined by gender, by being male. Intercourse as an act often expresses the power men have over women. Without being what the society recognizes as rape, it is what the society—when pushed to admit it—recognizes as dominance.

Intercourse often expresses hostility or anger as well as dominance.

Intercourse is frequently performed compulsively; and intercourse frequently requires as a precondition for male performance the objectification of the female partner. She has to look a certain way, be a certain type—even conform to preordained behaviors and scripts—for the man to want to have intercourse and also for the man to be able to have intercourse. The woman cannot exist before or during the act as a fully realized, existentially alive individual.

Despite all efforts to socialize women to want intercourse—e.g., women's magazines to pornography to *Dynasty*, incredible rewards and punishments to get women to conform and put out—women still want a more diffuse and tender sensuality that involves the whole body and a polymorphous tenderness.

There are efforts to reform the circumstances that surround intercourse, the circumstances that at least apparently contribute to its disreputable (in terms of rights and justice) legend and legacy. These reforms include: more deference to female sensuality prior to the act; less verbal assault as part of sexual expressiveness toward women; some lip service to female initiation of sex and female choice during lovemaking; less romanticizing of rape, at least as an articulated social goal.

Those who are political activists working toward the equality of women have other contextual reforms they want to make: economic equity; women elected to political office; strong, self-respecting role models for girls; emphasis on physical strength and self-defense, athletic excellence and endurance; rape laws that work; strategies for decreasing violence against women. These contextual reforms would then provide for the possibility that intercourse could be experienced in a world of social equality for the sexes. These reforms do not in any way address the question of whether intercourse itself can be an expression of sexual equality.

Life can be better for women—economic and political conditions improved—and at the same time the status of women can remain resistant, indeed impervious, to change: so far in history this is precisely the paradigm for social change as it relates to the condition of women. Reforms are made, important ones; but the status of women relative to men does not change. Women are still less significant, have less privacy, less integrity, less self-determination. This means that women have less freedom. Freedom is not an abstraction, nor is a little of it enough. A little more of it is not enough either. Having less, being less, impoverished in freedom and rights, women then inevitably have less self-respect: less self-respect than men have and less self-respect than any human being needs to live a brave and honest life. Intercourse as domination battens on that awful absence of self-respect. It expands to fill the near vacuum. The uses of women, now, in intercourse—not the abuses to the extent that they can be separated out—are absolutely permeated by the reality of male power over women. We are poorer than men in money and so we have to barter sex or sell it outright (which is why they keep us poorer in money). We are poorer than men in psychological well-being because for us self-esteem depends on the approval—frequently expressed through sexual desire—of those who have and exercise power over us. Male power may be arrogant or elegant; it can be churlish or refined: but we exist as persons to the extent that men in power recognize us. When they need some service or want some sensation, they recognize us somewhat, with a sliver of consciousness; and when it is over, we go back to ignominy, anonymous, generic womanhood. Because of their power over us, they are able to strike our hearts dead with contempt or condescension. We need their money; intercourse is frequently how we get it. We need their approval to be able to survive inside our own skins; intercourse is frequently how we get it. They force us to be compliant, turn us into parasites, then hate us for not letting go. Intercourse is frequently how we hold on: fuck me. How to separate the act of intercourse from the social reality of male power is not clear, especially because it is male power that constructs both the meaning and the current practice of intercourse as such. But it is clear that reforms do not change women's status relative to men, or have not yet. It is clear that reforms do not change the intractability of women's civil inferiority. Is intercourse itself then a basis of or a key to women's continuing social and sexual inequality? Intercourse may not cause women's orgasm or even have much of a correlation with it—indeed, we rarely find intercourse and orgasm in the same place at the same time—but intercourse and women's inequality are like Siamese twins, always in the same place at the same time pissing in the same pot.

Women have wanted intercourse to work and have submitted—with regret or with enthusiasm, real or faked—even though or even when it does not. The reasons have often been foul, filled with the spiteful but carefully hidden malice of the powerless. Women have needed what can be gotten through intercourse: the economic and psychological survival; access to male power through access to the male who has it; having some hold—psychological, sexual, or economic—on the ones who act, who decide, who matter. There has been a deep, consistent, yet of course muted objection to what Anais Nin has called "[t]he hunter, the rapist, the one for whom sexuality is a thrust, nothing more."[3] Women have also wanted intercourse to work in this sense: women have wanted intercourse to be, for women, an experience of equality and passion, sensuality and intimacy. Women have a vision of love that includes men as human too; and women want the human in men, including in the act of intercourse. Even without the dignity of equal power, women have believed in the redeeming potential of love. There has been—despite the cruelty of exploitation and forced sex—a consistent vision for women of a sexuality based on a harmony that is both sensual and possible. In the words of sex reformer Ellen Key:

> She will no longer be captured like a fortress or hunted like a quarry; nor will she like a placid lake await the stream that seeks its way to her embrace. A stream herself, she will go her own way to meet the other stream.[4]

A stream herself, she would move over the earth, sensual and equal; especially, she will go her own way.

Shere Hite has suggested an intercourse in which "thrusting would not be considered as necessary as it now is. . . [There might be] more a mutual lying together in pleasure, penis-in-vagina,

vagina-covering-penis, with female orgasm providing much of the stimulation necessary for male orgasm."[5]

These visions of a humane sensuality based in equality are in the aspirations of women; and even the nightmare of sexual inferiority does not seem to kill them. They are not searching analyses into the nature of intercourse; instead they are deep, humane dreams that repudiate the rapist as the final arbiter of reality. They are an underground resistance to both inferiority and brutality, visions that sustain life and further endurance.

They also do not amount to much in real life with real men. There is, instead, the cold fucking, duty-bound or promiscuous; the romantic obsession in which eventual abandonment turns the vagina into the wound Freud claimed it was; intimacy with men who dread women, coital dread—as Kafka wrote in his diary, "coitus as punishment for the happiness of being together"[6]

Fear, too, has a special power to change experience and compromise any possibility of freedom. A stream does not know fear. A woman does. Especially women know fear of men and of forced intercourse. Consent in this world of fear is so passive that the woman consenting could be dead and sometimes is. "Yeah," said one man who killed a woman so that he could fuck her after she was dead, "I sexually assaulted her after she was dead. I always see them girls laid out in the pictures with their eyes closed and I just had to do it. I dreamed about it for so long that I just had to do it."[7] A Nebraska appeals court did not think that the murder "was especially heinous, atrocious, cruel, or manifested exceptional depravity by ordinary standards of morality and intelligence," and in particular they found "no evidence the acts were performed for the satisfaction of inflicting either mental or physical pain or that pain existed for any prolonged period of time."[8] Are you afraid now? How can fear and freedom coexist for women in intercourse?

The role of fear in destroying the integrity of men is easy to articulate, to understand, hard to overstate. Men are supposed to conquer fear in order to experience freedom. Men are humiliated by fear, not only in their masculinity but in their rights and freedoms. Men are diminished by fear; compromised irrevocably by it because freedom is diminished by it. "Fear had entered his life," novelist Iris Murdoch wrote,

> and would now be with him forever. How easy it was for the violent to win. Fear was irresistible, fear was king, he had never really known this before when he had lived free and without it. Even unreasoning fear could cripple a man forever. . . . How well he understood how dictators flourished. The little grain of fear in each life was enough to keep millions quiet.[9]

Hemingway, using harder prose, wrote the same in book after book. But women are supposed to treasure the little grain of fear—rub up against it—eroticize it, want it, get excited by it; and the fear could and does keep millions quiet: millions of women; being fucked and silent; upright and silent; waiting and silent; rolled over on and silent; pursued and silent; killed, fucked, and silent. The silence is taken to be appropriate. The fear is not perceived as compromising or destroying freedom. The dictators do flourish: fuck and flourish.

Out of fear and inequality, women hide, use disguises, trying to pass for indigenous peoples who have a right to be there, even though we cannot pass. Appropriating Octavio Paz's description of the behavior of Mexicans in Los Angeles—which he might not like: "they feel ashamed of their origin. . . they act like persons who are wearing disguises, who are afraid of a stranger's look because it could strip them and leave them stark naked."[10] Women hide, use disguises, because fear has compromised freedom; and when a woman has intercourse—not hiding, dropping the disguise—she has no freedom because her very being has been contaminated by fear: a grain, a tidal wave, memory or anticipation.

The fear is fear of power and fear of pain: the child looks at the slit with a mirror and wonders how it can be, how will she be able to stand the pain. The culture romanticizes the rapist dimension of the first time: he will force his way in and hurt her. The event itself is supposed to be so distinct, so entirely unlike any other experience or category of sensation, that there is no conception that intercourse can be part of sex, including the first time, instead of sex itself. There is no slow opening up, no slow, gradual entry; no days and months of sensuality prior to entry and no nights and hours after entry. Those who learn to eroticize powerlessness will learn to eroticize the entry itself: the pushing in, the thrusting, the fact of entry with whatever force or urgency the act requires or the man enjoys. There is virtually no protest about entry as such from women; virtually no satire from men. A fairly formidable character in Don DeLillo's *White Noise*, the wife, agrees to read pornography to her husband but she has one condition:

> "I will read," she said. "But I don't want you to choose anything that has men inside women, quote-quote, or men entering women. 'I entered her.' 'He entered me.' We' re not lobbies or elevators. 'I wanted him inside me,' as if he could crawl completely in, sign the register, sleep, eat, so forth. I don't care what these people do as long as they don't enter or get entered."
>
> "Agreed."

"'I entered her and began to thrust.'"

"I'm in total agreement," I said.

"'Enter me, enter me, yes, yes.'"

"Silly usage, absolutely."

"'Insert yourself, Rex, I want you inside me, entering hard, entering deep, yes, now, oh.'"[11]

Her protests make him hard. The stupidity of the "he entered her" motif makes her laugh, not kindly. She hates it.

We are not, of course, supposed to be lobbies or elevators. Instead, we are supposed to be wombs, maternal ones; and the men are trying to get back in away from all the noise and grief of being adult men with power and responsibility. The stakes for men are high, as Norman O. Brown makes clear in prose unusually understated for him:

> Coitus successfully performed is incest, a return to the maternal womb; and the punishment appropriate to this crime, castration. What happens to the penis is coronation, followed by decapitation.[12]

This is high drama for a prosaic act of commonplace entry. Nothing is at risk for her, the entered; whereas he commits incest, is crowned king, and has his thing cut off. She might like to return to the maternal womb too—because life outside it is not easy for her either—but she has to be it, for husbands, lovers, adulterous neighbors, as well as her own children, boys especially. Women rarely dare, as we say, draw a line: certainly not at the point of entry into our own bodies, sometimes by those we barely know. Certainly they did not come from there, not originally, not from this womb belonging to this woman who is being fucked now. And so we have once again the generic meaning of intercourse—he has to climb back into some womb, maternal enough; he has to enter it and survive even coronation and decapitation. She is made for that; and what can it matter to him that in entering her, he is entering this one, real, unique individual.

And what is entry for her? Entry is the first acceptance in her body that she is generic, not individual; that she is one of a many that is antagonistic to the individual interpretation she might have of her own worth, purpose, or intention. Entered, she accepts her subservience to his psychological purpose if nothing else; she accepts being confused with his mother and his Aunt Mary and the little girl with whom he used to play "Doctor." Entered, she finds herself depersonalized into a function and worth less to him than he is worth to himself: because he broke through, pushed in, entered. Without him there, she is supposed to feel empty, though there is no vacuum there, not physiologically. Entered, she finds herself accused of regicide at the end. The king dead, the muscles of the vagina contract again, suggesting that this will never be easy, never be solved. Lovely Freud, of course, having discovered projection but always missing the point, wrote to Jung: "In private I have always thought of Adonis as the penis; the woman's joy when the god she had thought dead rises again is too transparent!"[13] Something, indeed, is too transparent; women's joy tends to be opaque.

Entered, she has mostly given something up: to Adonis, the king, the coronation, the decapitation for which she is then blamed; she has given up a dividing line between her and him. Entered, she then finds out what it is to be occupied: and sometimes the appropriate imagery is of evil and war, the great spreading evil of how soldiers enter and contaminate. In the words of Marguerite Duras, "evil is there, at the gates, against the skin."[14] It spreads, like war, everywhere: "breaking in every where, stealing, imprisoning, always there, merged and mingled. . . a prey to the intoxicating passion of occupying that delightful territory, a child's body, the bodies of those less strong, of conquered peoples."[15] She is describing an older brother she hates here ("I see wartime and the reign of my elder brother as one").[16] She is not describing her lover, an older man fucking an adolescent girl. But it is from the sex that she takes the texture of wartime invasion and occupation, the visceral reality of occupation: evil up against the skin—at the point of entry, just touching the slit; then it breaks in and at the same time it surrounds everything, and those with power use the conquered who are weaker, inhabit them as territory.

Physically, the woman in intercourse is a space inhabited, a literal territory occupied literally: occupied even if there has been no resistance, no force; even if the occupied person said yes please, yes hurry, yes more. Having a line at the point of entry into your body that cannot be crossed is different from not having any such line; and being occupied in your body is different from not being occupied in your body. It is human to experience these differences whether or not one cares to bring the consequences of them into consciousness. Humans, including women, construct meaning. That means that when something happens to us, when we have experiences, we try to find in them some reason for them, some significance that they have to us or for us. Humans find meaning in poverty and tyranny and the atrocities of history; those who have suffered most still construct meaning; and those who know nothing take their ignorance as if it were a precious, rare clay and they too construct meaning. In this way, humans assert that we have worth; what has happened to us matters; our time here on earth is not entirely filled with random events and spurious pain. On the contrary, we can understand some things if we try hard to learn empathy; we can seek freedom and honor and dignity; that we care about meaning gives us a human pride that has the fragility of a butterfly and the strength of tempered steel. The measure of women's oppression is that we do not take intercourse—entry, penetration, occupation—and ask or say what it means: to us as a dominated group or to us as a potentially free and self-determining people. Instead, intercourse is a loyalty test; and we are not supposed to tell the truth unless it compliments and upholds the dominant male ethos on sex. We know nothing, of course, about intercourse because we are women and women know nothing; or because what we know simply has no significance, entered into as we are. And men know everything—all of them—all the time—no matter how stupid or inexperienced or arrogant or ignorant they are. Anything men say on intercourse, any attitude they have, is valuable, knowledgeable, and deep, rooted in the cosmos and the forces of nature as it were: because they know; because fucking is knowing; because he knew her but she did not know him; because the God who does not exist framed not only sex but also knowledge that way. Women do not just lie about orgasm, faking it or saying it is not important. Women lie about life by not demanding to understand the meaning of entry, penetration, occupation, having boundaries crossed over, having lesser privacy: by avoiding the difficult, perhaps impossible (but how will we ever know?) questions of female freedom. We take oaths to truth all right, on the holy penis before entry. In so doing, we give up the most important dimension of what it means to be human: the search for the meaning of our real experience, including the sheer invention of that meaning—called creativity when men do it. If the questions make the holy penis unhappy, who could survive what the answers might do? Experience is chosen for us, then, imposed on us, especially in intercourse, *and so is its meaning.* We are allowed to have intercourse on the terms men determine, according to the rules men make. We do not have to have an orgasm; that terrible burden is on them. We are supposed to comply whether we want to or not. *Want* is active, not passive or lethargic. Especially we are supposed to be loyal to the male meanings of intercourse, which are elaborate, dramatic, pulling in elements of both myth and tragedy: the king is dead! long live the king!—and the Emperor wears designer jeans. We have no freedom and no extravagance in the questions we can ask or the interpretations we can make. We must be loyal; and on what scale would we be able to reckon the cost of that? Male sexual discourse on the meaning of intercourse becomes our language. It is not a second language even though it is not our native language; it is the only language we speak, however, with perfect fluency even though it does not say what we mean or what we think we might know if only we could find the right word and enough privacy in which to articulate it even just in our own minds. We know only this one language of these folks who enter and occupy us: they keep telling us that we are different from them; yet we speak only their language and have none, or none that we remember, of our own; and we do not dare, it seems, invent one, even in signs and gestures. Our bodies speak their language. Our minds think in it. The men are inside us through and through. We hear something, a dim whisper, barely audible, somewhere at the back of the brain; there is some other word, and we think, some of us, sometimes, that once it belonged to us.

There are female-supremacist models for intercourse that try to make us the masters of this language that we speak that is not ours.

They evade some fundamental questions about the act itself and acknowledge others. They have in common a glorious ambition to see women self-determining, vigorous and free lovers who are never demeaned or diminished by force or subordination, not in society, not in sex. The great advocate of the female-first model of intercourse in the nineteenth century was Victoria Woodhull. She understood that rape was slavery; not less than slavery in its insult to human integrity and human dignity. She acknowledged some of the fundamental questions of female freedom presented by intercourse in her imperious insistence that women had a *natural* right— a right that inhered in the nature of intercourse itself—to be entirely self determining, the controlling and dominating partner, the one whose desire determined the event, the one who both initiates and is the final authority on what the sex is and will be. Her thinking was not mean-spirited, some silly role reversal to make a moral point; nor was it a taste for tyranny hidden in what pretended to be a sexual ethic. She simply understood that women are unspeakably vulnerable in intercourse because of the nature of the act—entry, penetration, occupation; and she understood that in a society of male power, women were unspeakably exploited in intercourse. Society—men—had to agree to let the woman be the mind, the heart, the lover, the free spirit, the physical vitality behind the act. The commonplace abuses of forced entry, the devastating consequences of being powerless and occupied, suggested that the only condition under which women could experience sexual freedom in intercourse—real choice, real freedom, real happiness, real pleasure— was in having real and absolute control in each and every act of intercourse, which would be, each and every time, chosen by the woman. She would have the incontrovertible authority that would make intercourse possible:

To woman, by nature, belongs the right of sexual determination. When the instinct is aroused in her, then and then only should commerce follow. When woman rises from sexual slavery to sexual freedom, into the ownership and control of her sexual organs, and man is obliged to respect this freedom, then will this instinct become pure and holy; then will woman be raised from the iniquity and morbidness in which she now wallows for existence, and the intensity and glory of her creative functions be increased a hundred-fold. . . [17]

The consent standard is revealed as pallid, weak, stupid, second-class, by contrast with Woodhull's standard: that the woman should have authority and control over the act. The sexual humiliation of women through male ownership was understood by Woodhull to be a concrete reality, not a metaphor, not hyperbole: the man owned the woman's sexual organs. She had to own her sexual organs for intercourse to mean freedom for her. This is more concrete and more meaningful than a more contemporary vocabulary of "owning" one's own desire. Woodhull wanted the woman's desire to be the desire of significance; but she understood that ownership of the body was not an abstraction; it was concrete and it came first. The "iniquity and morbidness" of intercourse under male dominance would end if women could exercise a materially real self-determination in sex. The woman having material control of her own sex organs and of each and every act of intercourse would not lead to a reverse dominance, the man subject to the woman, because of the nature of the act and the nature of the sex organs involved in the act: this is the sense in which Woodhull tried to face the fundamental questions raised by intercourse as an act with consequences, some perhaps intrinsic. The woman could not forcibly penetrate the man.

The woman could not take him over as he took her over and occupy his body physically inside. His dominance over her expressed in the physical reality of intercourse had no real analogue in desire she might express for him in intercourse: she simply could not do to him what he could do to her. Woodhull's view was materialist, not psychological; she was the first publisher of the *Communist Manifesto* in the United States and the first woman stockbroker on Wall Street. She saw sex the way she saw money and power: in terms of concrete physical reality. Male notions of female power based on psychology or ideas would not have addressed for her the real issues of physical dominance and power in intercourse. The woman would not force or rape or physically own the man because she could not.

Thus, giving the woman power over intercourse was giving her the power to be equal. Woodhull's vision was in fact deeply humane, oriented toward sexual pleasure in freedom. For women, she thought and proclaimed (at great cost to herself), freedom must be literal, physical, concrete self-determination beginning with absolute control of the sexual organs; this was a natural right that had been perverted by male dominance—and because of its perversion, sex was for women morbid and degrading. The only freedom imaginable in this act of intercourse was freedom based on an irrevocable and unbreachable female will given play in a body honestly her own. This was an eloquent answer to reading the meaning of intercourse the other way: by its nature, intercourse mandated that the woman must be lesser in power and in privacy. Instead, said Woodhull, the woman must be king. Her humanity required sexual sovereignty.

Male-dominant gender hierarchy, however, seems immune to reform by reasoned or visionary argument or by changes in sexual styles, either personal or social. This may be because intercourse itself is immune to reform. In it, female is bottom, stigmatized. Intercourse remains a means or the means of physiologically making a woman inferior: communicating to her cell by cell her own inferior status, impressing it on her, burning it into her by shoving it into her, over and over, pushing and thrusting until she gives up and gives in—which is called *surrender* in the male lexicon. In the experience of intercourse, she loses the capacity for integrity because her body—the basis of privacy and freedom in the material world for all human beings—is entered and occupied; the boundaries of her physical body are—neutrally speaking—violated. What is taken from her in that act is not recoverable, and she spends her life— wanting, after all, to have something—pretending that pleasure is in being reduced through intercourse to insignificance. She will not have an orgasm—maybe because she has human pride and she resents captivity; but also she will not or cannot rebel—not enough for it to matter, to end male dominance over her. She learns to eroticize powerlessness and self-annihilation. The very boundaries of her own body become meaningless to her, and even worse, useless to her. The transgression of those boundaries comes to signify a sexually charged degradation into which she throws herself, having been told, convinced, that identity, for a female, is there—somewhere beyond privacy and self-respect.

It is not that there is no way out if, for instance, one were to establish or believe that intercourse itself determines women's lower status. New reproductive technologies have changed and will continue to change the nature of the world. Intercourse is not necessary to existence anymore. Existence does not depend on female compliance, nor on the violation of female boundaries, nor on lesser female privacy, nor on the physical occupation of the female body. But the hatred of women is a source of sexual pleasure for men in its own right. Intercourse appears to be the expression of that contempt in pure form, in the form of a sexed hierarchy; it requires no passion or heart because it is power without invention articulating the arrogance of those who do the fucking. Intercourse is the pure, sterile, formal expression of men's contempt for women; but that contempt can turn gothic and express itself in many sexual and sadistic practices that eschew intercourse per se. Any violation of a woman's body can become sex for men; this is the essential truth of pornography. So freedom from intercourse, or a social structure that reflects the low value of intercourse in women's sexual pleasure, or intercourse becoming one sex act among many entered into by (hypothetical) equals as part of other, deeper, longer, perhaps more sensual lovemaking, or an end to women's inferior status because we need not be forced to reproduce (forced fucking frequently justified by some implicit biological necessity to reproduce): none of these are likely social developments because there is a hatred of women, unexplained, undiagnosed, mostly unacknowledged, that pervades sexual practice and sexual passion. Reproductive technologies are strengthening male dominance, invigorating it by providing new ways of policing women's reproductive capacities, bringing them under stricter male scrutiny and control; and the experimental development of these technologies has been sadistic, using human women as if they were sexual laboratory animals—rats, mice, rabbits, cats, with kinky uteri. For increasing numbers of men, bondage and torture of the female genitals (that were entered into and occupied in the good old days) may supplant intercourse as a sexual practice. The passion for hurting women is a sexual passion; and sexual hatred of women can be expressed without intercourse.

There has always been a peculiar irrationality to all the biological arguments that supposedly predetermine the inferior social status of women. Bulls mount cows and baboons do whatever; but human females do not have estrus or go into heat. The logical inference is not that we are *always* available for mounting but rather that we are never, strictly speaking, "available." Nor do animals have cultures; nor do they determine in so many things what they will do and how they will do them and what the meaning of their own behavior is. They do not decide what their lives will be. Only humans face the often complicated reality of having potential and having to make choices based on having potential. We are not driven by instinct, at least not much. We have possibilities, and we make up meanings as we go along. The meanings we create or learn do not exist only in our heads, in ineffable ideas. Our meanings also exist in our bodies— what we are, what we do, what we physically feel, what we physically know; and there is no personal psychology that is separate from what the body has learned about life. Yet when we look at the human condition, including the condition of women, we act as if we are driven by biology or some metaphysically absolute dogma. We refuse to recognize our possibilities because we refuse to honor the potential humans have, including human women, to make choices. Men too make choices. When will they choose not to despise us?

Being female in this world is having been robbed of the potential for human choice by men who love to hate us. One does not make choices in freedom. Instead, one conforms in body type and behavior and values to become an object of male sexual desire, which requires an abandonment of a wide-ranging capacity for choice. Objectification may well be the most singly destructive aspect of gender hierarchy, especially as it exists in relation to intercourse. The surrender occurs before the act that is supposed to accomplish the surrender takes place. She has given in; why conquer her? The body is violated before the act occurs that is commonly taken to be violation. The privacy of the person is lessened before the privacy of the woman is invaded: she has remade herself so as to prepare the way for the invasion of privacy that her preparation makes possible. The significance of the human ceases to exist as the value of the object increases: an expensive ornament, for instance, she is incapable of human freedom—taking it, knowing it, wanting it, being it. Being an object—living in the realm of male objectification—is abject submission, an abdication of the freedom and integrity of the body, its privacy, its uniqueness, its worth in and of itself because it is the human body of a human being. Can intercourse exist without objectification? Would intercourse be a different phenomenon if it could, if it did? Would it be shorter or longer, happier or sadder; more complex, richer, denser, with a baroque beauty or simpler with an austere beauty; or bang bang bang? Would intercourse without objectification, if it could exist, be compatible with women's equality—even an expression of it—or would it still be stubbornly antagonistic to it? Would intercourse cause orgasm in women if women were not objects for men before and during intercourse? Can intercourse exist without objectification and can objectification exist without female complicity in maintaining it as a perceived reality and a material reality too: can objectification exist without the woman herself turning herself into an object—becoming through effort and art a thing, less than human, so that he can be more than human, hard, sovereign, king? Can intercourse exist without the woman herself turning herself into a thing, which she must do because men cannot fuck equals and men must fuck: because one price of dominance is that one is impotent in the face of equality?

To become the object, she takes herself and transforms herself into a thing: all freedoms are diminished and she is caged, even in the cage docile, sometimes physically maimed, movement is limited: she physically becomes the thing he wants to fuck. It is especially in the acceptance of object status that her humanity is hurt: it is a metaphysical acceptance of lower status in sex and in society; an implicit acceptance of less freedom, less privacy, less integrity. In becoming an object so that he can objectify her so that he can fuck her, she begins a political collaboration with his dominance; and then when he enters her, he confirms for himself and for her what she is: that she is something, not someone; certainly not someone equal.

There is the initial complicity, the acts of self-mutilation, self-diminishing, self-reconstruction, until there is no self, only the diminished, mutilated reconstruction. It is all superficial and unimportant, except what it costs the human in her to do it: except for the fact that it is submissive, conforming, giving up an individuality that would withstand object status or defy it. Something happens inside; a human forgets freedom; a human learns obedience; a human, this time a woman, learns how to goose-step the female way. Wilhelm Reich, that most optimistic of sexual liberationists, the only male one to abhor rape *really*, thought that a girl needed not only "a free genital sexuality" but also "an undisturbed room, proper contraceptives, a friend who is capable of love, that is, not a National Socialist. . ."[18] All remain hard for women to attain; but especially the lover who is not a National Socialist. So the act goes beyond complicity to collaboration; but collaboration requires a preparing of the ground, an undermining of values and vision and dignity, a sense of alienation from the worth of other human beings—and this alienation is fundamental to females who are objectified because they do not experience themselves as human beings of worth except for their value on the market as objects.

Knowing one's own human value is fundamental to being able to respect others: females are remade into objects, not human in any sense related to freedom or justice—and so what can females recognize in other females that is a human bond toward freedom? Is there anything in us to love if we do not love each other as the objects we have become? Who can love someone who is less than human unless love itself is domination per se? Alienation from human freedom is deep and destructive; it destroys whatever it is in us as humans that is creative, that causes us to want to find meaning in experiences, even hard experiences; it destroys in us that which wants freedom whatever the hardship of attaining it. In women, these great human capacities and dimensions are destroyed or mutilated; and so we find ourselves bewildered—who or what are these so-called persons in human form but even that not quite, not exactly, who cannot remember or manifest the physical reality of freedom, who do not seem to want or to value the individual experience of freedom? Being an object for a man means being alienated from other women—those like her in status, in inferiority, in sexual function. Collaboration by women with men to keep women civilly and sexually inferior has been one of the hallmarks of female subordination; we are ashamed when Freud notices it, but it is true. That collaboration, fully manifested when a woman values her lover, the National Socialist, above any woman, any one of her own kind or class or status, may have simple beginnings: the first act of complicity that destroys self-respect, the capacity for self-determination and freedom—readying the body for the fuck instead of for freedom. The men have an answer: intercourse is freedom. Maybe it is second-class freedom for second-class humans.

What does it mean to be the person who needs to have this done to her: who needs to be needed as an object; who needs to be entered; who needs to be occupied; who needs to be wanted more than she needs integrity or freedom or equality? If objectification is necessary for intercourse to be possible, what does that mean for the person who needs to be fucked so that she can experience herself as female and who needs to be an object so that she can be fucked?

The brilliance of objectification as a strategy of dominance is that it gets the woman to take the initiative in her own degradation (having less freedom is degrading). The woman herself takes one kind of responsibility absolutely and thus commits herself to her own continuing inferiority: she polices her own body; she internalizes the demands of the dominant class and, in order to be fucked, she constructs her life around meeting those demands. It is the best system of colonialization on earth: she takes on the burden, the responsibility, of her own submission, her own objectification. In some systems in which turning the female into an object for sex requires actual terrorism and maiming—for instance, footbinding or removing the clitoris—the mother does it, having had it done to her by her mother. What men need done to women so that men can have intercourse with women is done to women so that men will have intercourse; no matter what the human cost; and it is a gross indignity to suggest that when her collaboration is complete— unselfconscious because there is no self and no consciousness left— she is free to have freedom in intercourse. When those who domi- nate you get you to take the initiative in your own human destruction, you have lost more than any oppressed people yet has ever gotten back. Whatever intercourse is, it is not freedom; and if it cannot exist without objectification, it never will be. Instead occupied women will be collaborators, more base in their collaboration than other collaborators have ever been: experiencing pleasure in their own inferiority; calling intercourse freedom. It is a tragedy beyond the power of language to convey when what has been imposed on women by force becomes a standard of freedom for women: and all the women say it is so.

If intercourse can be an expression of sexual equality, it will have to survive—on its own merits as it were, having a potential for human expression not yet recognized or realized—the destruction of male power over women; and rape and prostitution will have to be seen as the institutions that most impede any experience of intercourse as freedom—chosen by full human beings with full human freedom. Rape and prostitution negate self-determination and choice for women; and anyone who wants intercourse to be freedom and to mean freedom had better find a way to get rid of them. Maybe life is tragic and the God who does not exist made women inferior so that men could fuck us; or maybe we can only know this much for certain—that when intercourse exists and is experienced under conditions of force, fear, or inequality, it destroys in women the will to political freedom; it destroys the love of freedom itself. We become female: occupied; collaborators against each other, especially against those among us who resist male domination—the lone, crazy resisters, the organized resistance. The pleasure of submission does not and cannot change the fact, the cost, the indignity, of inferiority.

MERCY

1990

One night I'm just there, where I live, alone, afraid, the men have been trying to come in. I'm for using men up as fast as you can; pulling them, grab, twist, put it here, so they dangle like twisted dough or you bend them all around like pretzels; you pull down, the asshole crawls. You need a firm, fast hand, a steady stare, calm nerve; grab, twist. First, fast; before they get to throw you down. You surprise them with your stance, warrior queen, quiet, mean, and once your hands are around their thing they're stupid, not tough; still mean but slow and you can get gone, it takes the edge off how mean he's going to be. Were you ever so alone as me? It doesn't matter what they do to you just so you get them first—it's your game and you get money; even if they shit on you it's your game; as long as it's your game you have freedom, you say it's fun but whatever you say you're in charge. Some people think being poor is the freedom or the game. It's being the one who says how and do it to me now; instead of just waiting until he does it and he's gone. You got to be mad at them perpetually and forever and fierce and you got to know that you got a cunt and that's it. You want philosophy and you're dumb and dead; you want true love and real romance, the same. You put your hand between them and your twat and you got a chance; you use it like it's a muscle, sinew and grease, a gun, a knife; you grab and twist and turn and stare him in the eye, smile, he's already losing because you got there first, between his legs; his thing's in your fist and your fist is closing on him fast and he's got a failure of nerve for one second, a pause, a gulp, one second, disarmed, unsure, long enough so he doesn't know, can't remember, how mean he is; and then you have to take him into you, of course, you've given your word; there on the cement or in a shadow or some room; a shadow's warm and dark and consoling and no one can close the door on you and lock you in; you don't go with him somewhere unless you got a feeling for him because you never know what they'll do; you go for the edge, a feeling, it's worth the risk; you learn what they want, early, easy, it's not hard, you can ride the energy they give out or see it in how they move or read it off their hips; or you can guide them, there's never enough blow jobs they had to make them tired of it if worse comes to worse and you need to, it will make him stupid and weak but sometimes he's mean after because he's sure you're dirt, anyone who's had him in her mouth is dirt, how do they get by, these guys, so low and mean. It's you, him, midnight, cement; viscous dark, slate gray bed, light falling down from tarnished bulbs above you; neon somewhere rattling, shaking, static shocks to your eye, flash, zing, zip, winding words, a long poem in flickering light; what is neon and how did it get into the sky at night? The great gray poet talked it but he didn't have to do it. He was a shithead. I'm the real poet of everyone; the Amerikan democrat on cement, with everyone; it wears you down, Walt; I don't like poetry anymore; it's semen, you great gray clod, not some fraternal wave of democratic joy. I was born in 1946 down the street from where Walt Whitman lived; the girl he never wanted, I can face it now; in Camden, the great gray city; on great gray cement, broken, bleeding, the girls squashed down on it, the fuck weighing down on top, pushing in behind; blood staining the gravel, mine not his; bullshitter poet, great gray bullshitter; having all the men in the world, and all the women, hard, real, true, it wears you down, great gray virgin with fantastic dreams, you great gray fool. I was born in

1946 down the street from where Walt Whitman lived, in Camden, Andrea, it means manhood or courage but it was pink pussy anyway wrapped in a pink fuzzy blanket with big men's fingers going coochie coochie coo. Pappa said don't believe what's in books but if it was a poem I believed it; my first lyric poem was a street, cement, gray, lined with monuments, broken brick buildings, archaic, empty vessels, great, bloodstained walls, a winding road to nowhere, gray, hard, light falling on it from a tarnished moon so it was silver and brass in the dark and it went out straight into the gray sky where the moon was, one road of cement and silver and night stained red with real blood, you're down on your knees and he's pushing you from inside, God's heartbeat ramming into you and the skin is scraped loose and you bleed and stain the stone under you. Here's the poem you got. It's your flesh scraped until it's rubbed off and you got a mark, you got a burn, you got stains of blood, you got desolation on you. It's his mark on you and you've got his smell on you and his bruise inside you; the houses are monuments, brick, broken brick, red, blood red. There's a skyline, five floors high, three floors high, broken brick, chopped off brick, empty inside, with gravel lots and a winding cement road, Dorothy tap-dances to Oz, up the yellow brick road, the great gray road, he's on you, twisted on top of you, his arms twisted in your arms, his legs twisted in your legs, he's twisted in you, there's a great animal in the dark, him twisting draped over you, the sweat silver and slick; the houses are brick, monuments around you, you're laid out dead and they're the headstones, nothing written on them, they tower over your body put to rest. The only signs of existence are on you, you carry them on you, the marks, the bruises, the scars, your body gets marked where you exist, it's a history book with the signs of civilized life, communication, the city, the society, *belles lettres*, a primitive alphabet of blood and pain, the flesh poem, poem of the girl, when a girl says yes, what a girl says yes to, what happens to a girl who is poesy on cement, your body the paper and the poem, the press and the ink, the singer and the song; it's real, it's literal, this song of myself, you're what there is, the medium, the message, the sign, the signifier; an autistic poem. Tattooed boys are your friends, they write the words on their skin; but your skin gets used up, scraped away every time they push you down, you carry what you got and what you know, all your belongings, him on you through time, in the scars—your meanings, your lists, your items, your serial numbers and identification numbers, social security, registration, which one you are, your name in blood spread thin on your skin, spread out on porous skin, thin and stretched, a delicate shade of fear toughened by callouses of hate; and you learn to read your name on your body written in your blood, the book of signs, manhood or courage but it's different when pussy does it. You don't set up house-keeping, a room with things; instead you carry it all on you, not on your back tied down, or on your head piled up; it's in you, carved in, the cold on you, you on cement, sexy abrasions, sexy blood, sexy black and blue, the heat's on you, your sweat's a wet membrane between you and the weather, all there is, and you have burns, scars, there's gray cement, a silver gray under a tarnished, brassy moon, there's a cement graveyard, brick gravestones, the empty brick buildings; and you're laid out, for the fucking. Walt was a fool, a virgin fool; you would have been ground down, it's not love, it's slaughter, you fucking fool. I'm the field, they fall on me and bruise the ground, you don't hear the earth you fall on crying out but a poet should know. Prophets are fucking fools. What I figured out is that writers sit in rooms and make it up. Marx made it up. Walt made it up. Fucking fools like me believe it; do it; foot soldiers in hell. Sleep is the worst time, God puts you in a fuck-me position, you can't run, you can't fight, you can't stay alive without luck, you're in the dark and dead, they can get you, have you, use you; you manage to disappear, become invisible in the dark, or it's like being hung out to dry, you're under glass, in a museum, all laid out, on display, waiting for whatever gang passes by to piss on you; it's inside, they're not supposed to come inside but there is no inside where they can't come, it's only doors and windows to keep them out, open sesame and the doors and windows open or they bash them open and no one stops them and you're inside laid out for them, come, hurt me now, I'm lying flat, helpless, some fucking innocent naked baby, a sweet, helpless thing all curled up like a fetus as if I were safe, inside her; but there's nothing between you and them; she's not between you and them. Why did God make you have to sleep? I was born in Camden; I'm twenty; I can't remember the last time I heard my name. My name is and will the real one please stand up, do you remember that game show on television, from when it was easy. Women will whisper it to you, even dirty street women; even leather women; even mean women. You have to be careful if you want it from the street women; they might be harder than you, know where you're soft, see through you, you're all different with them because maybe they can see through you. Maybe you're not the hardest bitch. Maybe she's going to take from you. I don't give; I take. It's when she's on me I hear my name; doesn't matter who she is, I love her to death, women are generous this way, the meanest of us, I say her name, she says mine, kisses brushing inside the ear, she's wet all over me, it's all continuous, you're not in little pieces, I hear my name like the sound of the ocean in a shell; whether she's saying it or not. We're twisted around each other inside slime and sweat and tear drops, we're the wave and the surf, the undercurrent, the pounding of the tidal wave halfway around the world banging the beach on a bright, sunny day, the tide, high tide, low tide, under the moon or under a black sky, we're the sand wet and hard deserted by the water, the sand under the water, gravel and shell and moving claws crawling. I remember this one woman because I wanted her so bad but something was wrong, she was lying to me, telling me my lie but no woman lies to me. There's this woman at night I remember, in a restaurant I go when I'm taking a break, kosher restaurant with old men waiters, all night it's open, big room, plain tables, high ceilings, ballroom high and wide, big, empty feeling, old, old building, in New York, wide downtown street, gray street, fluorescent lights, a greenish light on green walls, oil paint, green, the old men have thick Jewish accents, they're slow moving, you can feel their bones aching, I sit alone over coffee and soup and she's there at the next table, the room's empty but she sits at the table next to me, black leather pants, she's got black hair, painted black, like I always wanted, and I want her but I'm her prey because she wants a bowl of fucking soup, she's picked me, she's coming for me, how did that happen, how did it get all fucked up, she sees me as the mark because I've got the food which means I've got the money and I can't go with her now because she has an underlying bad motive, she wants to eat, and what I feel for her is complete sex, so I'm the dope; and I don't do the dopey part; it's my game and she's playing it on me; she's got muscles and I want to see the insides of her thighs, I want to feel them, I want her undressed, I want her legs around my shoulders, she smiles, asks me how I am; be a fool, tell her how you are. I look right through her. I stare right through her while I'm deciding what to do. I ain't giving; I take. I want to be with her, I want to be between her legs and all over her and her thighs a vise around my neck; I want my teeth in her; I want her muscles squeezing me to death and I want to push down on her shoulders and I want my thighs crushing down on her, all my weight on her hips, my skin, bluish, on the inside of my thighs feeling her bones; but I'm the mark, that's how she sees it, and maybe she's meaner than me, or crazy, or harder, or feels less, or needs less, so she's on top and she takes; how many times have I done what she's doing now and did they want me the way I want her; well, they're stupid and I'm not; it hurts not to take her with me, I could put my hand on her and she'd come, I stare right through her, I look right through her but I'm devouring her at the same time which means she knows I'm a fool; she's acting harmless but maybe it's a lie, my instincts say it's a lie, there's no harmless women left alive this time of night, not on these streets. You risk too much if you go with a woman who needs less than you do; if you don't have to, if you have a choice, you don't take risks—you could lose your heart or your money or your speed; fucking fool who has a choice and doesn't use it; it's stupid middle-class girls you have to find or street women past wanting, past ambition, they live on bits of this and pieces of that, they're not looking for any heavy score, they live almost on air, it's pat, habit, they don't need you, but sometimes they like a taste; survival's an art, there are nuances, she's a dangerous piece of shit, stunning black eyes, and I'm smitten, and I walk out, look behind me, she came out, watched me, didn't follow, made me nervous, I don't often pass up what I want, I don't like doing it, it leaves an ache, don't like to ache too long without distracting myself by activity, anything to pass the time, and it makes me restless and careless, to want someone like that; I wanted her, she wanted food, money, most of what happens happens for food, all kinds of food, deep hungers that rock you in their everloving arms, rocked to eternal sleep by what you need, the song of myself, I need; need her; remember her; need women; need to hear my name; wanted her; she wanted food. What's inside you gets narrow and mean—it's an edge, it cuts, it's a slice of sharp, a line at the blade's end, no surface, no waste, no tease, a thin line where your meanest edge meets the air; an edge, no blade you can see. If you could stomp on me, this is what you'd see—a line, touch it, you're slivers. I'd be cut glass, you'd be feet. You'd dance blood. The edge of the blade, no surface, just what cuts, a thin line, touch it, draw blood. Inside, nothing else is alive. Where's the love I dream of. I hole up, like a bug in a rug. There's women who bore me; wasted time; the taste of death; junkie time; a junkie woman comes to me, long, languid afternoons making love but I didn't like it, she got beat up by her boyfriend, she's sincerely in love, black and blue, loving you, and he's her source; pure love; true romance. Don't like mixing women with obligation—in this case, the obligation to redeem her from pain. I want to want; I like wanting, just so it gets fulfilled and I don't have to wait too long; I like the ache just long enough to make what touches it appreciated a little more, a little drama, a little pain. I don't like no beat-up piece of shit; junkie stooge. You don't want the edge of the blade to get dull; then you got dullness inside and this you can't afford. The woman's got to be free; a beast of freedom; not a predator needing a bowl of fucking soup, not a fool needing a fucking fix; she's got to give freedom off, exude it, she's got to be grand with freedom, all swelled up with it, a Madame Curie of freedom, or she's Garbo, or more likely, she's Che, she's got to be a monster of freedom, a hero of loveless love; Napoleon but they didn't lock her up or she got loose, now, for me; no beat up junkie fool; no beautiful piece looking for a hamburger. There's magnificent women out here. These lights light you up. You are on Broadway and there are stars of a high magnitude. There's the queen of them all who taught me—sweet name, Rebecca; ruthless crusher of a dyke; honest to God, she's wearing a gold lamé dress when I meet her in jail when I'm a kid, eighteen, a political prisoner as it were, as I saw myself, and she loves poetry and she sends me a pile of *New Yorker* magazines because, she says, I'm a poet; and I don't want her on me, not in jail, I'm too scared, too hurt, but she protects me anyway, and I get out fast enough that I don't have to do her, and I see her later out here and I remember her kindness, which it was, real kindness, taking care of me in that place, which was why I was treated right by the other inmates as it were; I see her on the street, gold lame against a window, I see her shimmering, and I go with her for thanks and because she is grand, and I find out you can be free in a gold lame dress, in jail, whoring, in black skin, in hunger, in pain, in strife, the strife of the streets, perpetual war, gritty, gray, she's the wild one with freedom in her soul, it translates into how you touch, what's in your fingers, the silk in your hands, the freedom you take with who you got under you; you got your freedom and you take theirs for when you are with them, you are a caretaker of the fragile freedom in them, because most women don't got much, and you don't be afraid to take, you turn their skin to flames, you eat them raw, your name's all over them, you wrap them up in you, crush them in you, and what you give is ambition, the ambition to do it big, do it great, big gestures, free—girls do it big, girls soar, girls burn, girls take big not puny; stop giving, child, better to be stole from than to give—stop giving away the little that you got. I stay with her until she's finished with me, she's doing her art on me, she's practicing freedom on me; I'm shaking from it, her great daring, the audacity of her body on mine; she's free on me and I learn from it on me how to do it and how to be it; flamboyant lovemaking, no apology, dead serious, we could die right after this and this is the last thing we know and it's enough, the last minute, the last time, the last touch, God comes down through her on me, the good God, the divine God; master lovemaker, lightning in a girl, I've got a new theology, She's a rough Girl; and what's between my legs is a running river, She made it then She rested; a running river; so deep, so long, clear, bright, smart, racing, white foam over a cliff and then a dead drop and then it keeps on going, running, racing, then the smooth, silk calm, the deep calm, the long, silk body, smooth. I heard some man say I put it in her smooth, smooth was a noun, and I knew right away he liked children, he's after children, there are such men; but it's not what I mean; I mean that together we're smooth, it's smooth, we're smooth on each other, it's a smooth ride; and if I died right after I wouldn't feel cheated or sorry and every time I'm happy I had her one more second and I feel proud she wants me; and she'll disappear, she'll take someone else, but I'll sit here like a dumb little shit until she does, a student, sitting, waiting at her feet, let her touch me once, then once more, I'm happy near her, her freedom's holding me tight, her freedom's on me, around me, climbing inside me, her freedom's embracing me; wild woman; a wild woman's pussy that will not die for some junkie prick; nor songwriter; nor businessman; nor philosopher. The men are outside, they want to come in, I hear them rattling around, death threats, destruction isn't quiet or subtle, imagine those for whom it is, safe, blessedly safe; so in my last minutes on this earth, perhaps, I am remembering Rebecca who taught me freedom; I would sit down quiet next to her, wait for her, watch her; did you ever love a girl? I've loved several; loved. Not just wanted but loved in thought or action. Wasn't raped by any of them. I mean, rape's just a word, it doesn't mean anything, someone fucks you, so what? I can't see complaining about it. But I wasn't hurt by any of them. I don't mean I wasn't hurt by love; shit, that's what love does, it drags your heart over a bed of nails, I was hurt by love, lazy, desperate drinks through long nights of pain without her, hurting bad. Wasn't pushed around. Saw others who were. It's not that women don't. It's just that it had my name on it, men said pussy or dyke or whatever stupid distortion but I saw freedom, I heard Andrea, I found freedom under her, wrapped around her, her lips on me and her hands on me, in me, her thighs holding on to me; there's always men around waiting to break in, throw themselves on top, pull you down; but women's different, it's a fast, gorgeous trip out of hell, a hundred-mile-an-hour ride on a different road in the opposite direction, it's when you see an attitude that sets you free, the way she moves breaks you out, or you touch her shoulder and exhilaration shoots through you like a needle would do hanging from your vein if it's got something good in it; it's a gold rush; your life's telling you that if you're between her legs you're free—free's not peaceful and not always kind, it's fast, a shooting star you ride, if you're stupid it shakes you loose and hurls you somewhere in the sky, no gravity, no fall, just eternal drift to nowhere out past up and down. You can live forever on the curve of her hip, attached there in sweat and desire taking the full measure of your own human sorrow; you can have this tearing sorrow with your face pushing on the inside of her thigh; you can have her lips on you, her hands pushing on you as if you're marble she's turning into clay, an electricity running all over you carried in saliva and spit, you're cosseted in electric shock, peeing, your hair standing up on end, muscles stretched, lit up; there's her around you and in you everywhere, the rhythm of your dance and at the same time she's like the placenta, you breathe in her, surrounded; it's something men don't know or they'd do it, they could do it, but instead they want this push, shove, whatever it is they're doing for whatever reason, it's an ignorant meanness, but with a woman you're whole and you're free, it ain't pieces of you flying around like shit, it ain't being used up, you got scars bigger than the freedom you get in everyday life; do it the way you're supposed to, you got twenty-four hours a day down on your knees sucking dick; that's how girls do hard time. There's not many women around who have any freedom in them let alone some to spare, extravagant, on you, and it's when they're on you you see it best and know it's real, now and all, there won't be anything wilder or finer, it's pure and true, you see it, you chase them, they're on you, you get enraptured in it, once you got it on you, once you feel it moving through you, it's a contagion of wanting more than you get being pussy for the boys, you catch it like a fever, it puts you on a slow burn with your skin aching and you want it more than you can find it because most women are beggars and slaves in spirit and in life and you don't ever give up wanting it. Otherwise you get worn down to what they say you are, you get worn down to pussy, bedraggled; not bewitched, bothered, bewildered; just some wet, ratty, bedraggled thing, semen caked on you, his piss running down your legs, worn out, old from what you're sucking, I'm pretty fucking old and I have been loved by freedom and I have loved freedom back. Did you ever have a nightmare? Men coming in's my nightmare; entering; I'm in, knock, knock. There's writers being assholes about outlaws; outlaw this, outlaw that, I'm bad, I'm sitting here writing my book and I'm bad, I'm typing and I'm bad, my secretary's typing and I'm bad, I got laid, the boys say, like their novels are letters home to mama, well, hell's bells, the boys got laid: more than once. It's something to write home about, all right; costs fifty bucks, too; they found dirty women they did it to, dirty women too fucking poor to have a typewriter to stuff up bad boy writer's ass. Shit. You follow his cock around the big, bad city: New York, Paris, Rome—same city, same cock. Big, bad cock. Wiping themselves on dirty women, then writing home to mama by way of Grove Press, saying what trash the dirty women are; how brave the bad boys are, writing about it, doing it, putting their cocks in the big, bad, dirty hole where all the other big, brave boys were; oh they say dirty words about dirty women good. I read the books. I had a typewriter but it was stolen when the men broke in. The men broke in before when I wasn't here and they took everything, my clothes, my typewriter. I wrote stories. Some were about life on other planets; I wrote once about a wild woman on a rock on Mars. I described the rock, the red planet, barren, and a woman with tangled hair, big, with muscles, sort of Ursula Andress on a rock. I couldn't think of what happened though. She was just there alone. I loved it. Never wanted it to end. I wrote about the country a lot, pastoral stuff, peaceful, I made up stories about the wind blowing through the trees and leaves falling and turning red. I wrote stories about teenagers feeling angst, not the ones I knew but regular ones with stereos. I couldn't think of details though. I wrote about men and women making love. I made it up; or took it from Nino, a boy I knew, except I made it real nice; as he said it would be; I left out the knife. The men writers make it as nasty as they can, it's like they're using a machine gun on her; they type with their fucking cocks—as Mailer admitted, right? Except he said balls, always a romancer. I can't think of getting a new typewriter, I need money for just staying alive, orange juice and coffee and cigarettes and milk, vodka and pills, they'll just smash it or take it anyway, I have to just learn to write with a pen and paper in handwriting so no one can steal it and so it don't take money. When I read the big men writers I'm them; careening around like they do; never paying a fucking price; days are long, their books are short compared to an hour on the street; but if you think about a book just saying I'm a prick and I fuck dirty girls, the books are pretty long; my cock, my cock, three volumes. They should just say: *I Can Fuck*. Norman Mailer's new novel. *I Can Be Fucked*. Jean Genet's new novel. *I'm Waiting To Be Fucked Or To*

Fuck, I Don't Know. Samuel Beckett's new novel. *She Shit.* James Joyce's masterpiece. *Fuck Me, Fuck Her, Fuck It.* The Living Theatre's new play. *Paradise Fucked.* The sequel. *Mama, I Fucked a Jewish Girl.* The new Philip Roth. *Mama, I Fucked a Shiksa.* The new, new Philip Roth. It was a bad day they wouldn't let little boys say that word. I got to tell you, they get laid. They're up and down these streets, taking what they want; two hundred million little Henry Millers with hard pricks and a mean prose style; Pulitzer prizewinning assholes using cash. Looking for experience, which is what they call pussy afterward when they're back in their posh apartments trying to justify themselves. Experience is us, the ones they stick it in. Experience is when they put down the money, then they turn you around like you're a chicken they're roasting; they stick it in any hole they can find just to try it or because they're blind drunk and it ain't painted red so they can't find it; you get to be lab mice for them; they stick the famous Steel Rod into any Fleshy Hole they can find and they Ram the Rod In when they can manage it which thank God often enough they can't. The prose gets real purple then. You can't put it down to impotence though because they get laid and they had women and they fucked a lot; they just never seem to get over the miracle that it's them in a big man's body doing all the damage; Look, ma, it's me. Volume Twelve. They don't act like human beings and they're pretty proud of it so there's no point in pretending they are; though you want to—pretend. You'd like to think they could feel something—sad; or remorse; or something just simple, a minute of recognition. It's interesting that you're so dangerous to them but you fucking can't hurt them; how can you be dangerous if you can't do harm; I'd like to be able to level them, but you can't touch them except to be fucked by them; they get to do it and then they get to say what it is they're doing—you're what they're afraid of but the fear just keeps them coming, it doesn't shake them loose or get them off you; it's more like the glue that keeps them on you; sticky stuff, how afraid the pricks are. I mean, maybe they're not afraid. It sounds so stupid to say they are, so banal, like making them human anyway, like giving them the insides you wish they had. So what do you say; they're just so fucking filled with hate they can't do anything else or feel anything else or write anything else? I mean, do they ever look at the fucking moon? I think all the sperm they're spilling is going to have an effect; something's going to grow. It's like they're planting a whole next generation of themselves by sympathetic magic; not that they're fucking to have babies; it's more like they're rubbing and heaving and pushing and banging and shoving and ejaculating like some kind of voodoo rite so all the sperm will grow into more them, more boys with more books about how they got themselves into dirt and got out alive. It's a thrilling story, says the dirt they got themselves into. It's bitterness, being their filth; they don't even remember right, you're not distinct enough, an amoeba's more distinct, more individuated; they go home and make it up after they did it for real and suddenly they ain't parasites, they're heroes—big dicks in the big night taming some rich but underneath it all street dirty whore, some glamorous thing but underneath filth; I think even if you were with them all the time they wouldn't remember you day-to-day, it's like being null and void and fucked at the same time, I am fucked, therefore I am not. Maybe I'll write books about history—prior times, the War of 1812; not here and now, which is a heartbreaking time, place, situation, for someone. You're nothing to them. I don't think they're afraid. Maybe I'm afraid. The men want to come in; I hear them outside, banging; they're banging against the door with metal things, probably knives; the men around here have knives; they use knives; I'm familiar with knives; I grew up around knives; Nino used a knife;

I'm not afraid of knives. Fear's a funny thing; you get fucked enough you lose it; or most of it; I don't know why that should be per se. It's all callouses, not fear, a hard heart, and inside a lot of death as if they put it there, delivered it in. And then out of nowhere you just drown in it, it's a million tons of water on you. If I was afraid of individual things, normal things—today, tomorrow, what's next, who's on top, what already has transpired that you can't quite reach down into to remember—I'd have to surrender; but it drowns you fast, then it's gone. I'd like to surrender; but to whom, where, or do you just put up a white flag and they take you to throw your body on a pile somewhere? I don't believe in it. I think you have to make them come get you, you don't volunteer, it's a matter of pride. Who do you turn yourself into and on what terms—hey, fellow, I'm done but that don't mean you get to hurt me more, you have to keep the deal, I made a deal, I get not to feel more pain, I'm finished, I'm not fighting you fucks anymore, I'll be dead if it's the way to accomplish this transformation from what I am into being nothing with no pain. But if you get dead and there's an afterlife and it's more of the same but worse—I would just die from that. You got all these same mean motherfuckers around after you're dead and you got the God who made it all still messing with you but now up close—He's around. You're listening to angels and you're not allowed to tell God He's one maggoty bastard; or you're running around in circles in hell, imprisoned by your fatal flaw, instead of being here on a leash with all your flaws, none fatal enough, making you a maggoty piece of meat. I want dead to mean dead; all done; finished; quiet; insensate; nothing; I want it to be peaceful, no me being pushed around or pushing, I don't want to feel the worms crawling on me or eating me or the cold of the wet ground or suffocating from being buried or smothering from being under the ground; or being stone cold from being dead; I don't want to feel cold; I don't want to be in eternal dark forever stone cold. Nothing by which I mean a pure void, true nonexistence, is different; it isn't filled with horror or dread or fear or punishment or pain; it's just an absence of being, especially so you don't have to think or know anything or figure out how you're going to eat or who's going to be on you next. It's not suffering. I don't have suffering in mind; not joy, not pain—no highs, no lows. Just not being; not being a citizen wandering around the universe in a body or loose, ethereal and invisible; or just not being a citizen here, now, under street lights, all illuminated, the light shining down. I hate the light shining down—display yourself, dear, show them; smile, spread your legs, make suggestive gestures, legs wide open—there's lots of ways to sit or stand with your legs wide open. Which day did God make light? You think He had the street lights in some big storeroom in the sky to send down to earth when women started crawling over sidewalks like cockroaches to stay alive? I think He did. I think it was part of the big plan—light those girls up, give them sallow light, covers pox marks, covers tracks, covers bruises, good light for covering them up and showing them at the same time, makes them look grotesque, just inhuman enough, same species but not really, you can stick it in but these aren't creatures that get to come home, not into a home, not home, not quite the same species, sallow light, makes them green and grotesque, creatures you put it in, not female ones of you, even a fucking rib of you; you got ones in good light for that. They stick it in boys too; anything under these lights is here to be used. You'd think they'd know boys was real, same species, with fists that work or will someday, but someday isn't their problem and they like the feel that the boy might turn mean on them—some of them like it, the ones that use the older ones. I read about this boy that was taken off the street and the man gave him hormones to make him grow breasts and lose his body hair or not get it, I'm not sure; it made me really sick because the boy was nothing to him, just some piece of something he could mess with, remake to what he wanted to play with, even something monstrous; I wanted to kill the guy; and I tried to figure out how to help the kid, but I just read it in *Time* or *Newsweek* so I wondered if I could find him or not. I guess it depends on how many boys there are being fed hormones by pedophiles. Once it's in *Newsweek*, I guess there are thousands. The kid's around here somewhere; it said Lower East Side; I hate it, what the man did to him. These Goddamn men would all be each other's meat if they weren't the butchers. They use fucking to slice you open. It's like they're hollow, there's nothing there, except they make big noise, this unbearable static, some screeching, high-pitched pain, and you can't see they're hollow because the noise diverts you to near madness; big lovemaker with fifty dollars to spend, seed to spill making mimetic magic, grind, bang, it's a boy, a big, bad boy who writes books, big, bad books. I see the future and it's a bunch of pricks making a literature of fucking, high art about sticking it in; I did it, ma; she was filth and I did it. Only you'll get a Mailer-Genet beast: I did it, ma, I did it to her, he did it to me. The cement will grow them; sympathetic magic works; the spilled seed, the grinding, bang bang, pushes the fuck out past the bounds of physical reality; it lurks in the biosphere; it will creep into weeping wombs; they'll be born, the next generation, out of what the assholes do to me; I've got enough semen dripping in me for a literary renaissance, an encyclo-pedia of novellas, a generation of genius; maybe some of them will paint or write songs. Mother earth, magic vessel, the altar where they worship, the sacred place; fifty dollars to burn a candle, or pills, or a meal and money; bang bang ain't never without consequences for the future of the race. No reason the race should be different from the people in it. There's no tomorrow I know of. I never seen one that ain't today. It's fine to be slutmama to a literary movement; the corporeal altar of sympathetic motherhood to a generation; his loins; my ass. Immortal, anonymous means to his end. It's what the hippie girls all glittering, flecked, stardust, want: to be procreatrix with flowering hips and tea made from plants instead of Lipton; they recline, posh and simple, all spread out draped in flowing cotton and color; they don't take money; well, they do, but they don't say so upfront—from my point of view they are mannerless in this regard; mostly they just hang on, like they have claws, it passes for spiritual, they just sit there until he comes back from wherever he's gone after coitus has made him triste, they say it's meditating but it's just waiting for some guy to show who's left; they ain't under the light, they are of it—luminescent fairy things from on high, just down for a fast, ethereal screw. I been to bed with them; usually a man and one of them, because they don't do women alone—too real for the nitrous oxide crowd, not Buddhistic enough—it's got an I want right between the legs and it's got your genitals leading your heart around or vice versa, who the hell knows, and it don't make the boy happy unless he gets to watch and the hippie girls do not irritate the love-boys by doing things that might not be directly and specifically for them. The hippie boys like bringing another woman into bed. You can shake some coke loose from them if you do it; or money, which they pretend is like nothing but they hold onto it pretty tight. Coke and orange juice is my favorite breakfast; they want you to do the coke with them because it makes them hard and high and ready but I like to take some off with me and do it alone or with someone I pick, not with someone in bed with some silly girl who ought to be a housewife but is seeing the big city and he's so hip he has to be able to roll over from one to another, dreaming it's another housewife, all girls are housewives to him; peace, flowers, love, clean my house, bake my bread. They try to tell you they see the real you, the sensitive you, inside, and the real you doesn't want money—she wants the good fucking he's got and to make strings of beads for him and sell them in flea markets for him; darling, it's sad. You convey to the guy that you're the real thing, what he never thought would be near him, street grime he won't be able to wash off, and he's so trembling and overwrought his prick starts shaking. There's some who do things real, don't spend their time posturing or preening; they just pull it out without philosophy. There's this one I had once, with a woman. I was on Demerol because I had an operation; my appendix came out but it had got all infected and it was a big slice in me and then they let me loose with a blood clot because there wasn't somewhere for me to stay and I didn't have money or no one to take care of me so they just let me out. My side didn't seem like it would stay sewed, it felt open, and there was a pain from the clot that was some evil drilling in my shoulder that they called reflexive pain which meant the pain was really somewhere else but I could only feel it in my shoulder. It hurt to breathe. You don't think about your shoulder or how it moves when you breathe unless some Nazi is putting a drill in it; I saw God the Nazi pushing His full weight on the drill and if I breathed it made more pressure from inside on where the drill was and there wasn't enough Demerol in the world. So I'm walking around, desperate and dreamy, in pain but liking the pills, and I see this shirt, fucking beautiful shirt, purple and turquoise and shades of blue all in flowers, silk, astonishing whirl of color; and the man's dark with long hair and a beard, some proto-type, no face, just hair; and I take him back but there's this girl with him too, and she's all hippie, endlessly expressing herself and putting little pats on my hand, teeny weeny little pats, her hand to mine: expressing affection for another woman; heavy shit. I can barely believe this one's rubbing her hands on me. And the guy starts fucking, and he's some kind of monster of fuck, he lasts forever and a day, it's night, it's dark, and hours go by, and I see the light coming up, and she and me are next to each other, and he's in me, then he's in her, then me, then her, and my side is splitting open and I'm not supposed to be moving around with the clot but you can't keep your hips still the whole time although my interest comes and goes, at some point the boy takes off the shirt and I'm wondering who he is and why he's here, and I don't have to worry about her sentimentality because the boy isn't seeking variety and he don't want to watch, this is a boy who wants to fuck and he moves good but he's boring as hell, the same, the same, and when the pain hits me I am pretty sure I am really going to die, that the clot is loose in my blood somewhere and it's going to go to my brain, and I'm trying to think this is real glorious, dying with some Olympian fuck, but the pain is some vicious, choked up tangle of blades in my gut, and I try to choreograph the pain to his fuck, and I try to rest when he's not in me, and I am praying he will stop, and I am at the same time trying to savor every second of my last minutes on earth, or last hours as it turns out, but intellectual honesty forced me to acknowledge I was bored, I was spending my last time bored to death, I could have been a housewife after all; and the light comes up and I think, well, dawn will surely stop him; but he fucks well into daylight, it's bright morning now with a disagreeably bright sun, profoundly intrusive, and suddenly there's a spasm, thank the Lord, and the boy is spent, it's the seventh day and this man who fucks must rest. And I thank God. I do. I say, thank you, Lord. I say, I owe You one. I say, I appear still to be alive, I know I was doing something proscribed and maybe I shouldn't address You before he even moves off me but I am grateful to You for stopping him, for making him tired, for wearing him out, for creating him in Your image so that, eventually, he had to rest. I can't move because my insides are messed up. My incision is burning as if there are lighted coals there and I'm afraid to see if it is open or if it will bleed now and my shoulder has stones crushed into it as if some demolition team was crushing granite, reflexive pain from some dead spot, I don't know where, and I truly think I might not ever move again and I truly think I might have opened up and I truly think I might still die; and I want to be alone; die alone or bleed alone or endure the pain alone; and I'm lying there thinking they will go now when the girl starts pawing me and says stupid, nice things and starts being all lovey dovey like we're both Gidget and she wants now to have the experience, if you will, of making love with a woman; this is in the too-little-too-late category at best; and I am fairly outraged and astonished because I hurt so much and my little sister in sensitivity thinks we should start dating. So I tell them to go; and she says but he doesn't like me better, maybe he needs you to be there—needs you, can you imagine—and I'm trying to figure out what it has to do with him, why it's what he wants when I want them to go; it's what I want; I never understand why it's always with these girls what he wants—if he's there and even if he ain't in sight or in the vicinity; he had his hours doing what he wants; and she tells me she's disappointed with me for not being loving and we could all share and this is some dream come true, the most amazing thing that's ever happened, to her or ever on earth, it's the proof that everything is possible, and the pain I'm in is keeping me from moving because I can't even sit up but I'm saying very quiet, get out now. And she's saying it's her first time with a woman and she didn't really get to do anything—tourist didn't get to see the Eiffel Tower—and I say yes, that's right, you didn't get nothing. So she's sad like some lover who was real left her and she's handling me like she read in some book, being a tender person, saying everything bland and stupid, all her ideals about life, everything she's hoped for, and she's preachy with the morality of sharing and unity and harmony and I expect her to shake her finger at me and hit my knuckles with a ruler and make me stand in a corner for not being some loving bitch. There's a code of love you have to learn by heart, which I never took to, and I'm thinking that if she don't take her treacle to another planet I'm going to stand up, no matter what the pain, and physically carry her out, a new little bride, over the threshold to outside. She's some sobbing ingenue with a delicate smile perpetually on her face shining through tears which are probably always with her and she's talking about universal love when all the boy did was fuck us to death as best he could, which in my case was close but no cigar and I couldn't bring myself to think it was all that friendly; and I had a short fuse because I needed another pill, I was a few behind and I was looking forward to making them up now in the immediate present, I could talk real nice to Demerol and I didn't want them there for when I got high again; so I said, you go, because he really likes you and you should stay with him and be with him and be good to him, so the dumb bitch leaves with the prince of peace over there, the boy's already smoking dope so he's already on another plane taking care of himself which is what he's really good at; and she's uncomprehending and she's mournful that I couldn't get the love part right but they went, I saw the boy's turquoise and purple silk shirt float by me and the drippy, sentimental girl in cotton floated out still soliciting love. I never understood why she thought you could ask for it. No one can ask it from me. I never can remember his face; peculiar, since his head was right above me for so long, his tongue in my mouth, he kissed the whole time he fucked, a nice touch, he was in her kissing me or in me kissing her so no one'd get away from him or decide to do something else; I just can't remember his face, as if I never saw it. He was a Taurus. I stayed away from them after that if I knew a man was one because they stay too long, slow, steady, forever. I never saw such longevity. She was Ellen, some flower child girl; doomed for housework. I'm not. I ain't cleaning up after them. I keep things as clean as I can; but you can't really stay clean; there's too much heat and dirt. It's a sweltering night. The little nymphs, imps, and pimps of summer flitter about like it's tea time at the Ritz. There's been uprisings on the streets, riots, lootings, burning; the air is crackling with violence, a blue white fire eating up the oxygen, it's tiny, sharp explosions that go off in the air around your head, firecrackers you can't see that go off in front of you when you walk, in front of your face, and you don't know when the air itself will become some white hot tornado, just enough to crack your head open and boil your brains. That's outside, the world. Summertime and the living is easy. You just walk through the fires between the flames or crawl on your belly under them; rough on your knees and elbows. You can be in the street and have a steaming mass, hot heat, kinetic, come at you, a crowd, men at the top of their energy, men spinning propelled by butane, and they bear down on you on the sidewalk, they come at you, martial chaos; they will march over you, you'll be crushed, bone marrow ground into a paste with your own blood, a smear left on a sidewalk. The crowd's a monster animal, a giant wolf, huge and frantic, tall as the sky, blood pulsing and rushing through it, one predator, bearing down, a hairy, freaky, hungry thing, bared teeth, ugly, hungry thing, it springs through the air, light and lethal, and you will fucking cringe, hide, run, disappear, to be safe—you will fucking hide in a hole, like some roachy thing you will crawl into a crack. You can hear the sound of them coming, there's a buzz coming up from the cement, it vibrates and kicks up dust, and somewhere a fire starts, somewhere close, and somewhere police in helmets with nightsticks are bearing down on the carnivorous beast, somewhere close and you can hear the skulls cracking open, and the blood comes, somewhere close there's blood, and you can hear guns, there's guns somewhere close because you smell the burning smell, it's heat rising off someone's open chest, the singed skin still smoking where the bullet went through; the wolf's being beat down—shot over and over, wounded, torn open—it's big manly cops doing it, steel faces, lead boots—they ain't harassing whores tonight. It looks like foreplay, the way the cops bear down on the undulating mass; I stroke your face with my nightstick; the lover tames the beloved; death does quiet you down. But a pig can't kill a wolf. The wolf's the monster prick, then the pigs come and turn the wolf into a girl, then it's payback time and the wolf rises again. In the day when the wolf sleeps there are still fires; anything can suddenly go up in flames and you can't tell the difference at first between a fire and a summer day, the sun on the garbage, the hot air making the ghetto buildings swell, the brick bulging, deformed and in places melting, all the solid brick wavy in the heat. At night the crowd rises, the wolf rises, the great predator starts a long, slow walk toward the bullets waiting for it. The violence is in the air; not symbol; not metaphor; it's thick and tasty; the air's charged with it; it crackles around your head; then you stay in or go out, depending on—can you stand being trapped inside or do you like the open street? I sleep days. It's safer. I sleep in daylight. I stay awake nights. I keep an eye out. I don't like to be unconscious. I don't like the way you get limp. I don't like how you can't hear what goes on around you. I don't like that you can't see. I don't like to be waiting. I don't like that you get no warning. I don't like not to know where I am. I don't like not to know my name. I sleep in the day because it's safer; at night, I face the streets, the crowd, the predator, any predator, head on. I'd rather be there. I want to see it coming at me, the crowd or anything else or anyone. I want it to look at me and I want a chance. There's gangs everywhere. There's arson or fires or wolf packs or packs of men; men and gangs. The men outside my door are banging; they want to come in; big group fuck; they tear me apart; boys' night out. It's about eight or nine at night and I'm going out soon, it's a little too early yet, I hear them banging on the door with knives and fists, I can't get out past them, there's only one way out; I can't get past them. Once night comes it's easy to seal you in. Night comes and you have the rules of the grave, different rules from daylight, they can do things at night, everyone can, they can't do in the day; they will break the door down, no one here calls the police, I don't have a gun, I have one knife, a pathetic thing, I sleep with it under my pillow. I figure if someone's right on top of me I can split him apart with it. I figure if he's already on top of me because I didn't hear him and didn't see him because I was unconscious and I wake up and he's there I can stick it in him or I can cut his throat. I figure it gives me time to come to, then I try for his throat, but if I'm too late, if I can't get it, if he's somehow so I can't get his throat, then I can get his back. Or I can finish myself off if there's no other way; I think about it each time I lie down to sleep, if I can do it, draw the knife across my throat, fast, I try to prepare myself to do it, in my mind I make a vow and I practice the stroke before I sleep. I think it's better to kill him but I just can't bear them no longer, really, and it's unknown if I could do it to me; so fast; but I keep practicing in my mind so if the time comes I won't even think. It would be the right thing. I don't really believe in hurting him or anyone. I have the knife; I can't stand to think about using it, what it would be like, or going to jail for hurting him, I never wanted to kill anybody and I'd do almost anything not to. I know the men outside, they're neighborhood, this block, they broke in before, in daylight, smashed everything, took everything, they ran riot in here, they tell me they're coming to fuck me, they say so out on the street, hanging on the stoop; they say so. They've broken in here before, that's when I started sleeping with the knife. Inside there's too many hours to dawn; too many hours of dark to hold them off; they'll get in; I know this small world as well as they do, I know what they can do and what they can't do and once it's night they can break the door down and no one will stop them; and the police don't come here; you never see a cop here; there's no way to keep them out and my blood's running cold from the banging, from the noise of them, fists, knives, I don't know what, sticks, I guess, maybe baseball bats, the arsenal of the streets. The telephone's worthless, they cut the wire when they broke in; but no one would come. This is the loneliest I ever knew existed; now; them banging. There's things you learn, tricks; no one can hurt me. I'm not some stupid piece of shit. You got a gang outside, banging, making threats. They want to come in; fuck. They'll kill me; fuck me dead or kill me after. It's like anything, you have to face what's true, you don't get to say if you want to handle it or not, you handle it to stay alive. So what's it to me; if I can just get through it; minimum damage, minimum pain, the goal of all women all the time and it's not different now. If you're ever attacked by a gang you have to get the leader. If you get him, disable him, pull him away from the others, kill him, render him harmless, the others are nothing. If you miss him, attack him but miss, wound him, irritate him, aggravate him, rile him, humiliate him without taking him out, you are human waste, excreta. So it's clear; there's one way. There's him. I have to get him. if I can pull him away from them, to me, I have a chance; a chance. I open the door. I think if I grab him between the legs I'm in charge; if I pull his thing.

I learn the limits of my philosophy. Every philosophy's got them. I ain't in charge. It's fast. It's simple. I open the door. It's a negotiation. The agreement is he comes in, they stay out; he doesn't bring the big knife he has in with him; it stays outside; if I mess with him, he will hurt me with it and turn me over to them; if anything bad happens to him or if I don't make him happy, he will turn me over to them. This is consent, right? I opened the door myself. I picked him. I just got to survive him; and tomorrow find a way out; away from here. He comes in; he's Pedro or Joe or Juan; he swaggers, touches every-thing, there's not much left he notes with humor; he wants me to cook him dinner; he finds my knife; he keeps it; he keeps saying what he'll do to me with it; I cook; he drinks; he eats; he keeps talking; he brags; he talks about the gang, keeps threatening me, what he'll do to me, what they'll do to me, aspects of lovemaking the gang would also enjoy and maybe he'll just let them in now or there's time after, they're waiting, right outside, maybe he'll call them in but they can come back tomorrow night too, there's time, no need to worry, nice boys in the gang, a little rough but I'll enjoy them, won't I? Then he's ready; he's excited himself; he's even fingered himself and rubbed himself. Like the peace boys he talks with his legs spread wide open, his fingers lightly caressing his cock, the denim pulled tight, exerting its own pressure. He goes to the bed and starts to undress and he runs one hand through the hair on his chest and he holds the knife in the other hand, he fingers the knife, he rubs his thumb over it and he caresses it and he keeps talking, seductive talk about how good he is and how good the knife is and I'm going to like them both and he's got a cross on a chain around his neck and it glistens in his hair, it's silver and his skin is tawny and his hair on his chest is black and curly and thick and it shines and I'm staring at it thinking it shouldn't be there, the shiny cross, I am having these highly moral thoughts against the blasphemy of the cross on his chest, I think it is wrong and concentrate on the immorality of wearing it now, doing this, why does he wear it, what does it mean, his shirt is off and his pants are coming off and he is rapturous with the knife in his hand and I look at the cross and I look at the knife and I think they are both for me, he will hold the knife, maybe I can touch the cross, I will try to touch it all through and maybe it will be something or mean something or I won't feel so frightened, so alone in this life now, and I think I will just touch it, and there's him, there's the cross, there's the knife, and I'm under them and I don't know, I will never remember, the hours are gone, blank, a tunnel of nothing, and I'm naked, the bell rings, it's light outside so it's been five hours, six, there's a knock on the door, insistent knocking, he says don't answer it, he says don't move, he holds the knife against me, just under my skin, the tip just under it, and I try to fight for my life, I say it's a friend who expects me to be here and will not go away and I will have to answer the door and I won't say anything and I won't tell or say anything bad, I will just go to the door to tell my friend to go away, to convince him everything's fine, and someone's knocking and he has a deep voice and I don't know what I will do when I reach the door or who it is on the outside or what will happen; but I'm hurt; dizzy; reeling; can't feel anything but some obscure pain somewhere next to me or across the room and I don't know what he's done, I don't look at any part of me, I cover myself a little with a sheet, I pull it over me and I don't look down, I have trouble keeping my head steady on my shoulders, I don't know if I can walk from the bed to the door, and I think I can open the door maybe and just keep walking but I am barely covered at all and maybe the gang's outside and you can't walk naked in a sheet, they'll just hurt you more; anyone will. I can't remember and I can barely carry my head up and I have this one chance; because I can't have him do more; you see? I got up, I put something around me, over me, a sheet or something, just held it together where I could, and I took some steps and I kept whispering to the man with the knife in my bed that I would just get rid of the man at the door because he wouldn't go away if I didn't come to the door and really I would just make him go away and I kept walking to the door to open it, not knowing if I would fall or if the man in the bed would stick the knife in me before I got there, or who was on the other side of the door and what he would do; would he run or laugh or walk away; or was it a member of the gang, wanting some. It was cool and clear and light outside and it was a man I didn't know except a little, a big man, so tall, so big, such a big man, and I whispered to him to help me, please help me, and I talked out loud that I couldn't come out now for breakfast like we had planned and I whispered to say that I was hurt and that the man inside was a leader of a gang and I indicated the big knife on the window ledge, out of my reach, a huge dagger, almost a sword, that I had got the man to leave outside and I whispered that he was in my bed now with a knife and out loud I tried to say normal things very loud but I was dizzy and I wasn't sure I could keep standing and the big man caught on quick and said normal things loud, questions so I could answer them and didn't have to think of new things because I'm shaking and I say the man's in my bed with a knife and please help me he was with a gang and I don't know where they are and maybe they're around and they'll show up and it's dangerous but please help me and the big man strides in, he doesn't take the big knife, I almost die from fear but he just does it, I used my chance and there's none left, he has long legs and they cover the distance to the bed in a second and the man in my bed is fumbling with the knife and the big man, so big, with long legs, says I'm his; his girl; his; this is an insult to him; an outrage to him; and the man in the bed with the knife says nothing, he grovels, he sweats, he asks forgiveness, he didn't mean no harm, you know how it is man; and hey they agree it's just a misunderstanding and they talk and the man in my bed with the knife is sweating and the man who saved me is known to be dangerous, he is known, a known very serious man, a quiet man, a major man, and he says he's my man and I'm his woman and he don't want me having no trouble with sniveling assholes and any insult he throws makes the man in my bed with the knife sweat more and grovel more and the big man, the man with the long legs, he speaks very soft, and he says that now the man in the bed with the knife will leave and the man in the bed with the knife fumbles to put his pants on and fumbles to put his shirt on and fumbles to get his shoes on and the big man, the man with the long legs, says quietly, politely, that nobody had ever better mess with me anymore and the man who was in my bed with the knife says yeah and sure and please and thank you and I am some kind of prom queen, bedecked, bejeweled, crowned princess, because the man with the long legs says I am his, and Pedro or Juan or Joe is obsequious and he says he is sorry and he says he didn't understand and he says he made a mistake and they chat and I'm shaking bad, I'm there covered a little, I'm shaking and I'm not really covered and I'm covered in sweat and I'm trying not to fall down faint and I'm shaking so much I'm nearly naked, I'm hurt, my head falls down and I see my skin, all bruised anywhere you can see as if I turned blue or someone painted me blue, and there's blood on me but I can't look or keep my eyes open, I'm just this side of dead but I'm holding on, I'm shaking but I got something covering me somewhere and I'm just not quite dead, I'm keeping something covering me somewhere, and Pedro or Juan or Joe leaves, he leaves mumbling an apology to the big man and I'm saying thank you to the big man with serious formality, quiet and serious and concentrating, and I'm something that ain't fresh and new, I'm something that ain't clean, and I don't know anything except he's got to go now because I have to curl up by myself to die now, it's time, I'm just going to put myself down on the bed, very careful, very slow, on my side with my knees raised a little, curled up a little, and I'm going to God, I am going to ask God to take me in now, I am going to forgive Him and I am going to put aside all my grudges against Him for all what He did wrong and for all the pain I ever had or saw and I am going to ask Him to take me away now from here and to somewhere else where I don't have to move ever again, where I can be curled up a little and nothing hurts and whatever hurts don't have to move and that I don't have to wake up no more but the big man ain't through and I say later or tomorrow or come back and he says I have to pay my debts and he talks and he threatens and he has a deep voice and he is big and he has long arms and he isn't leaving, he says, and he is strong and he pulls me down and gets on top of me and says I owe him and he fucks me and I say God You must stop him now but God don't stop him, God don't have no problem with this, God rides on the back of the man and I see Him there doing it and the man uses his teeth on me where men fuck and God's for him and I'm wondering why He likes people being hurt and I'm past hating Him and past Him and I can't beg Him no more for respite or help or death and the big man has his teeth between my legs, inside me and on the flesh all around, he's biting, not a little, deep bites, he's using his teeth and biting into the lips of my labia and I'm thinking this is not happening and it is not possible and it is not true and I am thinking it will stop soon because it must stop soon but it does not stop soon because the man has fucked but it means nothing to him except he had to do it so he did it but this is why he is here, the real reason, this biting in this place, he is wanting to do this other awful thing that is not like anything anyone ever did before and I say this is not happening and even You are not so cruel to let this man do this and keep doing it and not making him stop but the man has long arms and he's driven, a passionate man, and he holds me down and he has long legs and he uses his arms and legs to keep me pinned down and he is so big, so tall, he can have his face down there and still he covers me to hold me down, my shoulders, my breasts; but my head twists back and forth, side to side, like some loose head of a doll screwed on wrong. He is cutting me open with his teeth, he looks up at me, he bites more, he says lovers' things, he is the great lover and he is going slow, with his mouth, with his teeth, and then watching my head try to screw itself off my neck; and he gets in a frenzy and there's no words for this because pain is littler and sweeter and someday it ends but this doesn't end, will not end, it will never end, it's dull, dirty, rusty knives cutting my labial lips or the edge of a rusty tin can and it's inside me, his teeth reaching inside me turning me inside out, the skin, he is pulling me open and he is biting inside me and I'm thinking that pain is a river going through me but there's no words and pain isn't a river, there's just one great scream past sound and my mind moves over, it moves out of my head, I feel it escape, it runs away, it says no, not this, no and it says you cannot but the man does and my mind just fucking falls out of my brains and I am past being any-thing God can help anyway and He's making the man stronger, He's making the man happy, the man likes this, he is liking this, and he is proud to be doing it so good like a good lover, slow, one who lasts, one who takes time; and this is real; this happened and this will last forever, because I am just someone like anyone and there's things too bad for me and I didn't know you could be lying flat, blue skin with blood from the man with the knife, to find love again, someone cutting his way into you; and I'm just someone and it's just flesh down there, tender flesh, somewhere you barely touch and you wouldn't cut it or wound it; no one would; and I have pain all over me but pain ain't the word because there's no word, I have pain on me like it's my skin but pain ain't the word and it isn't my skin, blue with red. I'm just some bleeding thing cut up on the floor, a pile of something someone left like garbage, some slaughtered animal that got sliced and sucked and a man put his dick in it and then it didn't matter if the thing was still warm or not because the essential killing had been done and it was just a matter of time; the thing would die; the longer it took the worse it would be; which is true. He had a good time. He did. He got up. He was friendly. He got dressed. I wasn't barely alive. I barely moaned or whispered or cried. I didn't move. He left. The gang was somewhere outside. He left the door open, wide open, and it was going to be a hundred years before I could crawl enough to close it. There was daylight streaming in. It was tomorrow. Tomorrow had finally come, a long tomorrow, an eternal tomorrow, I'm always here, the girl lying here, can't run, can't crawl, where's freedom now, can't move, can't crawl, dear God, help me, someone, help me, this is real, help me; please, help me. I hate God; for making the pain; and making the man; and putting me here; under them all; anyone that wants.

LIFE AND DEATH

1997

MY LIFE AS A WRITER
1995

I come from Camden, New Jersey, a cold, hard, corrupt city, and—now having been plundered by politicians, some of whom are in jail—also destitute. I remember being happy there. First my parents and I lived on Princess Avenue, which I don't remember; then, with my younger brother, Mark, at my true home, 1527 Greenwood Avenue. I made a child's vow that I would always remember the exact address so I could go back, and I have kept that vow through decades of dislocation, poverty, and hard struggle. I was ten when we moved to the suburbs, which I experienced as being kidnapped by aliens and taken to a penal colony. I never forgave my parents or God, and my heart stayed with the brick row houses on Greenwood Avenue. I loved the stoops, the games in the street, my friends, and I hated leaving.

I took the story of the three little pigs to heart and was glad that I lived in a brick house. My big, bad wolf was the nuclear bomb that Russia was going to drop on us. I learned this at Parkside School from the first grade on, along with reading and writing. A bell would ring or a siren would sound and we had to hide under our desks. We were taught to cower and wait quietly, without moving, for a gruesome death, while the teacher, of course, stood at the head of the class or policed the aisles for elbows or legs that extended past the protection of the tiny desks. And what would happen to her when the bomb came? Never, I believe, has a generation of children been so relentlessly terrorized by adults who were so obviously and stupidly lying. Eventually, the dullest of us picked up on it; and I was far from the dullest.

I remember trying to understand what the bomb was and how it would come and why. I'd see blinding light and heat and fire; and when my brain got tired of seeing burning humans, empty cities, burning cement, I would console myself with the story of the three little pigs. I was safe because my house was brick.

It is that feeling of my brain meeting the world around me that I remember most about being a child. The feeling was almost physical, as if I could feel my brain being stretched inside my head. I could feel my brain reaching for the world. I knew my brain did more than think. It could see and imagine and maybe even create something new or beautiful, if I was lucky and brave. I always wanted engagement, not abstract knowledge.

I loved the world and living and I loved being immersed in sensation. I did not like boundaries or want distance from what was around me. I saw adults as gatekeepers who stood between me and the world. I hated their evasions, rules, lies, petty tyrannies. I wanted to be honest and feel everything and take everything on. I didn't want to be careful and narrow the way they were. I thought a person could survive anything, except maybe famine and war, or drought and war. When I learned about Auschwitz my idea of the unbearable became more specific, more informed, sober and personal.

I began to think about survival very early, because we were Jewish on the heels of the Holocaust; because of the ubiquitous presence of those Russian bombs; and also because my mother was ill with heart disease. She had scarlet fever when she was a child, and in her family, big and poor, both parents immigrants, one did not call the doctor for a girl. The scarlet fever turned into rheumatic fever, which injured her heart long before there was open-heart surgery. She had many heart failures, maybe heart attacks, and at least one stroke before I became officially adolescent. She would be short of breath, maybe fall down; then she'd be gone, to a hospital, but Mark and I never really had any way of knowing if she had died yet. We would be farmed out to relatives, separated most of the time. This could happen day or night, while doing homework or sleeping. We'd be told to get dressed fast because Mother was very sick and we couldn't stay here now; and Dad was at work or at the hospital and he would explain later: be quiet, don't ask questions, cooperate. We never knew anything we could count on. I usually didn't even know where Mark was. Or she might be sick, at home but in bed and off-limits, maybe dying. Sometimes I would be allowed to sit on her bed for a little while and hold her hand.

She was Sylvia, and I loved her madly when I was a child, which she never believed, not even by the time she did die, in 1991 at the age of seventy-six. I did stop loving her when I was older and exhausted by her repudiations of me; but it would not be wrong to say that as a child I was in love with her, infatuated. I remember loving her long, dark hair, and the smell of coffee, which she drank perpetually when she was able to walk around, and the smoke from her cigarettes. Maybe it was my child's fear of death, or her sudden, brutal absences, that made me adore her without ever flinching when she pushed me away. I wanted to be around her, and I would have been her slave had she been generous enough to accept me. She was my first great romance.

But I was the wrong child for my mother to have had. She preferred dull obedience to my blazing adoration. She valued conformity and never even recognized the brazen emotional ploys of a child to hold on to her. My emotions were too extravagant for her own more literal sensibility. One could follow her around like a lovesick puppy, but if the puppy peed on the floor, she thought its intention was to spite her. She saw malice in almost anything I said or did. When I would be stretching my brain in curiosity—and dancing my brain in front of her to dazzle her—she thought it was defiance. When I asked her questions, which was a way for me to be engaged with her, she considered the questions proof of rebellion, a wayward delinquency, maybe even treason to her authority. I could never excite her or make myself understood or even comfort her. I do remember her reading to me sometimes at night when I couldn't sleep, and I remember feeling very happy.

She often told me that she loved me but did not like me. I came to believe that whatever she meant by love was too remote, too cold, too abstract or formulaic to have anything to do with me as an individual, as I was. She said that a mother always loved her child; and since this was an important rule in her world, she probably followed it. I never understood what she meant even when I was fully grown up—which feelings this generic and involuntary love might include. But to the extent that she knew me, there was no doubt that she did not like me, and also that I could not be the child that she would find likable. I wasn't, I couldn't be, and I didn't want to be. She understood only that I didn't want to be.

I had to be independent, of course. I had to learn to live without her or without anyone special. I had to learn to live from minute to minute. I had to learn to be on my own, emotionally alone, physically alone. I had to learn to take care of myself and sometimes my brother and sometimes even her. I never knew what would happen next, or if she'd be sick or dying, or where I'd be sleeping at night. I had to get strong and grow up. I'd try to understand and I'd ask God how He could make her so sick. Somehow, in stretching my brain to beat back the terror, I'd assert my own desire to live, to be, to know, to become. I had many a Socratic dialogue in my head before I ever read one. I had a huge inner life, not so strange, I think, for a child, or for a child who would become a writer. But the inner lives of children were not an acknowledged reality in those days, in the fifties, before I was ten and we moved to the suburbs, a place of sterility and desolation where no one had an inner life ever.

I have idyllic memories of childhood in Camden: my brother, my father, and me having tickling fights, wrestling, on the living room floor; me in my cowgirl suit practicing my fast draw so I could be an Amerikan hero; a tiny sandbox on our front lawn where all the children played, boys and girls together, our Eden until a certain year when the girls had to wear tops—I may have been five but I remember screaming and crying in an inarticulate outrage. We girls played with dolls on the stoops, washed their hair, set it, combed it out, dressed the dolls, tried to make stories of glamour in which they stood for us. I remember being humiliated by some girl I didn't like for not washing my doll's hair right—I think the doll was probably drowning. Later, my grandfather married her mother across the street, and I had to be nice to her. I was happier when we moved from dolls to canasta, gin rummy, poker, and strip poker. The children on the street developed a collective secret life, a half dozen games of sex and dominance that we played, half in front of our mother's eyes, half in a conspiracy of hiding. And we played Red Rover and Giant Steps, appropriating the whole block from traffic. And there was always ball, in formal games, or alone to pass the time, against brick walls, against the cement stoops. I liked the sex-and-dominance games, which could be overtly sadomasochistic, because I liked the risk and the intensity; and I liked ordinary games like hide-and-seek. I loved the cement, the alleys, the wires and telephone poles, the parked cars that provided sanctuary from the adults, a kind of metallic barrier against their eyes and ears; and I loved the communal life of us, the children, half *Lord of the Flies*, half a prelude to *Marjorie Morningstar*. To this day, my idea of a good time is to sit on a city stoop amid a profusion of people and noise as dark is coming on.

I would say that it was Sylvia who started fighting with me when I was an exuberant little pup and still in love with her. But eventually I started fighting back. She experienced my inner life as a reproach. She thought I was arrogant and especially hated that I valued, my own thoughts. When I kept what I was thinking to myself, she thought I was plotting against her. When I told her what I thought, she said I was defiant and some species of bad: evil, nasty, rotten. She often accused me of thinking I was smarter than she. I probably was, though I didn't know it; but it wasn't my fault. I was the child, she the adult, but neither of us understood that.

Our fights were awful and I don't doubt that, then as now, I fought to win. I may have been around eight when I dug in; and we were antagonists. I may have been a little older. Of course, I still wanted her to take me back and love me, but each crisis made that harder. Because of the wrenching separations, the pressing necessity of taking care of myself or Mark or her, the loneliness of living with relatives who didn't particularly want me, I had to learn to need my mother less. When we fought she said I was killing her. At some point, I don't know exactly when, I decided not to care if she did die. I pulled myself away from her fate and tried to become indifferent to it. With a kind of emotional jujitsu, I pushed my mother away in my mind and in how I lived. I did this as a child. I knew that she might really die, and maybe I would be the cause, as they all kept saying. I also knew I was being manipulated. I had to make a choice: follow by rote her ten thousand rules of behavior for how a girl must act, think, look, sit, stand—in other words, cut out my own heart; or withstand the threat of her imminent death—give up the hope of her love or her friendship or her understanding. I disciplined myself to walk away from her in every sense and over time I learned how. She told me I had a hard heart.

I made good grades, though I had trouble conforming in class as I got older because of the intellectual vacuity of most of my teachers. I followed enough of the social rules to keep adults at bay. There weren't therapists in schools yet, so no adult got to force-fuck my mind. I was smart enough to be able to strategize. I wasn't supposed to take long, solitary walks, but I took them. I wasn't supposed to go to other parts of our neighborhood, but I went. I had friends who were not Jewish or white at a time when race and religion lines were not crossed. I knew boys who were too old for me. I read books children weren't allowed to read. I regarded all of this as my private life and my right. My mother simply continued to regard me as a liar and a cheat with incomprehensible but clearly sinister tendencies and ideas.

When I was ten we moved to Delaware Township in New Jersey, a place *New York Times* writer Russell Baker described in a column as "nowhere along the highway," after which the outraged citizens changed the name to Cherry Hill. It was an empty place with sporadic outbreaks of ranch-type and split-level housing projects. There were still wild cherry trees and some deer. With the deer came hunters who stalked them across flat fields of ragweed and poison ivy. It was virtually all-white, unlike Camden where the schools were racially and ethnically mixed even as residential blocks were segregated according to precise calibrations: Polish Catholics on one block, Irish Catholics on another. It was intellectually arid, except for a few teachers, one of whom liked to play sex-and-seduction games with smart little girls. It was wealthy while we were quite poor. We moved there because my mother could not climb steps and the good Lord had never made a flatter place than Delaware Township/Cherry Hill. I lived for the day that I would leave to go to New York City, where there were poets and writers and jazz and people like me.

———

Harry, my daddy, was not a rolling stone. He wasn't at home because he worked two jobs most of the time and three jobs some of the time. He was a schoolteacher during the day and at night he unloaded packages at the post office. Later he became a guidance counselor at a boys' academic high school in Philadelphia and also in a private school for dropouts trying to get their high school diplomas. I don't know what the third job was, or when he had it. My brother and I would go stretches of many days without seeing him at home; and when we were in other people's houses, it could be weeks. There were times when he would go to college classes on Saturdays in an effort to get his Ph.D. degree, but he never had the time to write a dissertation, so he never got the degree. My dream was that when I grew up I would be able to give him the money to write his dissertation; but I never did make enough money and he says he is too old now anyway (though he still goes to the library every week). He was different from other men in how he acted and how he thought. He was gentle and soft-spoken. He listened with careful attention to children and women. He wanted teachers to unionize and the races to integrate. He was devoted to my mother and determined that she would get the very best medical care, a goal entirely out of reach for a low-paid schoolteacher, except that he did it. He borrowed money to pay medical bills. He borrowed money to take my mother to heart specialists. He borrowed money for professional nurses and to get housecleaning help and some child care and sometimes to hire a cook. He kept us warm and fed and sheltered, even though not always at home or together. He was outspoken and demonstrative in expressing affection, not self-conscious or withdrawn as most men were. He was nurturant and emotionally empathetic. He crossed a gender line and was stigmatized for it; called a sissy and a fairy by my buddies on the street who no doubt heard it from their parents. He loved my mother and he loved Mark and me; but especially me. I will never know why. He said I was the apple of his eye from the time I was born and I believe him. I did nothing to earn it and it was the one great gift of my life. On Sundays he slept late but he and I would watch the Sunday news shows together and analyze foreign crises or political personalities or social conflicts. We would debate and argue, not the vicious arguments I had with my mother but heightened dialogue always touching on policy, ideas, rights, the powerful and the oppressed, discrimination and prejudice. I don't know how he had the patience; but patience was a defining characteristic. He enjoyed my intelligence and treated me with respect. I think that to be loved so unconditionally by a father and treated with respect by him was not common for a girl then. I think he kept my mother alive and I think he kept Mark and me from being raised in foster care or as orphans.

He was appalled by the conflict between me and my mother, and certainly by the time I was a teen-ager he held me responsible for it. He knew I was adult inside. He let me know that my mother's well-being would always come first with him. And I remember that he hated it when I would cry. He must have thought it cowardly and pitiful and self-indulgent. I made many eloquent but to him unpersuasive declarations about my right to cry.

I trusted and honored him. I guess that I trusted him to love me even more than to take care of us. In an honors history seminar in high school, the class was asked to name great men in history. I named my father and was roundly ridiculed by advocates for Thomas Jefferson and Napoleon. But I meant it—that he had the qualities of true greatness, which I defined as strength, generosity, fairness, and a willingness to sacrifice self for principle. His principle was us: my mother, Mark, and me. When I was an adult we had serious ruptures and the relationship broke apart several times—all occasions of dire emergency for me. I think that he did abandon me when I was in circumstances of great suffering and danger. He was, I learned the hard way, only human. But what he gave me as a child, neither he nor anyone else could take away from me later. I learned perseverance from his example, and that endurance was a virtue. Even some of his patience rubbed off on me for some few years. I saw courage in action in ordinary life, without romance; and I learned the meaning of commitment. I could never have become a writer without him.

———

I wrote my first novel during science class in seventh grade in the suburbs. My best friend, a wild, beautiful girl who wanted to be a painter, sat next to me and also wrote a novel. In the eighth grade, my friend gone from school to be with a male painter in his late twenties or thirties, I wrote a short story for English class so disturbing to my teacher that she put her feelings of apprehension into my permanent record. The ethos was to conform, not to stand out. She knew the writing was good, and that troubled her. There was too much vibrancy in the language, too much imagination in the physical evocations of place and mood. Highly influenced by the television series *The Twilight Zone* and grief-stricken at the loss of my soulmate girlfriend, I wrote a story about a wild woman, strong and beautiful, with long hair and torn clothes, on another planet, sitting on a rock. My story had no plot really, only longing and language. I remember getting lost in descriptions of the woman, the sky, the rock, maybe wind and dirt. In formal terms, I believe I kept circling back to the woman on the rock through repeating images and phrases that worked almost like music to my ear—a way of creating movement yet insisting on the permanence of some elements of the scenario. I had a picture in my mind, which was involuntary. I don't know why it was there or how it got there. The picture was stubborn: it didn't move or change. I could see it as if it were real with my eyes open, though it was conceptual and in my head. It wasn't in front of my eyes; it was behind them. I had huge emotions of pain and loss. I had the need to keep moving through life, not be held back or stopped by anything I felt. I remember finding words that resonated with the emotions I felt: not words that expressed those emotions or described them, but words that embodied them without ever showing them. It was the unrevealed emotion—attached to the words but invisible in them, then used to paint the picture in my head in language that was concrete and physical—that gave the prose an intensity so troubling to my teacher. Was she troubled by the homoeroticism of the story? I don't believe she recognized it.

In the eighth grade, of course, I did not have any consistent internal standards for how prose must be or what prose must do. But I did know much more about what I wanted from language when, thirty years later, I brought that same picture, the same wild woman on the same rock, into my novel *Mercy*, first published in

1990 in England. The rock was Masada: a steep, barren mountain surrounded by desert, a refuge in ancient Palestine for a community of Jews known as zealots who committed, as the traditional story goes, mass suicide rather than surrender to the occupying Roman army. Ten men used their swords to slit the throats of everyone else; then one man killed the nine men and himself.

Mercy's narrator is a contemporary figure who in one of the novel's endings (it has two) sees herself as the wild woman on Masada at the time of the so-called suicides: "A child can't commit suicide. You have to murder a child. I couldn't watch the children killed; I couldn't watch the women taken one last time; throats bared; heads thrown back, or pushed back, or pulled back; a man gets on top, who knows what happens next, any time can be the last time, slow murder or fast, slow rape or fast, eventual death, a surprise or you are waiting with a welcome, an open invitation; rape leading, inexorably, to death; on a bare rock, invasion, blood, and death. Masada; hear my heart beat; hear me; the women and children were murdered."

I wasn't missing my old girlfriend. I didn't have the same picture in my head because I was feeling what I had felt in the eighth grade. In my experience nothing in writing is that simple. Both memory and consciousness are deeper and wider than the thinking mind, which might find meaning in such a facile association.

I felt, certainly, a much larger abandonment, a more terrifying desolation, essentially impersonal: how the lives of women and children were worthless to men and God. In the despair of that recognition, the barren landscape of the rock became a place to stare men and God in the face, and my wild woman the one to do it. When the picture first came into my head, I dismissed it but it would not go. When I started to work with it in words, I saw

Masada, I saw her, and I saw the murders. I, the writer, became a witness. Real history out in the world and a picture etched in my brain but forgotten for three decades converged in words I felt compelled to keep bringing together. Each word brought with it more detail, more clarity. My narrator, who is a character in my book, knows less than I do. She is inside the story. Deciding what she will see, what she can know, I am detached from her and cold in how I use her. I do not ever think she is me. She is not my mouthpiece. She does not directly speak my views or enumerate my ideas or serve as a mannequin in words displaying my wounds of body or soul. I am more than the sum of all her parts; and she can live in the reader's mind but the reader's mind cannot know me through knowing her. I have never been to Masada. However dull it may seem, I am the person who sits at the typewriter writing words, rewriting them, over and over, night in and night out (since I work at night), over months or years. *Mercy* took three years to write.

In using the picture in my head from my eighth-grade story, I broke the picture open into a universe of complex and concrete detail dreadful with meaning, in particular about incest and the power of the father—the patriarchal right of invasion into the bodies of women and children. At the end of writing *Mercy*'s Masada chapter, I felt as if I had finally seen that earlier picture whole. When I was younger I could only see a fragment, or a line drawing, but now I had seen everything that had been implicit in the picture from the beginning, from its first appearance in my mind, as if I had uncovered something pre-existing. It was always real and whole; what I had done as a writer was to find it and describe it, not invent it. In the eighth grade, I had not known how to use my mind or language to explicate the picture in my head, which was a gift or a visitation; I couldn't see the human destiny that had been acted out on that barren rock. But the time between my childhood and now had collapsed. The time between Masada and now had collapsed.

This strange but not unusual aftermath of creating helps to explain why so many writers disclaim responsibility for their characters and ideas. The character made me do it, most writers say. But the truth is that one starts out with a blank page, and each and every page is blank until the writer fills it. In the process, the mind uses itself up, each cognitive capacity—intellect, imagination, memory, intuition, emotion, even cunning—used to the absolute utmost, a kind of strip-mining of one's mental faculties. At the same time, with the mind as scavenger and plunderer, one cannibalizes one's own life. But one's own life for the writer includes everything she can know, not just what happened to her in the ordinary sense. If I know about you—a gesture, an emotion, an event—I will use you if I need your gesture, your emotion, your event. What I take will seem to me to be mine, as if I know it from the inside, because my imagination will turn it over and tear it apart. Writers use themselves and they use other people. Empathy can be invasive. Friendship is sometimes a robbery-in-progress. This omniscient indifference takes a certain coldness, and a certain distance, which writers have and use.

Facts and details are the surface. The writer needs the facts and everything underneath them. One wanders, bodiless, or goes on search-and-destroy missions using one's mind. One needs a big earth, rich soil, deep roots: one digs and pulls and takes.

But after, when the writing is finished, one looks at the finished thing and has a feeling or conviction of inevitability: I found it, not I made it. It—the story, the novel—had its own laws; I simply followed them—found them and followed them; was smart enough and shrewd enough to find them and follow them; wasn't sidetracked or diverted, which would mean failure, a lesser book. Even with nonfiction, which in the universe of my writing has the same cognitive complexity as fiction, in the aftermath one feels that one has chiseled a pre-existing form (which necessarily has substance attached to it) out of a big, shapeless stone: it was there, I found it. This is an affirmation of skill but not of invention. At best, one feels like a sculptor who knows how to liberate the shape hidden in the marble or clay—or knew the last time but may not know the next, may be careless, may ruin the stone through distraction or stupidity. Once finished, the process of writing becomes opaque, even to the writer. I did it but how did I do it? Can I ever do it again? The brain becomes normal. One can still think, of course, but not with the luminosity that makes intelligence so powerful a tool while writing, nor can one think outside of literal and linear time anymore.

Writing is alchemy. Dross becomes gold. Experience is transformed. Pain is changed. Suffering may become song. The ordinary or horrible is pushed by the will of the writer into grace or redemption, a prophetic wail, a screed for justice, an elegy of sadness or sorrow. It is the lone and lonesome human voice, naked, raw, crying out, but hidden too, muted, twisted and turned, knotted or fractured, by the writer's love of form, or formal beauty: the aesthetic dimension, which is not necessarily familiar or friendly. Nor does form necessarily tame or simplify experience. There is always a tension between experience and the thing that finally carries it forward, bears its weight, holds it in. Without that tension, one might as well write a shopping list.

My fiction is not autobiography. I am not an exhibitionist. I don't show myself. I am not asking forgiveness. I don't want to confess. But I have used everything I know—my life—to show what I believe must be shown so that it can be faced. The imperative at the heart of my writing—what must be done—comes directly from my life. But I do not show my life directly, in full view; nor even look at it while others watch.

Autobiography is the unseen foundation of my nonfiction work, especially *Intercourse* and *Pornography: Men Possessing Women*. These two nonfiction books are not "about" me. There is no first-person writing in them. Conceptually, each involved the assimilation of research in many intellectually distinct areas using analytical skills culled from different disciplines. The research materials had nothing to do with me personally. They were freestanding, objectively independent (for instance, not interviews conducted by me). Yet when I wrote *Intercourse* and *Pornography: Men Possessing Women*, I used my life in every decision I made. It was my compass. Only by using it could I find north and stay on course. If a reader could lift up the words on the page, she would see—far, far under the surface—my life. If the print on the page turned into blood, it would be my blood from many different places and times. But I did not want the reader to see my life or my blood. I wanted her to see intercourse or pornography. I wanted her to know them the way I know them: which is deeply.

I'd like to take what I know and just hand it over. But there is always a problem for a woman: being believed. How can I think I know something? How can I think that what I know might matter? Why would I think that anything I think might make a difference, to anyone, anywhere? My only chance to be believed is to find a way of writing bolder and stronger than woman hating itself—smarter, deeper, colder. This might mean that I would have to write a prose more terrifying than rape, more abject than torture, more insistent and destabilizing than battery, more desolate than prostitution, more invasive than incest, more filled with threat and aggression than pornography. How would the innocent bystander be able to distinguish it, tell it apart from the tales of the rapists themselves if it were so nightmarish and impolite? There are no innocent bystanders. It would have to stand up for women—stand against the rapist and the pimp—by changing women's silence to speech. It would have to say all the unsaid words during rape and after; while prostituting and after; all the words not said. It would have to change women's apparent submission—the consent read into the silence by the wicked and the complacent—into articulate resistance. I myself would have to give up my own cloying sentimentality toward men. I'd have to be militant; sober and austere. I would have to commit treason: against the men who rule. I would have to betray the noble, apparently humanistic premises of civilization and civilized writing by conceptualizing each book as if it were a formidable weapon in a war. I would have to think strategically, with a militarist's heart: as if my books were complex explosives, mine fields set down in the culture to blow open the status quo. I'd have to give up Baudelaire for Clausewitz.

Yes, okay, I will. Yes, okay: I did. In retrospect, that is just what I did: in *Mercy* and *Intercourse* and *Pornography: Men Possessing Women* and *Ice and Fire*.

———

It was in Amsterdam in 1972 that I made the vow, which I have kept, that I would use everything I know in behalf of women's liberation. I owed the women's movement a big debt: it was a feminist who helped me escape the brutality of my marriage. Escape is not a one-time run for your life: you keep running and hiding; he shows up out of nowhere and beats you, menaces you, threatens, intimidates, screams a foul invective at you in broad daylight on crowded streets, breaks into wherever you find to live, hits you with his dirty fists, dirtied by your pain, your blood.

I left the marital home toward the end of 1971, some two months after I turned twenty-five. I fled the country in which I had been living for five years in November 1972. I have no continuous memory of the events of that year. Even with the events I can remember, I have no sense of their sequence. I was attacked, persecuted, followed, harassed, by the husband I had left; I often lived the life of a fugitive, except that it was the more desperate life of a battered woman who had run away for the last time, whatever the outcome.

I have written about the experience of being a battered wife in three nonfiction essays: "A Battered Wife Survives" (1978) and "What Battery Really Is" (1989), both of which are included in the U.S. edition of *Letters From a War Zone*, and "Trapped in a Pattern of Pain," published in the *Los Angeles Times*, June 26, 1994. I wrote "A Battered Wife Survives" to celebrate my thirty-first birthday. I still shook and trembled uncontrollably, but not all the time; had nightmares and flashbacks, but less. I had published two books: *Woman Hating* (1974) and *Our Blood* (1976). I had survived and was not alone in a universe of pain and fear. The other two essays were written in behalf of other battered women: Hedda Nussbaum and Nicole Brown Simpson. I felt the need to try to make people understand how destructive and cruel battery is—and how accepted, how normal, how supported by society. With enormous reluctance, I revisited the site of this devastation in my own life. I had to say what battery was from the point of view of the woman being hurt, since I knew.

Everything I have written in these nonfiction essays about myself is true. It would be wrong, however, to read my fiction as if it were a factual narrative, a documentary in words. Literature is always simpler and easier than life, especially in conveying atrocity. As the infrequency of my nonfiction essays about battery suggests, I am extremely reluctant to write about it: partly because I cant bear to think about it; partly because I feel physically ill when I literally trip over absent memory, great and awful blank areas of my life that I cannot recover—I am shaky with dread and vertigo; and partly because I still hide.

But the year of running, hiding, to stay alive is essential to the story of how I became a writer, or the writer I am, for better or worse. He kept our home; I was pushed out. This was fine, since I just wanted not to be hit. I had no money. I was isolated as battered women usually are but also I was a foreigner with no real rights except through my husband. My parents refused to have me back. His family was his—I was too afraid of him ever to tell them anything, though I believe they knew. I slept first on the floor of a friend's room—his friend, too—with her two dogs. Later, I slept where I could. I lived this way before I was married but not with an assassin after me, nor having sustained such brutality that my mind didn't quite work—it failed me in everyday situations, which it no longer recognized; it failed me with ordinary people who couldn't grasp my fear.

A feminist named Ricki Abrams helped me: gave me asylum, a dangerous kindness in the face of a battering man; helped me find shelter repeatedly; and together she and I started to plan the book that became *Woman Hating*.

I lived on houseboats on the canals—a majestic one near the Magere Brug, a stunningly beautiful bridge, a plainer one infested with mice. I slept in someone's kitchen. I lived for a while in the same house as Ricki, a narrow, teetering building on a cobblestone street that ringed a canal in Amsterdam's historically preserved old city. I hid on a farm far outside Amsterdam with a commune of hippies who made their own cloth with a spinning wheel and a loom. I slept in a cold and deserted mansion near the German border. In one emergency, when my husband had broken into where I was living, had beaten me and threatened to kill me, I spent three weeks sleeping in a movie theater that was empty most of the time. Experimental movies were shown in a big room where I hid. The whole building was empty otherwise. On some nights small audiences of artistes would sit and watch formless flashes of light. When the avant-garde cleared out, I was allowed to open a cot. I lived in a state of terror. Every trip outside might mean death if he found me.

No one knew about battery then, including me. It had no public name. There were no shelters or refuges. Police were indifferent. There was no feminist advocacy or literature or social science. No one knew about the continuing consequences, now called post-traumatic stress syndrome, which has a nice dignity to it. How many times, after all, can one say terror, fear, anguish, dread, flashbacks, shaking, uncontrollable trembling, nightmares, he's going to kill me?

At the time, so far as I knew, I was the only person this had ever happened to; and the degradation had numbed me, disoriented me, changed me, lowered me, shamed me, broken me.

It was Ricki who first gave me feminist books to read. I remember especially *Sexual Politics* by Kate Millett (whose class at Barnard Ricki had taken), *The Dialectic of Sex* by Shulamith Firestone, and the anthology *Sisterhood Is Powerful* edited by Robin Morgan. I had left the United States in 1968 a second time (the first being in 1965, after a rapelike trauma in Manhattan's Women's House of

Detention, where I was taken after an arrest for protesting the Vietnam War). I had not read or heard about these books. I argued with them in Amsterdam. I argued with Ricki. Oppression meant the U.S. in Vietnam, or apartheid in South Africa, or legal segregation in the U.S. Even though I had been tortured and was fighting for my life, I could not see women, or myself as a woman, as having political significance. I did know that the battery was not my fault. I had been told by everyone I asked for help the many times I tried to escape—strangers and friends—that he would not be hitting me if I didn't like it or want it. I rejected this outright. Even back then, the experience of being battered was recognizably impersonal to me. Maybe I was the only person in the world this had ever happened to, but I knew it had nothing to do with me as an individual. It just never occurred to me that I was being hit because I was a woman.

Woman Hating was not a book written out of an ideology. It came out of an emergency, written half underground and in hiding. I wanted to find out what had happened to me and why. I knew *only* that it was impersonal. I made a list of what I thought might bear on what had happened to me, and that list became the table of contents in the published book. I looked at fairy tales—what did they teach about being female; at pornography—I was part of a generation that used it—what did it say about being female; at Chinese footbinding and the persecution of the witches—why was there culturally normalized violence against females; at androgyny—the myths and contemporary ideas of a community not organized on the principle of gender, the falseness of gender itself. I wanted to examine the culture: sex roles; sex; history; mythology; community.

Somehow, I had been given a key and access to a space in the basement of Paradiso, one of the clubs the Dutch government sponsored for counterculture, hashish-smoking, rock-and-roll-addicted hippies. The basement under the huge church building was dark and dank with a colony of misfits and homeless, mentally disoriented strangers, most of whom were hiding from someone, often the police. I was allowed to work there on the book—I had a desk and chair—but I was not supposed to sleep there, and I tried not to. My cohabitants did not inspire confidence, and my husband, who worked upstairs at night when Paradiso was open, was dangerous for sure. Like other escaping battered women (I have since learned), I lived in a shared or overlapping social and economic world with the batterer; I tried to believe it would be all right.

The book Ricki and I were going to write together became, of course, very important to me. I don't know if the attempt was interrupted by the violence or the violence was interrupted by the attempt. I know that I devoted myself to the book, even though it was hard for me to concentrate because I lived in constant fear. I held on to the book as if it were a life raft, even though I was drowning in poverty and fear. There were times of hope, near normalcy. At one point my husband got a new apartment and offered me our old one. I took it, for all the obvious reasons. He left a mattress; someone gave me a small radio; and I lived on potatoes. Then he started breaking in; and it was there that he bloodied me and said he would kill me, run me down when he saw me, and I knew it was true finally, and I had to hide in the movie theater after that for three weeks, the time it took to get a restraining order. My lawyer, assigned by the court, at first didn't believe me or didn't care when I told him about the beatings or how dangerous my husband was; but later my husband apparently roughed up the lawyer's secretary. This time, when driven from the apartment by my husband's threats to a phone in a store around the block, the lawyer told me to go somewhere else for a while, though he didn't know where or how and didn't care. I had had to go to the store to use the phone because the apartment phone was in my husband's name, and he had it disconnected and it was a two-year wait for a new line. As I came out of the back room of the store where the phone was, the woman who owned the store opened her cash register, grabbed a handful of bills, pushed them at me, and said: "Run for your life. Now." I did.

Through all this, I held on to this idea of a book; and I kept working on it. Ricki and I did research together and some writing together. But then she pulled away from it. The book itself, in taking on counterculture pornography, brought us into conflict with friends and acquaintances in the exilic, counterculture community in Amsterdam. Some of these folks produced a pornography tabloid called *Suck*. Ricki and I drafted a chapter on *Suck* and gave it to them to read. I, at least, believed that they would see the insult to women in what they were publishing, and that there was danger in some of their photographs—I remember in particular a photo of an Asian woman inserting a huge, glass, bowl-shaped jar into her rectum. I had begun to identify with other women. Our friends, the makers of the pornography, reacted with outrage to our effrontery in challenging them. They said they had always been for civil rights (against segregation based on race) and this was sex—what kind of chicks were we anyway? We thought we were perfectly fine chicks at the time, even though the word "chick" itself was beginning to have an ugly sound to it. Ricki decided that she couldn't take the social ostracism these folks threatened. We agreed that I would finish the book and get it published. I had to get out of there anyway or I'd be killed. I knew I had to disappear and that there could be no mistakes. I planned a secret escape and in November 1972 I disappeared suddenly.

The vow that I made—out loud, to myself but with Ricki as witness—was that I would become a real writer and I would use everything I knew to help women. I didn't know how much I knew, how valuable it would be; nor did she. But we both did understand that in 1972 what I knew was not part of feminism: what I knew about male dominance in sex or rape in marriage, for instance. The knowledge about male dominance in sex came not only from this one marriage but from several years of prostituting before I got married. I called it "being on the streets," and it consisted of equal parts whoring, poverty and homelessness, and just being a tough girl. I had never kept it a secret, not from my husband, not from any friend. Ricki and I both understood that I had experience that could be knowledge. I made a vow to use it for women.

———

Writers need to be damned hard to kill. So do women, of course. I have never believed in suicide, the female poet's alternative to standing her ground and facing down the power of men. I don't like it that Plath and Sexton wrote strong and beautiful poems capturing the horror and meanness of male dominance but would not risk losing socially conventional femininity by sticking around to fight it out in the realm of politics, including the politics of culture. I always wanted to live. I fought hard to live. This means I did something new. I have been bearing the unbearable, and facing men down, for a long time now.

I began messing with men when I was in high school, though, sadly, they began messing with me earlier than that—I was raped at nine, though not legally, since fingers and a hand were used for penetration, not the officially requisite penis. That ended up in my hand as he twisted and contorted with a physical omnipresence that pinned me and manipulated me at the same time. This breach of a child's body does count. It does register. The boundary of the body itself is broken by force and intimidation, a chaotic but choreographed violence. The child is used intentionally and reduced to less than human by the predator's intelligence as well as his behavior. The commitment of the child molester is absolute, and both his insistence and his victory communicate to the child his experience of her—a breachable, breakable thing any stranger can wipe his dick on. When it is family, of course, the invasion is more terrible, more intimate, escape more unlikely. I was lucky—it was a stranger. I was lucky by the standards of today: neither kidnapped nor killed. The man became part of the dark—not "the dark" in its usual symbolic sense, bad, with a racist tinge, but part of the literal dark: his body, almost distinct, got folded into every dark room like the one in which he hurt me and he got folded into the dark of every night I had to get through, with eyes open, waiting. I didn't like to sleep, because then I couldn't guard my mother against death. So I kept my eyes open. I could feel that the night was occupied with tangible creatures, and the man, hiding, was one of them.

As a child with an immense ambition to live, to know, to feel, I moved toward everything that frightened me: men, night, the giving up of my own body. I wanted to be an artist, by which I meant a writer. I despised commercial writing. My heroes were Rimbaud and Baudelaire. I had a paperback of Baudelaire's poems with me, in French with an English prose translation, when the man molested me. A few years later I had a high school teacher who said that most girls of my social class who worked (the ideal was not to work) became hairdressers, but I was so smart that I could become a prostitute, which at least was interesting. He was my tutor in sex; a guide; a charlatan and an exploiter. But he made the sameness of art and opening my legs palpable, urgent: there wasn't one without the other. I thought he was a philosopher and someday we would found a school of philosophy; I would be his acolyte. He introduced me to Camus and Sartre. I was a motherless child with spirit and intelligence in a world that abhorred both in girls. I wanted knowledge but distrusted formal education because the adults were enforcers and transparently wanted to break my spirit; except for the seducer. He wanted to appropriate it for his own purposes but I didn't begin to imagine that. I would find ways to go to New York City to find poems and on the bus I would find a way to get money from old guys who liked teen-age girls to touch them. I'd use the money to go to Greenwich Village and buy mimeographed collections of poems. I loved Allen Ginsberg especially. More than anyone he expressed the sense of pain I felt, the anger and rebellion, but also the undifferentiated infatuation I felt for the world of possibility around me. I had no sense of evil and I didn't believe that harm could defeat me—I'd make poems out of it. High school was hell, to be endured, the teachers behavior-police who took books away and tried to shut the mind down. For instance, a tenth-grade teacher in a study hall confiscated my copy of *Hamlet*, which I had been reading. She said we weren't allowed to read it until the twelfth grade. I told her that I had already read it several times so why take it from me? She did take it and countered with her certainty that one day she would read about me in the newspapers. In those days only politicians and criminals made news. Girls didn't become politicians. I was bad for reading *Hamlet*. Each day the enforcers pushed me into a sustained rage laced with contempt; and each day the seducer manipulated my anger and loneliness, pushed me further into experiencing intelligence as a sexualized mark of Cain and artistic ambition as a sexualized delinquency.

Meanwhile, my father worked hard so that I could have a formal education that would be excellent, not mediocre, on the college level. The high school guidance counselors wanted me to go to a state college for girls to get a teaching degree "to fall back on when your husband dies." My intelligence had no significance to them; my desire to write, which I confessed, was beneath consideration. My father knew I would not stay in any college that was high school redux. In September 1964 I went to Bennington College on scholarships and loans, loans he took out, not me. I did have jobs there for money but not enough to carry any of the real economic burden. I stayed there one year, left, returned for two years, left, mailed in my thesis from Amsterdam. In 1969 my father, fittingly, attended my graduation and picked up my diploma. I am considered a graduate of the class of 1968, however, because that is how Bennington keeps track of students. In those years, so many students left—some of the richer ones to Austin Riggs, a mental institution not too far away, some taking other detours—that the college always reckoned you a member of the class in which you entered and optimistically added four years to signify graduation; it would be hard for an already overtaxed administration to know who returned when, for how long, and to what end.

Bennington had a reputation for academic excellence and a bohemian environment. In fact, Bennington trained mistresses, not wives, for artists, not businessmen. To illustrate the ambience: the year before my first year, seniors in literature had, as a group project, recreated the brothel scene in Joyce's *Ulysses*, themselves the whores. A lot of the faculty preyed on the nearly all-female student body; and the deep conviction of most of the faculty that these girls would never become artists themselves was openly articulated when, in my third year of attendance, coeducation was discussed and eventually adopted. Students, including me, got to hear how useless the mostly male faculty felt teaching girls. We never became anything, they said, each a dozen times in a dozen ways. We seemed to be fine for fucking and serial marriage, some faculty actually going through as many as four marriages with successive students and countless adulteries. But we could never become what in our hearts we thought we were: creative, ambitious, risk-taking doers and thinkers and makers. I had three brilliant teachers at Bennington, each of whom was ethically scrupulous with respect to me; and I owe them a lot. They taught me with an astonishing intellectual generosity; they supported my aspirations; they even protected me, from other faculty and sometimes from myself. They extended friendship without the sexualization. The rest of it was intellectually boring. After my first few weeks there, my philosophy professor telephoned me at the student house where I lived and asked me please not to leave: she knew I was bored. I distracted myself with drugs, sex, and politics.

Bennington had a nine-week work period in the winter—a long two months—and long Thanksgiving, Christmas, and spring breaks, a big problem for a girl with no real home and no money. For my first work period in December 1964 I took marginal political jobs in New York City and fucked for food and shelter and whatever cash I needed. I worked with the Student Peace Union and the War Resisters League opposing the war in Vietnam. I had other jobs, too, for instance as a receptionist at a New York University institute for remedial reading. In February 1965 I was arrested outside the United States Mission to the United Nations for protesting Amerika's involvement in Vietnam. I had a book of poems by Charles Olson with me when I was arrested. I spent four days in the Women's

House of Detention before I was released on my own recognizance. While in jail, in addition to the many strip-searches by hand that police and nurses made into my vagina and anus, I was brutalized by two male doctors who gave me an internal examination, the first one I ever had. They pretty much tore me up inside with a steel speculum and had themselves a fine old time verbally tormenting me as well. I saw them enjoy it. I witnessed their pleasure in doing it. I couldn't understand why they would like to hurt me. I began to bleed right after. When I came out of jail I was mute from the trauma. I wandered around the city, homeless and resourceless, silent and confused, for several days, until I showed up at the apartment of a stranger who had taken a bag I had packed for jail from me when, toward the end of the day, it seemed as if we would not be arrested. I sort of vaguely remembered her name and looked it up in the phone book when I needed underwear badly enough. She was the writer Grace Paley and this was before she herself had gone to jail to protest Vietnam. She made me come in and sit; I stared silently. Grace got me to talk but instead of normal talk I said what had happened to me. I didn't even know the words for speculum or internal examination, so I was exceptionally blunt and used my hands. She thought that what had been done to me was horrible and she immediately called a woman reporter to say that this monstrous thing had been done to this girl. The reporter said: so what? But that night I went to the Student Peace Union office and typed letters to newspapers to tell what had happened to me in the jail: blunt letters. The antiwar boys, whose letters I typed during the day, whose leaflets I mimeographed, laughed at me; but I mounted a protest against the prison. *The New York Times*, the *Daily News*, and the *New York Post* carried the story. The city was forced to conduct a grand jury investigation. An assistant to the governor also investigated. A liberal Republican, John V. Lindsay, challenged entrenched Democratic incumbent Robert Wagner for mayor partly by holding Wagner responsible for the corruption in the jail and promising to shut it down. Lindsay won. Television news shows did documentaries on the prison, which had a long history of brutalizing women, some of whom had died. Eventually, the grand jury vindicated the prison, and the governor's assistant was defunded by the legislature. My parents were ashamed of my arrest and of the way in which I had been hurt. They were enraged with me and pretty much abandoned me. I left school, my parents, the country. I went to Greece with less than $100 in my pocket. I gave most of it to an old woman, Mildred, whom I met on a train. She said she had lost hers but had money waiting in Athens. I showed up at the appointed place, at the appointed time, but she never came. That night, my nineteenth birthday, I picked up a Greek army officer: I needed food and money. Since the hill overlooking Athens was beautiful and the night sublime, it was easy to pretend this was romance. I remember saying to him after, "You really hate women, don't you?" I hadn't anticipated woman hating but I recognized it in his abrupt post-coital tristesse. I learned not to voice the observation however many times I made it, whatever the post-coital mood. Men don't like to be seen or remarked on by what my friend Judith Malina, director of the Living Theatre, calls "talking women." I wrote poems and a novel called *Notes on Burning Boyfriend*, a surrealistic screed against the Vietnam War built on the self-immolation of protester Norman Morrison. I published a small collection of poems and Genet-like prose called *Child* (Heraklion, Crete, 1966). It wasn't until I published *Woman Hating* in 1974 that I became a talking woman who could say with some authority: you really hate women, don't you?

The authority was never my own plain experience. I always thought other people's lives were worth more than mine. As a matter of temperament I had an interest in the collective or communal, not the personal. I thought psychology was a phony science, and I still do. I didn't think something was important simply because it happened to me, and certainly the world concurred. I had learned that I would not be believed. I knew that from the world's point of view, though never my own, I was trash, the bottom. The prison authorities said I lied and the grand jury claimed to believe them, not me. No one really believed me about my husband. I had a deep experience of the double standard but no systematic understanding of it. The writers I had loved and wanted to emulate—Baudelaire or Artaud or Dostoevsky or Henry Miller or Jean Genet—were apparently enno-bled by degradation. The lower they sunk the more credibility they had. I was lowered and disgraced, first by what was being called sexual liberation, then by the violence of domestic sexual servitude, without any concomitant increase in expertness: I paid my dues, baby, I know the price of the ticket but so what? When I emerged as a writer with *Woman Hating*, it was not to wallow in pain, or in depravity, or in the male romance with prostitution; it was to demand change. I wanted to change the power structure in the social world that had made degradation a destiny for many of us, or lots of us, or maybe even all of us—for women. I didn't want to write the female suicide's poem; nor did I want to write another male-inspired lyric celebrating the sewer. I wanted to resist male dominance for myself and to change the outcome for other women. I did not want to open my legs again, this time in prose. I did not believe that to do so would persuade or bring change. I found, then and over the next twenty years, a stubborn refusal to credit a woman with any deep knowledge of the world itself, the world outside the domain of her own introspection about romantic love, housekeeping, a man. This refusal was so basic and so widespread that it could stay an unspoken assumption. Women who wanted to write about social issues did it through anecdote. Books that could only have been written out of an extensive and significant knowledge of what it meant to be pornographized or sexually colonized—my books—were dismissed by patriarchy's intellectual ruling class as Victorian or puritanical—empirical synonyms for ignorant.

Instead of using my own experience as the immediate subject of discourse, I used a more complex method of exposing bone and blood: I found the social phenomena that could be pulled apart to show what I knew to be the essential heart of the experience—rape, prostitution, battery, for instance; woman hating, sexualized insult, bias, discrimination—and I found the language to carry it: to carry it far, way past where critics could reach or, frankly, most men could imagine. I had the luck of having my books last over enough time to reach women—not elite women but grassroots women and marginalized women. Slowly women began to come to me to say, yes, that's right; and I learned more from them, went deeper. I used writing to take language where women's pain was—and women's fear—and I kept excavating for the words that could bear the burden of speaking the unspeakable: all that hadn't been said during the rape or after, while prostituting or after; truths that had not been said ever or truths that had not been said looking the rapist, the batterer, the pimp, the citizen-john in the eye. This has been my contribution to literature and to the women's movement.

———

I saw my mother's strength. Illness seems a visitation, a particular affliction to test the courage of the stricken person, a personal challenge from God. It is hard to know what one can learn from the example even of someone as heroic as my mother surely was. In my mother, I saw Herculean strength in the face of pain, sickness, incapacitation, and the unknown. I have never thought that much of it rubbed off, because I am a coward in that realm: any minor illness makes me feel as if life has stopped. The heroic person, as I saw from my mother, never accepts even the suggestion that life might stop. She keeps pulling the burden, illness as a stone weight; she never stops pulling. Nothing in my mother's life suggested that women were wimps.

In school—grade school and college—my female friends were rebels with deep souls: bad children in adulthood; smart adults in childhood; precocious; willful; stubborn; not one age or one sex or with one goal easily advanced by a conforming marriage and inevitable motherhood. Despite the best efforts of parents, teachers, to bind our feet Chinese-style, we kept kicking. Ain't none of us got out with unbroken feet; we all got some bones bent in half; we got clipped and pushed and stepped on hard to make us conform; and in our different ways we kept walking, even on the broken bones. It was a time when girls were supposed to be virgins when we married. The middle-class ideal was that women were not supposed to work; such labor would reflect badly on our husbands. Anyone pregnant outside of marriage was an outcast: a delinquent or an exile; had a criminal abortion or birthed a child that would most likely be taken away from her for adoption, which meant forever then. In disgrace, she would be sent away to some home for pregnant girls, entirely stigmatized; her parents ashamed, shocked; she herself a kind of poison that had ruined the family's notion of its own goodness and respectability. She would be socially reprehensible and repulsive—and the social ostracism would be absolute. I had close friends who resisted, who never quite gave in, despite appearances to the contrary. The cost was high sometimes; but it is my impression that my friends, like most women, paid the highest price when they did give in, not when they resisted. The cost needs to be spread out over time: the many marriages and the midlife depression. On the streets there were women who were both strong and fragile at the same time: immensely strong to bear the continuing sexual invasion, consistent brutality, and just plain bad weather (no joke); immensely strong to accept responsibility as the prostituting persona—I want this, I do this, I am this, ain't nothin' hurts me; and much too fragile to face either the cost of prostituting or its etiology. The cost was physical disintegration and mental splitting apart. The cost was getting dirtier and lonelier and anesthetizing pain with more and meaner drugs. The cost was accepting the physical violence of the johns, moving through it as if it didn't matter or hadn't happened, never facing that one had been hurt, then hurt again, nor asking why. Some girls were straight-out battered and forced. But even without a violent man in sight, the etiology always had to do with sexual abuse, in the present or in the past; also with homelessness and poverty; with the willingness of men to use any girl for small change; with abandonment—the personal abandonment of family, the social abandonment choreographed by the users. It may be harder to face abandonment than to endure exploitation; and there were no models for articulating the realities and consequences of sexual abuse. The point of dealing with political oppression has never been that the oppressed are by nature weak, therefore pitiful: the more injustice on one's back, the stronger one must be. Strong girls become strong women and use that strength to endure; but fighting injustice requires a dynamic strength disciplined to resistance, focused on subverting illegitimate power, eventually to level it. In a system valuing men over women, girls with piss and vinegar carried a heavier burden than girls brimming over with sugar and spice; the stronger were punished more, and still are. In this world, female friendships, deep and sustained loves, romances and infatuations, also love affairs, helped keep one's heart alive, one's sense of self, however unratified by the larger universe, animated and sensate. The political use of female strength to change society for the benefit of women is a different choice: a harder, better choice than endurance, however noble (or stylish) the endurance.

In my early adult life as a writer, there were three women especially who helped me and taught me and believed in me: Grace Paley, Barbara Deming, and Muriel Rukeyser. Each one sort of took me in and took me to her heart for some significant period of my life. Each one was mother and sister and friend. Each one was a distinguished and powerful writer, a social rebel, an original moral thinker. Each lived a life that combined writing and political action. Each put herself on the line for the oppressed, the powerless; was repelled by exploitation and injustice; and was devoted to women— had deep and intimate friendships with women and fought for women's rights. I met Grace in 1965, shortly after I got out of the Women's House of Detention. She fed me and gave me a bed to sleep in; I went to her when I was distressed, exhausted, in trouble—or more trouble than usual. She helped me when I came back from Greece; then again later when I came back from Amsterdam. I met Barbara in 1965 a few months after I met Grace, on a television program about the Women's House of Detention, where she too had spent some time as a political protester (see "Letter to M.," *Lavender Culture*, edited by Jay and Young); and then we met again and became close after *Woman Hating* was published. In 1976, my friend John Stoltenberg (about whom more later) and I went down to Sugarloaf Key in Florida to live on shared land with Barbara and her lover, Jane Verlaine. I couldn't tolerate the subtropical climate so after five months John and I moved north to the Berkshires. I met Muriel in 1972 after I had returned to New York City from Amsterdam at an antiwar meeting. She tried very hard to help me survive as a writer, including by hiring me as her assistant (see "Introduction," *Letters From a War Zone*). My apprenticeship to her had a slightly formal quality, because she paid me for the duration. She opened her home to me and her heart; she advised me and counseled me; and she made sure I had a bare minimum of money. She was attuned to the concrete necessities. A woman who has been poor and entirely on her own, as Muriel had been, knows that one's life can slip through a crack; good intentions can't match the value of a dime.

These friendships were of enormous importance to me; I doubt I would have survived without them. But the friendships went far beyond any utility for survival. Each of these women had faith in me—and I never quite knew why; and each of these women loved me—and I never knew why. It was a lucky orphan who found each of these women and it was a lucky striving writer who found each of these writers. They are all taken more seriously now than they were then; but I had the good sense to know that each was an Amerikan original, wise with common sense and plan talk, gritty with life; they were great craftswomen, each a citizen and a visionary. I know what I took; I hope I gave enough back.

———

It is hard to say what keeps a writer writing in the face of discouragement. It helps to have had a difficult childhood; to have a love of writing itself, without regard to the outcome; and eventually to have an audience, however small, that wants you, wants those troublesome books, is like a lover to you, very intimate with enormous expectations—embraces you through the language you find and the truth you are willing to tell. I have had that audience, which I meet when I travel to lecture or to give readings, a U.S. underground unrecognized by the media in small towns, on college campuses, at political rallies, tender, luminous, brave women of all ages, and mostly but not exclusively young men who want fairness for women. They have shown me respect and love.

One can be derailed by savage reviews, certainly poverty, a ubiquitous cultural contempt, violent words or violent gestures or violent acts, invisibility as a writer or, in the Amerikan tradition, too much fame or notoriety. My own view is that survival is a matter of random luck: the right blow, the one that will finish you, does not hit you at the right time in the right place. I have not made money or had an easy time publishing my work, which has been anathematized. I had a hard childhood, which is good; and I have the audience that wants my work, which is essential; and I love to write regardless of the outcome in publishing, which is damned lucky or I'd have died of a broken heart. But especially I have had the love of John Stoltenberg, with whom I have lived now for twenty years, and the love and friendship of Elaine Markson, who has been my agent for the past twenty-two years. They are fierce and brilliant friends. Neither has been intimidated by the anger against my work or against me. Each has stayed with me when I thought they would leave or should leave. I love John with my heart and soul; but what is more extraordinary is the way in which he has loved me (see his "Living With Andrea Dworkin," *Lambda Book Review*, May/June 1994). I never promised him anything; but he promised me right from the beginning that he would stay with me for the rest of his life. I am just entertaining the idea that he might. He undertook to live the life I needed. He has taken on my hardships as his own; indeed, they have become his own. We share the circumstances created by the antagonism to my work on Grub Street. We share the politics of radical feminism and a commitment to destroying male dominance and gender itself. We share a love of writing and of equality; and we share each and every day. He is a deeply kind person, and it is through the actual dailiness of living with him that I understand the spiritual poverty and the sensual stupidity of eroticizing brutality over kindness. Elaine has been a loyal friend and colleague in circumstances both complex and difficult. She has stayed loyal to me and to my work through years when she didn't make enough in commissions to cover the postage she spent sending out my manuscripts. Pornographers and their flunkies have tried to bully and intimidate her; so have publishers, as if silencing me would further freedom of speech. She has kept sending out manuscripts of mine for years as publishers stubbornly refused them. It was she who finally made it possible for me to publish my work in England when U.S. publishers were a dead end. *Ice and Fire*, published by Seeker & Warburg in the United Kingdom in 1986, was the first of several books to have widespread British distribution while remaining unsold in the U.S. I had written a good first draft in 1983, which Elaine tried to sell in the U.S., then a final version in 1984. *Ice and Fire* was finally published here in 1987— by an English company—but was never brought out in a paperback edition. The paperback is still in print in England. These are trying difficulties that no slick, money-driven agent would tolerate. Elaine will tell you that she doesn't always agree with me; but why should she—and why should anyone assume that she does? The assumption comes from the lazy but popular stigmatizing ploy of guilt by association, a form of hysteria that pervades any discussion of me or my work in publishing circles. She refuses to give in to this discrediting ruse. Her faith in me has sometimes had to stand in for my faith in myself: I have become shaky but she stands firm. Many times, in the quiet of the room where I work, I have had to face the fact that I would not still be writing—given how hard the hard times have been—were it not for Elaine's passionate commitment and integrity. We've walked many miles together.

So the right blow may still strike in the right place at exactly the right time: to break my writer's heart and stop me in my tracks. I do believe that survival is random, not a result of virtue or talent. But so far, especially in knowing John and Elaine, I have been blessed with monumental grace and staggering good luck.

———

On April 30, 1992, at the age of forty-two, my brother Mark died of cancer. This was exactly eighteen years after the publication date of *Woman Hating*, an anniversary that will never make me happy again.

He was living in Vienna when he died, a molecular biologist, married to his wife of ten years, Eva Rastl, also a molecular biologist, forty at the time of his death.

He was chair of the department of molecular biology at the Ernst Boehringer Institute of Vienna. He and Eva worked together there and also earlier at Columbia University in New York City. He had done postdoctoral work in biochemistry at the Carnegie Institution in Baltimore, the National Cancer Institute in Bethesda, and the University of California at Davis. At the time Mark got ill, he and Eva were doing research on the metabolism of cancer cells.

They were wonderful together, sharing love, friendship, and work. She, a Catholic from Austria, he, Jewish, born in Camden in 1949, reconciled cultural differences and historical sorrow through personal love, the recognition of each other as individuals, and the exercise of reason, which they both, as scientists, valued. A belief in reason was key to a world view that they had in common.

When my brother died, part of me died. This is not hyperbole or cliche. I could feel some of the light that is life going dead inside me and when he died, it went out. He was a gentle boy, the one life I knew from infancy. I had a utopian memory of loving him, a kind of ecstatic love for him that was nonverbal, inexplicable, untouched by growing older. Although we were separated from the time I left home to go to college—there was a period of eleven years when I didn't see him at all, although we wrote each other—the closeness of early childhood never changed, his emotional importance to me, mine to him. But he didn't remember his early childhood or his later childhood; he didn't remember anything from childhood. This terrified me. Because we had usually been sent to stay at separate places when my mother was ill, I had no idea what might have happened to him. As an adult, he had recurrent nightmares that he couldn't understand. I was able to explain or identify the elements of one of them for him. He saw a big man dressed in black carrying a black bag and coming into the house at night—then he woke up in fear. This was my mother's doctor, a cold, frightening figure. I always thought of him as death but I did know who he was. My brother didn't. The childhood years were still blank when he died. He was the kind child, the nurturer of my parents. As they grew older, he took care of them, with his company, his true concern. My mother died a year before Mark, and I don't believe he recovered from her death before his own. Like my father, like John, he was a good and giving man.

I saw him about three weeks before he died. He had asked me to come to Vienna in October 1990 to visit. I didn't want to go to Austria ever, but put these feelings aside to see him. Told in November 1991 he had cancer, he submitted to a major operation in which a large part of his esophagus near his stomach was removed. He recovered from the surgery but lost the use of his larynx. There were signs that the malignant cells had spread. I found myself the bearer of this knowledge, a confidant for Eva, the one who had to keep my father hoping and eventually the one who had to tell him that Mark would die soon, probably within a few days. In our childhood, Mark and I had learned to be alone with our troubles whatever they were. Mark undertook to die the same way. Eva was with him and they were close, tender, inseparable; but he didn't want family or friends to make the journey to see him. I told him that I was coming to Vienna and he didn't have to see me but I would be there; I had made the arrangements. I believe he was glad, but he got sicker much faster than he or Eva or I anticipated. When I went he was unbearably ill. He had asked me to bring him Skippy peanut butter, which was our staple as children. He was starving to death, a not unusual effect of cancer, and so Eva and I hoped he would eat it. But he couldn't. I also took him marbles, especially cats' eyes, which we had played with when we were children. Marbles and bottlecaps were currency among the kids in our neighborhood. Once he had stolen all mine and my mother had let him keep them because he was a boy—they were boys' wealth, not girls'. He smiled when I told him but I don't think he remembered. He kept the marbles near him.

I sat with him during the day for as long as he would let me. Sometimes he could whisper—it was air, not sound, shaped by his mouth. But sometimes he was too weak for that, and I sat at a table in the same room—a modern living room with a large picture window that looked out on trees and bushes, a room filled with daylight—and read, or tried to read. I think it was only after he died and Eva sent me some photographs of him from those days of my visit that I realized how frail he had been, how much I hadn't seen—how hard it had been for him to appear clean and groomed and calm and smiling. The cancer had spread to his liver. Tumors were growing on his neck, which he kept covered, and on other parts of his body.

Then I'd go back to my hotel and I would wail; I'd scream and cry and wail. I would call John—it would still be late afternoon in Vienna, too expensive to call—and I'd howl and keen and cry wildly, again and again, until I was worn out. Then I'd take a walk in the park across from my hotel. The cold air would be bracing, and my head would stop hurting. Then I would return to my room and sit down to write. I had brought a legal pad with me and also an article that John Irving had recently published in *The New York Times Book Review* castigating feminists for opposing pornography, charging that we were purveyors of a new puritanism (see John Irving, "Pornography and the New Puritans," March 29, 1992). I knew that to survive the pain I felt on seeing my brother dying I would have to find a way to use the pain. I truly thought that otherwise it would kill me. I decided, coldly and purposefully, to confront the most painful theme in my own life—repeated sexual abuse. The logic of my answer to Mr. Irving was that no one with the kind of experience I had could be called a puritan; and maybe I and other women actually knew more about sexual violence than he did; and it was the pornographers, not feminists, who punished women in the public square, as puritans had, for being sexual. The narrative was a first-person detailed telling of rapes and assaults (see *The New York Times Book Review*, May 3, 1992). The day my piece was published as a nearly full-page letter edited from the article I had intended, my father and I were on a plane to Vienna to bury Mark at the Central Cemetery. The chief rabbi of Vienna conducted the service. My father simply refused to sit with the men, as is Orthodox practice, and sat with Eva and me. My brother wasn't religious but he loved walking in that great European graveyard. He was someone who walked miles for pleasure; and the Central Cemetery, miles from where he lived, had been one of his favorite places to walk to, then wander in. What does a man with no memory of childhood think of on long, solitary walks to the civilized, well-tended graves of the Austrians, the abandoned, overgrown graves of the Jews? My brother had taken me there on my first trip to Vienna—he had wanted me to see this place that was special to him. I had reacted with horror to the sight of the neglected Jewish graves, the latest stone I saw dated 1938. On my 1992 trip back to Vienna when Mark was sick, I saw on television that the mayor of Vienna had just made a speech acknowledging the importance of Jews, always, to life in Vienna, to its greatness as a city, and that a committee of non-Jewish Austrians was trying to make some restitution by cleaning up the abandoned graves and trying to find out what had happened to the families. Because of this change, we felt able to bury Mark in the Central Cemetery, in the contemporary Jewish burial ground, where he could rest near Eva, though she cannot be buried with him. I have gone back to visit his grave. Eva says it has helped her to have Mark buried there.

I am less alive because I lost my brother. Yet I used what I felt while I watched him dying to write something I considered necessary. I think this is a deep and perhaps terrible truth about writing. Surely, it is a deep and terrible truth about me. As long as I can, I will take what I feel, use it to face what I am able to know, find language, and write what I think must be written for the freedom and dignity of women.

I. BEFORE THE TRIAL

Its the Perpetrator, Stupid

You wont ever know the worst that happened to Nicole Brown Simpson in her marriage, because she is dead and cannot tell you. And if she were alive, remember, you wouldn't believe her.

You heard Lorena Bobbitt, after John Wayne Bobbitt had been acquitted of marital rape. At her own trial for malicious wounding, she described beatings, anal rape, humiliation. She had been persistently injured, hit, choked by a husband who liked hurting her. John Wayne Bobbitt, after a brief tour as a misogynist-media star, beat up a new woman friend.

It is always the same. It happens to women as different as Nicole Simpson, Lorena Bobbitt—and me. The perpetrators are men as different as O.J. Simpson, John Wayne Bobbitt, and the former flower-child I am still too afraid to name.

There is terror, yes, and physical pain. There is desperation and despair. One blames oneself, forgives him. One judges oneself harshly for not loving him enough. "It's your fault," he shouts as he is battering in the door, or slamming your head against the floor. And before you pass out, you say yes. You run, but no one will hide you or stand up for you—which means standing up to him. You will hide behind bushes if there are bushes; or behind trash cans; or in alleys; away from the decent people who aren't helping you. It is, after all, your fault.

He hurts you more: more than last time and more than you ever thought possible; certainly more than any reasonable person would ever believe—should you be foolish enough to tell. And, eventually, you surrender to him, apologize, beg him to forgive you for hurting him or provoking him or insulting him or being careless with something of his—his laundry, his car, his meal. You ask him not to hurt you as he does what he wants to you.

The shame of this physical capitulation, often sexual, and the betrayal of your self-respect will never leave you. You will blame yourself and hate yourself forever. In your mind, you will remember yourself—begging, abject. At some point, you will stand up to him verbally, or by not complying, and he will hit you and kick you; he may rape you; he may lock you up or tie you up. The violence becomes contextual, the element in which you try to survive.

You will try to run away, plan an escape. If he finds out, or if he finds you, he will hurt you more. You will be so frightened you think dying might be okay.

If you have no money, can't find shelter, have no work, you will go back and ask him to let you in. If you work, he will find you. He may ask you back and make promises filled with repentance. He may beat you and force you back. But if you do stay away and make a break, he will strike out of nowhere, still beat you, vandalize your home, stalk you.

Still, no one stops him. You aren't his wife anymore, and he still gets to do it.

Nicole Simpson, like every battered woman, knew she would not be believed. She may have been shrewd enough to anticipate the crowds along the Orange County freeways cheering on O.J. Every battered woman has to be careful, even with strangers. His friends won't stop him. Neither will yours.

Nicole Simpson went to many experts on domestic violence for help but none of them stopped *him*. That's what it takes: the batterer has to be stopped. He will not stop himself. He has to be imprisoned, or killed, or she has to escape and hide, sometimes for the rest of her life, sometimes until he finds another woman to "love." There is no proof that counseling the batterer stops him.

It was Nicole who asked the police to arrest Simpson in 1989, the ninth time the police had been called. Arrest needs to be mandatory. The 1989 assault on Nicole Simpson should have resulted in O.J. Simpson's ninth arrest. We don't know by what factor to multiply the number nine: how many episodes of being beaten women endure, on average, per phone call to the police. In 1993 alone, there were 300, 000 domestic violence calls to the police in New York City.

Wife-beating is not Amerika's dirty little secret, as the press and Health and Human Services Secretary Donna Shalala say. Feminists have spent two decades exposing wife abuse with insistence and accuracy, organizing refuges and escape routes and changing law enforcement practices so that, increasingly, wife-beating is recognized as a violent crime.

Wife-beating is commonplace and ordinary because men believe they have rights over women that women dispute. The control men want of women, the domination men require over women, is expressed in this terrible brutality. For me, it was for a four-year period, twenty-five years ago in another country. For 4 million women in the United States, one every fifteen seconds, it was yesterday and today.

What no one will face is this: the problem is not with the woman; it is with the perpetrator. She can change every weakness, transform every dependency. She can escape with the bravado of a

Jesse James or the subtle skill of a Houdini. But if the husband is committed to violence and she is not, she cannot win her safety or her freedom. The current legal system, victim advocates, counseling cannot keep her safe in the face of his aggression.

Accounts of wife-beating have typically been met with incredulity and disdain, best expressed in the persistent question, "*Why doesn't she leave?*" But after two decades of learning about battery, we now know that more battered women are killed after they leave than before.

Nicole Simpson was living in her own home when she was murdered. Her divorce had been finalized in 1992. Whether or not her ex-husband committed the murder, he did continue to assault her, threaten her, stalk her, intimidate her. His so-called desire for reconciliation masks the awfulness of her situation, the same for every woman who escapes but does not disappear. Having ended the marriage, Nicole Simpson still had to negotiate her safety with the man who was hurting her.

She had to avoid angering him. Any hint that her amiability was essentially coerced, any threat of public exposure, any insult to his dignity from his point of view, might trigger aggression. This cause-and-effect scenario is more imagined than real, since the perpetrator chooses when he will hurt or threaten or stalk. Still, the woman tries. All the smiling photographs of them together after the divorce should evoke alarm, not romantic descriptions of his desire to reconcile. Nicole Simpson followed a strategy of appeasement, because no one stood between her and him to stop him.

Escape, in fact, is hell, a period of indeterminate length reckoned in years, not months, when the ex-husband commits assaults intermittently and acts of terrorism with some consistency. Part of the torment is that freedom is near but he will not let the woman have it. Many escaped women live half in hiding. I am still afraid of my ex-husband each and every day of my life—and I am not afraid of much.

Maybe you don't know how brave women are—the ones who have stayed until now and the ones who have escaped, both the living and the dead. Nicole Simpson is the hero. The perpetrator is the problem, stupid.

II. DURING THE TRIAL

In Nicole Brown Simpson's Words

Words matter. O.J. Simpson's defense team asked Judge Lance A. Ito to order the prosecution to say *domestic discord* rather than *domestic violence* or even *spousal abuse*—already euphemisms for wife-beating—and to disallow the words *battered wife* and *stalker*. Ito refused to alter reality by altering language but some media complied—for example, *Rivera Live*, where *domestic discord* became a new term of art. The lawyer who successfully defended William Kennedy Smith on a rape charge also used that term systematically.

Where is the victim's voice? Where are her words? "I'm scared," Nicole Brown told her mother a few months before she was killed. "I go to the gas station, he's there. I go to the Payless Shoe Store, and he's there. I'm driving, and he's behind me."

Nicole's ordinary words of fear, despair, and terror told to friends, and concrete descriptions of physical attacks recorded in her diary, are being kept from the jury. Insignificant when she was alive—because they didn't save her—the victim's words remain insignificant in death: excluded from the trial of her accused murderer, called "hearsay" and not admissible in a legal system that has consistently protected or ignored the beating and sexual abuse of women by men, especially by husbands.

Nicole called a battered-women's shelter five days before her death. The jury will not have to listen—but we must. Evidence of the attacks on her by Simpson that were witnessed in public will be allowed at trial. But most of what a batterer does is in private. The worst beatings, the sustained acts of sadism, have no witnesses. Only she knows. To refuse to listen to Nicole Brown Simpson is to refuse to know.

There was a time when the law, including the FBI, and social scientists maintained that wife-beating did not exist in the United States. Eventually the FBI did estimate that a woman is beaten every fifteen seconds in the U.S., and the Justice Department concluded the same in 1984.

Such a change happens this way. First, there is a terrible and intimidating silence—it can last centuries. Inside that silence, men have a legal or a tacit right to beat their wives. Then, with the support of a strong political movement, victims of the abuse speak out about what has been done to them and by whom. They break the silence. One day, enough victims have spoken—sometimes in words, sometimes by running away or seeking refuge or striking back or killing in self-defense—that they can be counted and studied: social scientists find a pattern of injury and experts describe it.

The words of experts matter. They are listened to respectfully, are often paid to give evidence in legal cases. Meanwhile, the voice of the victim still has no social standing or legal significance. She still has no credibility such that each of us—and the law—is compelled to help her.

We blame her, as the batterer did. We ask why she stayed, though we, of course, were not prepared to stand between her and the batterer so that she could leave. And if, after she is dead, we tell the police that we heard the accused murderer beat her in 1977, and saw her with black eyes—as Nicole's neighbors did—we will not be allowed to testify, which may be the only justice in this, since it has taken us seventeen years to bother to speak at all. I had such neighbors.

Every battered woman learns early on not to expect help. A battered woman confides in someone, when she does, to leave a trail. She overcomes her fear of triggering violence in the batterer if he finds out that she has spoken in order to leave a verbal marker somewhere, with someone. She thinks the other person's word will be believed later.

Every battered woman faces death more than once, and each time the chance is real: the batterer decides. Eventually, she's fractured inside by the continuing degradation and her emotional world is a landscape of desperation. Of course, she smiles in public and is a good wife. He insists—and so do we.

The desperation is part fear—fear of pain, fear of dying—and part isolation, a brutal aloneness, because everything has failed— every call for help to anyone, every assumption about love, every hope for self-respect and even a shred of dignity. What dignity is there, after all, in confessing, as Nicole did in her diary, that O.J. started beating her on a street in New York and, in their hotel room, "continued to beat me for hours as I kept crawling for the door." He kept hitting her while sexually using her, which is rape—because no meaningful consent is possible or plausible in the context of this violence.

Every battered woman's life has in it many rapes like this one. Sometimes, one complies without the overt violence but in fear of it. Or sometimes, one initiates sex to try to stop or head off a beating. Of course, there are also the so-called good times—when romance overcomes the memory of violence. Both the violation and the complicity make one deeply ashamed. The shame is corrosive. Whatever the batterer left, it attacks. Why would one tell? How can one face it?

Those of us who are not jurors have a moral obligation to listen to Nicole Simpson's words: to how O.J. Simpson locked her in a wine closet after beating her and watched TV while she begged him to let her out; to how, in a different hotel room, "O.J. threw me against the walls. . . and on the floor. Put bruises on my arm and back. The window scared me. Thought he'd throw me out." We need to hear how he "threw a fit, chased me, grabbed me, threw me into walls. Threw all my clothes out of the window into the street three floors below. Bruised me." We need to hear how he stalked her after their divorce. "Everywhere I go," she told a friend, "he shows up. I really think he is going to kill me."

We need, especially, to hear her call to a battered-women's shelter five days before her murder. In ruling that call inadmissible, Ito said: "To the man or woman on the street, the relevance and probative value of such evidence is both obvious and compelling. . . . However, the laws and appellate-court decisions that must be applied. . . held otherwise." The man and woman on the street need to hear what was obvious to her: the foreknowledge that death was stalking her.

We need to believe Nicole's words to know the meaning of terror—it isn't a movie of the week—and to face the treason we committed against her life by abandoning her.

When I was being beaten by a shrewd and dangerous man twenty-five years ago, I was buried alive in a silence that was unbreachable and unbearable. Imagine Nicole being buried alive, then dead, in noise—our prowoman, pro-equality noise; or our pro-family, pro-law-and-order noise. For what it's worth—to Nicole nothing—the shame of battery is all ours.

Domestic Violence: Trying to Flee

Five days before Nicole Brown Simpson was murdered on June 12, 1994, she called a battered women's shelter in terror that her ex-husband was going to kill her. The jury was not told this, because she couldn't be cross-examined. Guess not. Most of the rest of the evidence of beating and stalking, from 1977 to May 1994, was also excluded.

O.J. Simpson had stalked her not once, as represented to the jury, but over at least a two-year period. Prosecutors had been permitted to introduce seven incidents of stalking, but they chose to admit only one into evidence. The jury, predominantly women, was not responding to the wife abuse evidence, said observers. In fact, during an interview late last week, one woman juror called the domestic abuse issue "a waste of time." Polls during the trial confirmed women were indifferent to the beatings Nicole Simpson endured.

As a woman who escaped an assassin husband and is still haunted by fear and flashbacks, I agreed with Deputy District Attorney Christopher A. Darden that, in 1989, Nicole Simpson knew someday her husband would kill her. She'd told many people, including her sister, Denise, that he'd kill her and get away with it. In fact, you can take a battered woman's knowledge of her abuser's capacity to inflict harm and evade consequences to the bank.

But five days before Nicole Simpson was murdered, she knew, for sure, she would die. How? Why? Something had happened: a confrontation, a threatening phone call, an unwanted visit, an aggressive act from Simpson directed at her. She told no one, because, after seventeen years of torment, she knew there was no one to tell. The police virtually everywhere ignore assault against women by their male intimates, so that any husband can be a brutal cop with tacit state protection; in Los Angeles, the police visited Nicole Simpson's abuser at home as fans.

Remember the video showing Simpson, after the ballet recital, with the Brown family—introduced by the defense to show Simpson's pleasant demeanor. Hours later, Nicole Simpson was dead. In the video, she is as far from Simpson, physically, as she can manage. He does not nod or gesture to her. He kisses her mother, embraces and kisses her sister, and bear-hugs her father. They all reciprocate. She must have been the loneliest woman in the world.

What would Nicole Simpson have had to do to be safe? Go underground, change her appearance and identity, get cash without leaving a trail, take her children and run—all within days of her call to the shelter. She would have had to end all communication with family and friends, without explanation, for years, as well as leave her home and everything familiar.

With this abuser's wealth and power, he would have had her hunted down; a dream team of lawyers would have taken her children from her. She would have been the villain—reckless, a slut, reviled for stealing the children of a hero. If his abuse of her is of no consequence now that she's been murdered, how irrelevant would it have been as she, resourceless, tried to make a court and the public understand that she needed to run for her life?

Nicole Simpson knew she couldn't prevail, and she didn't try. Instead of running, she did what the therapists said: be firm, draw a line. So she drew the sort of line they meant: he could come to the recital but not sit with her or go to dinner with her family—a line that was no defense against death. Believing he would kill her, she did what most battered women do: kept up the appearance of normality. There was no equal justice for her, no self-defense she felt entitled to. Society had already left her to die.

On the same day the police who beat Rodney G. King were acquitted in Simi Valley, a white husband who had raped, beaten, and tortured his wife, also white, was acquitted of marital rape in South Carolina. He had kept her tied to a bed for hours, her mouth gagged with adhesive tape. He videotaped a half hour of her ordeal, during which he cut her breasts with a knife. The jury, which saw the videotape, had eight women on it. Asked why they acquitted, they said he needed help. They looked right through the victim— afraid to recognize any part of themselves, shamed by her violation. There were no riots afterward.

The governing reality for women of all races is that there is no escape from male violence, because it is inside and outside, intimate and predatory.

While race-hate has been expressed through forced segregation, woman-hate is expressed through forced closeness, which makes punishment swift, easy, and sure. In private, women often empathize with one another, across race and class, because their experiences with men are so much the same. But in public, including on juries, women rarely dare. For this reason, no matter how many women are battered—no matter how many football stadiums battered women could fill on any given day—each one is alone.

Surrounded by family, friends, and a community of affluent acquaintances, Nicole Simpson was alone. Having turned to police, prosecutors, victims aid, therapists, and a women's shelter, she was still alone. Ronald L. Goldman may have been the only person in seventeen years with the courage to try to intervene physically in an attack on her; and he's dead, killed by the same hand that killed her, an expensively gloved, extra-large hand.

Though the legal system has mostly consoled and protected batterers, when a woman is being beaten, it's the batterer who has to be stopped; as Malcolm X used to say, "by any means necessary"—a principle women, all women, had better learn. A woman has a right to her own bed, a home she can't be thrown out of, and for her body not to be ransacked and broken into. She has a right to safe refuge, to expect her family and friends to stop the batterer—by law or force—before she's dead. She has a constitutional right to a gun and a legal right to kill if she believes she's going to be killed. And a batterer's repeated assaults should lawfully be taken as intent to kill.

Everybody's against wife abuse, but who's prepared to stop it?

ISRAEL

WHOSE COUNTRY IS IT ANYWAY?

1990

It's mine. We can put the question to rest. Israel belongs to me. Or so I was raised to believe.

I've been planting trees there since I can remember. I have memories of my mother's breast—of hunger (she was sick and weak); of having my tonsils out when I was two and a half—of the fear and the wallpaper in the hospital; of infantile bad dreams; of early childhood abandonment; of planting trees in Israel. Understand: I've been planting trees in Israel since before I actually could recognize a real tree from life. In Camden where I grew up we had cement. I thought the huge and splendid telephone pole across the street from our brick row house was one—a tree; it just didn't have leaves. I wasn't deprived: the wires were awesome. If I think of "tree" now, I see that splintery dead piece of lumber stained an uneven brown with its wild black wires stretched out across the sky. I have to force myself to remember that a tree is frailer and greener, at least prototypically, at least in temperate zones. It takes an act of adult will to remember that a tree grows up into the sky, down into the ground, and a telephone pole, even a magnificent one, does not.

Israel, like Camden, didn't have any trees. We were cement; Israel was desert. They needed trees, we didn't. The logic was that we lived in the United States where there was an abundance of everything, even trees; in Israel there was nothing. So we had to get them trees. In synagogue we would be given folders: white paper, heavy, thick; blue ink, light, reminiscent of green but not green.

White and blue were the colors of Israel. You opened the folder and inside there was a tree printed in light blue. The tree was full, round, almost swollen, a great arc, lush, branches coming from branches, each branch growing clusters of leaves. In each cluster of leaves, we had to put a dime. We could use our own dimes from lunch money or allowances, but they only went so far; so we had to ask relatives, strangers, the policeman at the school crossing, the janitor at school—anyone who might spare a dime, because you had to fill your folder and then you had to start another one and fill that too. Each dime was inserted into a little slit in the folder right in the cluster of leaves so each branch ended up being weighed down with shining dimes. When you had enough dimes, the tree on the folder looked as if it was growing dimes. This meant you had collected enough money to plant a tree in Israel, your own tree. You put your name on the folder and in Israel they would plant your tree and put your name on it. You also put another name on the folder. You dedicated the tree to someone who had died. This tree is dedicated to the memory of. Jewish families were never short on dead people but in the years after my birth, after 1946, the dead overwhelmed the living. You touched the dead wherever you turned. You rubbed up against them; it didn't matter how young you were. Mass graves; bones; ash; ovens; numbers on forearms. If you were Jewish and alive, you were—well, almost—rare. You had a solitary feeling even as a child. Being alive felt wrong. Are you tired of hearing about it? Don't be tired of it in front of me. It was new then and I was a child. The adults wanted to keep us from becoming morbid, or anxious, or afraid, or different from other children. They told us and they didn't tell us. They told us and then they took it back. They whispered and let you overhear, then they denied it. Nothing's wrong. You're safe here, in the United States. Being a Jew is, well, like being an Amerikan: the best. It was a great secret they tried to keep and tried to tell at the same time. They were adults—they still didn't believe it really. You were a child; you did.

My Hebrew school teachers were of two kinds: bright-eyed Jewish men from New Jersey, the suburbs mostly, and Philadelphia, a center of culture—mediocre men, poor teachers, their aspirations more bourgeois than Talmudic; and survivors from ancient European ghettos by way of Auschwitz and Bergen-Belsen—multilingual, learned, spectral, walleyed. None, of course, could speak Hebrew. It was a dead language, like Latin. The new Israeli project of speaking Hebrew was regarded as an experiment that could only fail. English would be the language of Israel. It was only a matter of time. Israel was the size of New Jersey. Israel was a miracle, a great adventure, but it was also absolutely familiar.

The trick in dedicating your tree was to have an actual name to write on your folder and know who the person was to you. It was important to Amerikan Jews to seem normal and other people knew the names of their dead. We had too many dead to know their names; mass murder was erasure. Immigrants to the United States had left sisters, brothers, mothers, aunts, uncles, cousins behind, and they had been slaughtered. Where? When? It was all blank. My father's parents were Russian immigrants. My mother's were Hungarian. My grandparents always refused to talk about Europe. "Garbage," my father's father said to me, "they're all garbage." He meant all Europeans. He had run away from Russia at fifteen— from the Czar. He had brothers and sisters, seven; I never could find out anything else. They were dead, from pogroms, the Russian Revolution, Nazis; they were gone. My grandparents on each side ran away for their own reasons and came here. They didn't look back. Then there was this new genocide, new even to Jews, and they couldn't look back. There was no recovering what had been lost, or who. There couldn't be reconciliation with what couldn't be faced. They were alive because they were here; the rest were dead because they were there: who could face that? As a child I observed that Christian children had lots of relatives unfamiliar to me, very old, with honorifics unknown to me—great-aunt, great-great-grand-mother. Our family began with my grandparents. No one came before them; no one stood next to them. It's an incomprehensible and disquieting amnesia. There was Eve; then there is a harrowing blank space, a tunnel of time and nothing with enormous murder; then there's us. We had whoever was in the room. Everyone who wasn't in the room was dead. All my mourning was for them—all my trees in the desert—but who were they? My ancestors aren't individual to me: I'm pulled into the mass grave for any sense of identity or sense of self. In the small world I lived in as a child, the consciousness was in three parts: (1) in Europe with those left behind, the dead, and how could one live with how they had died, even if why was old and familiar; (2) in the United States, the best of all possible worlds—being more-Amerikan-than-thou, more middle-class however poor and struggling, more suburban however urban in origins, more nor-mal, more conventional, more conformist; and (3) in Israel, in the desert, with the Jews who had been ash and now were planting trees. I never planted a tree in Camden or anywhere else for that matter. All my trees are in Israel. I was taught that they had my name on them and that they were dedicated to the memory of my dead.

One day in Hebrew school I argued in front of the whole class with the principal; a teacher, a scholar, a survivor, he spoke seven languages and I don't know which camps he was in. In private, he would talk to me, answer my questions, unlike the others. I would see him shaking, alone; I'd ask why; he would say sometimes he couldn't speak, there were no words, he couldn't say words, even though he spoke seven languages; he would say he had seen things; he would say he couldn't sleep, he hadn't slept for nights or weeks. I knew he knew important things. I respected him. Usually I didn't respect my teachers. In front of the whole class, he told us that in life we had the obligation to be first a Jew, second an Amerikan, third a human being, a citizen of the world. I was outraged. I said it was the opposite. I said everyone was first a human being, a citizen of the world—otherwise there would never be peace, never an end to nationalist conflicts and racial persecutions. Maybe I was eleven. He said that Jews had been killed throughout history precisely because they thought the way I did, because they put being Jews last; because they didn't understand that one was always first a Jew—in history, in the eyes of the world, in the eyes of God. I said it was the opposite: only when everyone was human first would Jews be safe. He said Jews like me had had the blood of other Jews on their hands throughout history; that had there been an Israel, Jews would not have been slaughtered throughout Europe; that the Jewish homeland was the only hope for Jewish freedom. I said that was why one had an obligation to be an Amerikan second, after being a human being, a citizen of the world: because only in a democracy without a state religion could religious minorities have rights or be safe or not be persecuted or discriminated against. I said that if there was a Jewish state, anyone who wasn't Jewish would be second-class by definition. I said we didn't have a right to do to other people what had been done to us. More than anyone, we knew the bitterness of religious persecution, the stigma that went with being a minority. We should be able to see in advance the inevitable consequences of having a state that put us first; because then others were second and third and fourth. A theocratic state, I said, could never be a fair state—and didn't Jews need a fair state? If Jews had had a fair state wouldn't Jews have been safe from slaughter? Israel could be a beginning: a fair state. But then it couldn't be a Jewish state. The blood of Jews, he said, would be on my hands. He walked out. I don't think he ever spoke to me again.

You might wonder if this story is apocryphal or how I remember it or how someone so young made such arguments. The last is simple: the beauty of a Jewish education is that you learn how to argue if you pay attention. I remember because I was so distressed by what he said to me: the blood of Jews will be on your hands. I remember because he meant what he said. Part of my education was in having teachers who had seen too much death to argue for the fun of it. I could see the blood on my hands if I was wrong; Jews would have nowhere; Jews would die. I could see that if I or anyone made it harder for Israel to exist, Jews might die. I knew that Israel had to succeed, had to work out. Every single adult Jew I knew wanted it, needed it: the distraught ones with the numbers on their arms; the immigrant ones who had been here, not there; the cheerful more-Amerikan-than-thou ones who wanted ranch houses for themselves, an army for Israel. Israel was the answer to near extinction in a real world that had been demonstrably indifferent to the mass murder of the Jews. It was also the only way living Jews could survive having survived. Those who had been here, not there, by immigration or birth, would create another here, a different here, a purposeful sanctuary, not one stumbled on by random good luck. Those who were alive had to find a way to deal with the monumental guilt of not being dead: being the chosen this time for real. The building of Israel was a bridge over bones; a commitment to life against the suicidal pull of the past. How can I live with having lived? I will make a place for Jews to live.

I knew from my own urgent effort to try to understand racism—from the Nazis to the situation I lived in, hatred of black people in the United States, the existence of legal segregation in the South—that Israel was impossible: fundamentally wrong, organized to betray egalitarian aspirations—because it was built from the ground up on a racial definition of its desired citizen; because it was built from the ground up on exclusion, necessarily stigmatizing those who were not Jews. Social equality was impossible unless only Jews lived there. With hostile neighbors and a racial paradigm for the state's identity, Israel had to become either a fortress or a tomb. I didn't think it made Jews safer. I did understand that it made Jews different: different from the pathetic creatures on the trains, the skeletons in the camps; different; indelibly different. It was a great relief—to me too—to be different from the Jews in the cattle cars. Different mattered. As long as it lasted, I would take it. And if Israel ended up being a tomb, a tomb was better than unmarked mass graves for millions all over Europe—different and better. I made my peace with different; which meant I made my peace with the State of Israel. I would not have the blood of Jews on my hands. I wouldn't help those who wanted Israel to be a place where more Jews died by saying what I thought about the implicit racism. It was shameful, really: distance me, Lord, from those pitiful Jews; make me new. But it was real and even I at ten, eleven, twelve needed it.

You might notice that all of this had nothing to do with Palestinians. I didn't know there were any. Also, I haven't mentioned women. I knew they existed, formally speaking; Mrs. So-and-So was everywhere, of course—peculiar, all held in, reticent and dutiful in public. I never saw one I wanted to become. Nevertheless, adults kept threatening that one day I had to be one. Apparently it was destiny and also hard work; you were born one but you also had to become one. Either you mastered exceptionally difficult and obscure rules too numerous and onerous to reveal to a child, even a child studying Leviticus; or you made one mistake, the nature of which was never specified. But politically speaking, women didn't exist, and frankly, as human beings women didn't exist either. You could live your whole life among them and never know who they were.

———

I was taught about *fedayeen*: Arabs who crossed the border into Israel to kill Jews. In the years after Hitler, this was monstrous. Only someone devoid of any humanity, any conscience, any sense of decency or justice could kill Jews. They didn't live there; they came from somewhere else. They killed civilians by sneak attack; they didn't care whom they killed just so they killed Jews.

I realized only as a middle-aged adult that I was raised to have prejudice against Arabs and that the prejudice wasn't trivial. My parents were exceptionally conscious and conscientious about racism and religious bigotry—all the homegrown kinds—hatred of blacks or Catholics, for instance. Their pedagogy was very brave. They took a social stance against racism, for civil rights, that put them in opposition to many neighbors and members of our family. My mother put me in a car and showed me black poverty. However poor I thought we were, I was to remember that being black in the United States made you poorer. I still remember a conversation with my father in which he told me he had racist feelings against blacks. I said that was impossible because he was for civil rights. He explained the kinds of feelings he had and why they were wrong. He also explained that as a teacher and then later a guidance counselor he worked with black children and he had to make sure his racist feelings didn't harm them. From my father I learned that having these feelings didn't justify them; that "good" people had bad feelings and that didn't make the feelings any less bad; that dealing with racism was a process, something a person tangled with actively. The feelings were wrong and a "good" person took responsibility for facing them down. I was also taught that just because you feel something doesn't make it true. My parents went out of their way to say "some Arabs," to emphasize that there were good and bad people in every group; but in fact my education in the Jewish community made that caveat fairly meaningless. Arabs were primitive, uncivilized, violent. (My parents would never have accepted such characterizations of blacks.) Arabs hated and killed Jews. Really, I learned that Arabs were irredeemably evil. In all my travels through life, which were extensive, I never knew any Arabs: and ignorance is the best friend of prejudice.

In my mid-thirties I started reading books by Palestinians. These books made me understand that I was misinformed. I had had a fine enough position on the Palestinians—or perhaps I should say "the Palestinian question" to convey the right ring of condescension—once I knew they existed; long after I was eleven. Maybe twenty years ago, I knew they existed. I knew they were being wronged. I was for a two-state solution. Over the years, I learned about Israeli torture of Palestinian prisoners; I knew Jewish journalists who purposefully suppressed the information so as not to "hurt" the Jewish state. I knew the human rights of Palestinians in ordinary life were being violated. Like my daddy, on social issues, the policy questions, I was fine for my kind. These opinions put me into constant friction with the Jewish community, including my family, many friends, and many Jewish feminists. As far as I know, from my own experience, the Jewish community has just recently—like last Tuesday—really faced the facts—the current facts. I will not argue about the twisted history, who did what to whom when. I will not argue about Zionism except to say that it is apparent that I am not a Zionist and never was. The argument is the same one I had with my Hebrew school principal; my position is the same—either we get a fair world or we keep getting killed. (I have also noticed, in the interim, that the Cambodians had Cambodia and it didn't help them much. Social sadism takes many forms. What can't be imagined happens.) But there are social policy questions and then there is the racism that lives in individual hearts and minds as a prejudgment on a whole people. You believe the stereotypes; you believe the worst; you accept a caricature such that members of the group are comic or menacing, always contemptible. I don't believe that Amerikan Jews raised as I was are free of this prejudice. We were taught it as children and it has helped the Israeli government justify in our eyes what they have done to the Palestinians. We've been blinded, not just by our need for Israel or our loyalty to Jews but by a deep and real prejudice against Palestinians that amounts to race-hate.

The land wasn't empty, as I was taught: oh yes, there are a few nomadic tribes but they don't have homes in the normal sense—not like we do in New Jersey; there are just a few uneducated, primitive, dirty people there now who don't even want a state. There were people and there were even trees—trees destroyed by Israeli soldiers. The Palestinians are right when they say the Jews regarded them as nothing. I was taught they were nothing in the most literal sense. Taking the country and turning it into Israel, the Jewish state, was an imperialist act. Jews find any such statement incomprehensible. How could the near-dead, the nearly extinguished, a people who were ash have imperialized anyone, anything? Well, Israel is rare: Jews, nearly annihilated, took the land and forced a very hostile world to legitimize the theft. I think Amerikan Jews cannot face the fact that this is one act—the one act—of imperialism, of conquest that we support. We helped; we're proud of it; here we stand. This is a contradiction of every idea we have about who we are and what being a Jew means. It is also true. We took a country from the people who lived there; we the dispossessed finally did it to someone else; we said, they're Arabs, let them go somewhere Arab. When Israelis say they want to be judged by the same standards applied to the rest of the world, not by a special standard for Jews, in part they mean that this is the way of the world. It may be a first for Jews, but everyone else has been doing it throughout recorded history. It is recorded history. I grew up in New Jersey, the size of Israel; not so long ago, it belonged to Indians. Because Amerikan Jews refuse to face precisely this one fact—we took the land—Amerikan Jews cannot afford to know or face Palestinians: initially, even that they existed.

As for the Palestinians, I can only imagine the humiliation of losing to, being conquered by, the weakest, most despised, most castrated people on the face of the earth. This is a feminist point about manhood.

When I was growing up, the only time I heard about equality of the sexes was when I was taught to love and have fidelity to the new State of Israel. This new state was being built on the premise that men and women were equal in all ways. According to my teachers, servility was inappropriate for the new Jew, male or female. In the new state, there was no strong or weak or more or less valuable according to sex. Everyone did the work: physical labor, menial labor, cooking—there was no, as we say now, sex-role stereotyping. Because everyone worked, everyone had an equal responsibility and an equal say. Especially, women were citizens, not mothers.

Strangely, this was the most foreign aspect of Israel. In New Jersey, we didn't have equality of the sexes. In New Jersey, no one thought about it or needed it or wanted it. We didn't have equality of the sexes in Hebrew school. It didn't matter how smart or devout you were: if you were a girl, you weren't allowed to do anything important. You weren't allowed to want anything except marriage, even if you were a talented scholar. Equality of the sexes was something they were going to have in the desert with the trees; we couldn't send them any because we didn't have any. It was a new principle for a new land and it helped to make a new people; in New Jersey, we didn't have to be quite that new.

When I was growing up, Israel was also basically socialist. The kibbutzim, voluntary collectives, were egalitarian communities by design. The kibbutzim were going to replace the traditional nuclear family as the basic social unit in the new society. Children would be raised by the whole community—they wouldn't "belong" to their parents. The communal vision was the cornerstone of the new country.

Here, women were pretty invisible, and material greed, a desire for middle-class goods and status, animated the Jewish community. Israel really repudiated the values of Amerikan Jews—somehow the adults managed to venerate Israel while in their own lives transgressing every radical value the new state was espousing. But the influence on the children was probably very great. I don't think it is an accident that Jewish children my age grew up wanting to make communal living a reality or believing that it could be done; or that the girls did eventually determine, in such great numbers, to make equality of the sexes the dynamic basis of our political lives.

While women in the United States were living in a twilight world, appendages to men, housewives, still the strongest women I knew when I was a child worked for the establishment, well-being, and preservation of the State of Israel. It was perhaps the only socially sanctioned field of engagement. My Aunt Helen, for instance, the only unmarried, working woman I knew as a child, made Israel her life's cause. Not only did the strong women work for Israel, but women who weren't visibly strong—who were conformist—showed some real backbone when they were active on behalf of Israel. The equality of the sexes may have had a resonance for them as adults that it couldn't have had for me as a child. Later, Golda Meir's long tenure as prime minister made it seem as if the promise of equality was being delivered on. She was new, all right; forged from the old, visibly so, but herself made new by an act of will; public, a leader of a country in crisis. My Aunt Helen and Golda Meir were a lot alike: not defined in terms of men; straightforward when other women were coy; tough; resourceful; formidable. The only formidable women I saw were associated with and committed to Israel, except for Anna Magnani. But that's another story.

Finally in 1988, at forty-two, on Thanksgiving, the day we celebrate having successfully taken this land from the Indians, I went to Israel for the first time. I went to a conference billed as the First International Jewish Feminist Conference. Its theme was the empowerment of Jewish women. Its sponsors were the American Jewish Congress, the World Jewish Congress, and the Israel Women's Network, and it was being organized with a middle-class agenda by middle-class women, primarily Amerikan, who were themselves beholden to the male leadership of the sponsoring groups. So the conference looked to secular Israeli feminists organizing at the grassroots level—and so it was. Initially, the secular Israeli feminists intended to organize an alternate feminist conference to repudiate the establishment feminist conference, but they decided instead to have their own conference, one that included Palestinian women, the day after the establishment conference ended.

The establishment conference was designed not to alienate Orthodox Jewish women. As far as I could see, secular Jewish women, especially Israelis, were expendable. What the hell? They could be counted on to keep working—keep those battered women's shelters going, keep those rape crisis centers open—without being invited *into* the hotel. They couldn't afford to come anyway. The wealthier excluded the poor and struggling; the timid (mainstream) excluded the grassroots (really mainstream but as socially invisible and despised as the women they represent and serve); the religious excluded the secular; Jewish excluded Palestinian; and, to a considerable degree, Amerikans, by virtue of their money and control of the agenda, excluded Israelis—feminists, you know, the ones who do the work in the country, on the ground. Lesbians were excluded until the last minute by not being specifically included; negotiations with those organizing what came to be called the post-conference put a lesbian on the program speaking as such, though under a pseudonym because she was Israeli and it was too dangerous for her to be known by her real name. War-and-peace issues were underplayed, even as the establishment conference was held in the occupied West Bank; even though many feminists—organizers and theorists—consider both militarism and masculinity feminist issues—intrinsically feminist, not attached to the agenda because of a particular political emergency.

I went because of grassroots Israeli feminists: the opportunity to meet with them in Haifa, Tel Aviv, and Jerusalem; to talk with those organizing against violence against women on all fronts; to learn more about the situation of women in Israel. I planned to stay on—if I had, I also would have spoken at and for the rape crisis center in

Jerusalem. In Haifa, where both Phyllis Chesler and I spoke to a packed room (which included Palestinian women and some young Arab men) on child custody and pornography in the United States, women were angry about the establishment conference—its tepid feminist agenda, its exclusion of the poor and of Palestinian feminists. One woman, maybe in her sixties, with an accent from Eastern Europe, maybe Poland, finally stood up and said approximately the following: "Look, it's just another conference put on by the Amerikans like all the others. They have them like clockwork. They use innocents like these"—pointing to Phyllis and me—"who don't know any better." Everyone laughed, especially us. I hadn't been called an innocent in a long time, or been perceived as one either. But she was right. Israel brought me to my knees. Innocent was right. Here's what compromised my innocence, such as it was.

I. THE LAW OF RETURN

Jewish women attended the establishment conference from many countries, including Argentina, New Zealand, India, Brazil, Belgium, South Africa, and the United States. Each woman had more right to be there than any Palestinian woman born there, or whose mother was born there, or whose mother's mother was born there. I found this morally unbearable. My own visceral recognition was simple: I don't have a right to this right.

The Law of Return says that any Jew entering the country can immediately become a citizen; no Jew can be turned away. This law is the basis for the Jewish state, its basic principle of identity and purpose. Orthodox religious parties, with a hefty share of the vote in recent elections, wanted the definition of "Jewish" narrowed to exclude converts to Judaism not converted by Orthodox rabbis, according to Orthodox precepts. Women at the establishment conference were mobilized to demonstrate against this change in the Law of Return. The logic used to mobilize the women went as follows: "The Right is doing this. The Right is bad. Anything the Right wants is bad for women. Therefore, we, feminists, must oppose this change in the Law of Return." Fight the Right. In your heart you know the fight is for the sake of women, but don't tell anyone else: not Shamir, not the Orthodox rabbis, not the press; but especially not the Amerikan Jewish boys who are sponsoring your conference, who are in Israel right then and there to lobby Shamir and to keep an eye on the girls. Fight the Right. Find an issue important to Jewish men and show up as the women's auxiliary. Make them proud. And don't offend them or upset them by making them stand with you—if they want you there—for the rights of women.

Protesting the change in the Law of Return was presented at the establishment conference as "taking a first step" against the power of the Orthodox rabbis. Because the power of these men over the lives of Jewish women in Israel is already vast and malignant, "taking a first step" against them—without mentioning any of the ways in which they are already tyrants over women—wasn't just inadequate; it was shameful. We needed to take a real step. In Israel, Jewish women are basically—in reality, in everyday life—governed by Old Testament law. So much for equality of the sexes. The Orthodox rabbis make most of the legal decisions that have a direct impact on the status of women and the quality of women's lives. They have the final say on all issues of "personal status," which feminists will recognize as the famous private sphere in which civilly subordinate women are traditionally imprisoned. The Orthodox rabbis decide questions of marriage, adultery, divorce, birth, death, legitimacy; what rape is;

and whether abortion, battery, and rape in marriage are legal or illegal. At the protest, feminists did not mention women. How did Israel get this way—how did these Orthodox rabbis get the power over women that they have? How do we dislodge them, get them *off* women? Why isn't there a body of civil law superseding the power of religious law that gives women real, indisputable rights of equality and self-determination in this country that we all helped build? I'm forty-four; Israel is forty-two; how the hell did this happen? What are we going to do about it now? How did Jewish feminists manage not to "take a first step" until the end of 1988—and then not mention women? The first step didn't amount to a feminist crawl.

II. THE CONDITION OF JEWISH WOMEN IN ISRAEL IS ABJECT

Where I live things aren't too good for women. It's not unlike Crystal Night all year long given the rape and battery statistics—which are a pale shadow of the truth—the incest, the pornography, the serial murders, the sheer savagery of the violence against women. But Israel is shattering. Sisters: we have been building a country in which women are dog shit, something you scrape off the bottom of your shoe. We, the "Jewish feminists." We who only push as far as the Jewish men here will allow. If feminism is serious, it fights sex hierarchy and male power and men don't get to stand on top of you, singly or in clusters, for forever and a day. And you don't help them build a country in which women's status gets lower and lower as the men get bigger and bigger—the men there and the men here. From what I saw and heard and learned, we have helped to build a living hell for women, a nice Jewish hell. Isn't it the same everywhere? Well, "everywhere" isn't younger than I am; "everywhere" didn't start out with the equality of the sexes as a premise. The low status of women in Israel is not unique but we are uniquely responsible for it. I felt disgraced by the way women are treated in Israel, disgraced and dishonored. I remembered my Hebrew school principal, the Holocaust survivor, who said I had to be a Jew first, an Amerikan second, and a citizen of the world, a human being last, or I would have the blood of Jews on my hands. I've kept quiet a long time about Israel so as not to have the blood of Jews on my hands. It turns out that I am a woman first, second, and last—they are the same; and I find I do have the blood of Jews on my hands—the blood of Jewish women in Israel.

(. . .)

I remember the heat of the Jerusalem sun. Hundreds of women dressed in black were massed on the sidewalks of a big public square in Jerusalem. Women in Black began in Jerusalem at the same time as the intifada, with seven women who held a silent vigil to show their resistance to the occupation. Now the hundreds of women who participate each week in three cities are met with sexual derision and sometimes stones. Because the demonstrations are women-only, they are confrontational in two ways: these are Israelis who want peace with Palestinians; these are women who are standing on public ground. Women held signs in Hebrew, Arabic, and English saying: END THE OCCUPATION. An Arab vendor gave some of us, as many as he could reach, gifts of grapes and figs to help us fight the heat. Israeli men went by shouting insults—men called out insults from passing cars—the traffic was bumper to bumper, with the men trying to get home before Sabbath eve, when Jerusalem shuts down. There were also men with signs who screamed that the women were traitors and whores.

Along with most of the demonstrators, I had come from the postconference organized by the grassroots, secular feminists. The post-conference was chaired by Nabila Espanioli, a Palestinian woman who spoke Hebrew, English, and Arabic. Palestinian women came out of the audience to give first-person testimony about what the occupation was doing to them. They especially spoke about the brutality of the Israeli soldiers. They talked about being humiliated, being forcibly detained, being trespassed on, being threatened. They spoke about themselves and about women. For Palestinian women, the occupation is a police state and the Israeli secret police are a constant danger; there is no "safe space." I already knew that I had Palestinian blood on my hands. What I found out in Israel is that it isn't any easier to wash off than Jewish blood—and that it is also female.

I had met Nabila my first night in Israel, in Haifa, at the home of an Israeli woman who gave a wonderful welcoming party. It was a warm, fragrant night. The small, beautiful apartment open to the night air was filled with women from Jerusalem, Tel Aviv, Haifa—feminists who fight for women, against violence. It was Sabbath eve and there was a simple feminist ceremony—a breaking of bread, one loaf, everyone together; secular words of peace and hope. And then I found myself talking with this Palestinian woman. She talked a mile a minute about pornography. It was her field of study and she knew it inside out, recognized herself in it, under it, violated by it. She told me it was the focus of her resistance to both rape and sexualized racism. She, too, wanted freedom and it was in her way. I thought: with this between us, who can pull us apart? We see women with the same eyes.

In Israel, there are the occupied and the occupied: Palestinians and women. In the Israel I saw, Palestinians will be freer sooner. I didn't find any of my trees.

MY SUICIDE

1999

This text of My Suicide *is an excerpt from Dworkin's manuscript as edited for the stage by Adam Thorburn and titled* Aftermath.

(1)

I was in Paris. I had become old, fifty-two, and I was tired. I had fought the battles of my time: I fought the Vietnam War, the civilian side of it, against the government, and I had won. But the War was about everything—race, war, nuclear war, sex, gender, a word unused even though the fights were more about gender because I was a girl who argued. I haven't been near my family in three decades except in hospital rooms, where my mother died, where my father now languishes.

I've loved my father my whole life. He's the best person I've ever known. Soon he will die. His father, Morris, lived to be 105. In his last twenty years I never saw my grandfather; I liked him but I never saw him, which brings up what my mother had said when his wife, my Grandma Rose, died: you cry when they die but when they're alive you don't want to be around them. I was nine then and I've never forgotten her charge, nor the others she made against me over a lifetime. When I got too tired of it I stopped loving my mother, one of the great accomplishments of my life. To stop loving your mother creates a cold place in your heart and you write from there. I wish I could be cold all the way through.

Vicious but the truth was vicious: I didn't want to be around my family; they were all worse than strangers to me. I despised their houses and their rules. I disliked their lack of courtesy. I hated the family gatherings. I hated the mass think of them all. I would go on long walks alone to places that were new to me, I would have poetic melancholy spiked with Salinger, I would make friends with the juvenile delinquent boys, I was tough but no one knew. Girls couldn't be tough but I was. I kept it hidden.

I am a fierce enemy of death. Its inevitability is cruel and wrong. One friend says that death is a form of violence and that it must be ended and we can end it and will end it. Even I didn't buy that, and I'm still a sixties child in my heart. I pretty much can be sold anything, which is how both Ronald Reagan and Bill Clinton got to be president. I mean, not me, I didn't vote for Reagan. I did vote for Clinton the first time. They really got me with his anti-war stuff. But the second time, no. He had thrown women off of welfare and how were they going to live? All they talked about was pregnant teenagers and how they were sowing seeds of destruction. Did all these men use contraception every single time they fucked? If they didn't they should shut up because they could have become pregnant if they were women. Fuck and lie is the name of the game. Fuck and lie.

I like Paris because I can moon about Robespierre and Danton. To drink a coffee where Rimbaud was, that's thrilling. There's talk he had been gang-raped and that was what turned him wild and dissolute and ultimately empty. I believe that. It's the gang-rape that screams out in the poems, the force behind every word, the punch in the face he delivers. I can go to a movie house called Danton or go to where Rodin and Delacroix lived. I can see Picassos but I hate Picasso. He won't last. He was so awful and his paintings are so ugly. You can't be proud to do nothing during the Nazi occupation, just paint, just watch your own ass. What kind of an artist didn't get in trouble with the Nazis? Maybe they looked at his women and thought they were Jews.

I thought art would save me, Van Gogh, Camus. I thought that I could stand anything if there was music playing. I was naïve. Each better day was supposed to come. I could walk down the street and believe that each man was someone I could love with sex, each one, the perfect us, the real we. I'd look at the dirty and think so what, or the maimed, or the mean. It's pride. The Christians say pride's a sin and I think so. Why do I think it's my job to love these loveless men? Because I think I can suffer and it will make me better. I think I can love where there is no love. I think I can't be defeated if I can only accept enough suffering. I can take it. This is the belief of my people, Jews and women. Women have this kind of pride, to think I can take any pain and still love, I don't matter, as if it's selfless rather than prideful. It's the worst kind of pride, the way girls and women do it, the way I did it. I didn't stop them from hurting me. I've wanted to do good and to be good and not to be afraid. I wasn't until I found pure terror each time one took me from myself. I'm sick with pain, a kind of grief, for all the times I've died without dying. I am crushed under the responsibilities of survival. I need to know everything about terror. I need to see every exploitation and trace the map of it with my own fingers. As I once said to a friend, why couldn't I be an expert on Shakespeare like you? Why am I an expert on debasement and filth?

I have really bad pheromones. This is true, I have a friend who's seen it more than once: huge roaches on New York sidewalks run towards me, I change direction and they do too and keep rushing towards me. The bad men and the bad bugs, or I was a monster in my last life and I'm paying now. I don't want any more lives or any afterlife.

I used to think that at the moment you died God would answer all your questions, everything you had ever wondered about, from how the universe was made to is there life on other planets to what ever happened to the lover I really loved or so-and-so who I never saw again. I could see in that split second of first nonexistence that I'd be rising up away from the planet and God would raise me up by the shoulders and in his touch would be all the answers and then nothing, a million years of nothing.

I think God is a really ruthless artist and earth is an early draft. This draft was bad, overloaded with gratuitous cruelty. Love doesn't work. Pride is a sin. Nothing we do is right. Each person is like a deep lake under which there is slime and mud and ooze. You go near the person and the lake's so beautiful, so calm, and then you go in and the water pulls you down into the slime. You die there, at the nadir of this person.

(2)

I hate each day. I see the sun coming and I'm ready to end. Story over. Leave me be. I have trouble putting one foot in front of another. My body is a curse to me. How could it so betray me?

It's very clear in my mind. I'm in bed. My bed. I take a big butcher knife and I plunge it into my heart, break through the ribs. I'm not sure I can do it. Maybe I'm not strong enough, physically, upper-body strength. There would be so much blood. I'd close my cats out, of course, but they would smell the blood, and my desertion would hurt them. I'd make sure Paul was away for long enough so I could bleed to death. There are smarter things to do but the meaning of this would be plain. I would get to live truthfully at the end. I should cut veins or jugular but it wouldn't be big enough. I need a complete end, all the blood gone.

To live would be even more wrong. I would be ashamed always. It is likely I would never talk to anyone again. I can't talk now. I can't say the words. How do you say I was raped without slaying the person you're talking to, making them responsible for knowing, and if they want to make it better they can't. There's nothing they can do. No heart-to-heart will help. The minute after you're alone, back alone, and there's nothing but the grief.

I met this woman. She said, I was in Paris. I was fifty-two. I was reading a book in a Zen garden in a hotel. *French Literary Fascism.* I was having a kir royale. I had two. The second one didn't taste right. I felt a little sick or jetlagged or something. I can remember standing in front of the elevator and thinking, please, God, let me get to my room, please let me get there. I ordered dinner from room service. Next there was a boy in my room. He had a pass key. I tried to rise up. I did but barely and then I fell against the opposite wall. Then I signed the room service check. I was barely able to balance myself. Then I went back to the bed. I didn't lock the door. I came to about four or five hours later. I didn't know where I was. I had internal pain. I was hurting bad. I went to the toilet and found blood on my hand, fresh, bright red, not menstrual blood, not clotted blood. I'm past bleeding. I looked for where the blood was coming. My hand got covered in it again. I found huge, deep scratches on my right leg. I couldn't stop the bleeding of it so I tried to keep it clean. A few hours later I took a shower. I had a big and strange bruise on my left breast, right next to the aureole, not a regular bruise, more like a sucking bruise, huge black and blue with solid white skin in the center, as if someone had sucked it up and chewed it. She said she didn't feel good the next day or the day after that. She said she had been drugged and raped. She said she thought that the bartender had done it, because he had made the drinks and he was on the phone at room service and he flirted grandly with her saying it would be his great privilege to make her dinner that evening. She thought the boy was supposed to report that she had passed out. She thought the bartender had raped her. She didn't know if the boy had been there or not but she thought yes. She couldn't remember but she thought they had pulled her down on the bed so that her vagina was at the bottom's edge. She thought that the deep, bleeding scratches, right leg, and the big bruise, left breast, were the span of a man on top of her. She had been wearing sweat pants that just fell right down. She had been wearing an undershirt. Usually she covered herself but she had felt too sick to manage it before the boy came in with the dinner. She said that she didn't have intercourse normally in her own life. She said that she had gotten an internal infection in the aftermath. She said it was horrible not knowing. She said there was literally no memory of what the man and the boy had done. She said that it was like being operated on. She speculated that her body must have been completely relaxed, no muscles straining, no physical resistance or even tension. She said the hours were gone, missing. She said that her mind had gone over and over it for weeks and weeks turning into months and months. She said she couldn't find it because it wasn't there, in her brain. She said that she had lost all hope. She said that she couldn't have defended herself. She said that she had long before decided no one would ever rape her again and either she or he would die. She said that they had wanted to fuck a dead woman. She said that it was like being in a coma. She said being forced and being conscious was better because then you knew, even if no one ever believed you, you knew. She said she hated every day and to see the sun rise and she couldn't put one foot in front of the other and she wanted to put a butcher knife into her heart behind her ribs. She said she was consumed by grief and sorrow. She said that she could resist now by not dying but that might be too hard. She said that her body was a curse and had betrayed her. She said she couldn't figure out why they would want to do this to her—why they would want to do *this* and why to *her*. She said she had always had an appetite for life but now she hated it. There's never a day that she doesn't hate, she said. There isn't a minute or an hour that she doesn't hate, she said.

How can you say those words? I can't say them and I can't say anything else. I don't know why the world didn't stop right then. I don't know how the sun can still rise and the earth can still turn. I think everyone should have stopped everything because I was fifty-two and this happened to me. I think every person should have been in mourning. I think no one should work or spend money or love anyone ever again. I say my bad pheromones or karma brought the rapist to me. I blame me no matter what it takes, no matter how abstract or abstruse I need to be. I say, I didn't. I didn't wear a short skirt, I didn't drink a lot even though it was alcohol and I rarely drink, I didn't drink it with a man, I sat alone and read a book, I didn't go somewhere I shouldn't have been, I didn't flirt, I didn't. It was still daylight. They took my body from me and used it. They came inside me. My muscles were completely relaxed, there was no resistance. Once you're put under you can't stop the surgeon. You don't remember the surgery. But afterward the body is cut. After this there was blood and scratches that were more like deep clawing and a huge bruise on the left breast near the aureole with white skin in the middle as if it had been sucked and chewed. I then had seventy-two hours to get a blood test and a urine test to nail down the presence of the drug but I didn't know and seventy-two hours wasn't enough time, I couldn't say for sure, I couldn't place the bartender in the bedroom at all but I know he did it but how do I know that? Now there is scarring where the scratches were. But I had decided: no more rape, no matter what the cost no more rape. I was old and tired and I was taking myself out of the rape pool. My immorality was evident: pick someone else. I can't have this happen to me.

(3)
When I was young I had optimism in the face of everything. Boys threw a Christmas tree at me and my head bled. I liked to take long, solitary walks, so they hurt me. But I still would go wherever I wanted and do whatever I wanted. I can't understand how she, that bright girl, became me, dull and tired and sick of life.

I wanted to go to Mississippi for civil rights work. I wanted to make abortion legal, segregation illegal, and stop the War. Those were my dreams, plus a book, that I would write a book. It glimmered in my mind. I wanted to make life better. My mother once said that I was lucky that the sixties happened because, she said, the others are just following leaders but you would have been this way even if you were alone. I didn't sing Christmas carols in public school. I didn't comply with the atom bomb scares. You couldn't make me if I didn't believe in it.

I had girlfriends I loved. Madeleine and I made love and drew with pastels. She was so beautiful and so smart. I loved Rebecca and Jackie. I never could know enough people because each one was another world, a whole vision of something, a center of a universe. I wanted to touch everything and do everything. This was my optimism. It's in the body. It's a form of energy that demands connection. It's an affirmation of pure faith that this day and the next one would be miracles. It's a refusal to be afraid of life. Girls aren't supposed to have it—nerve or courage or adventure or curiosity or direct contact. The girl touches life, it goes through her, you can't separate her from it, she insists on everything out of her reach, she makes the world bigger for herself, maybe it's even greed, I'm not sure.

I could never get enough of anything I wanted. I thought moderation was a form of stupidity. I don't think that now but I have the habit of too much of everything and I can't change it. I want to spend all the money and read all the books and stay in all the hotels and go everywhere and eat everything and cry real hard and long and I don't want to be touched, not by girl or boy, male or female, man or woman, friend or foe.

I get infatuated but I'm leaving that behind, infatuation won't outlast death. I love Paul but I'm too sad. He's more sad. I've hurt him too much. I want women. I have a flat-out appetite now. But I'm not touching anyone. Everyone's cruel. Everyone lies. Fucks and lies. Touching is even harder than talking and I'm buried alive. Silence is on top of me, covering me, keeping me under. Rape is on my skin and inside me.

I can't do this. I can't be this person who was raped. I can't.

(4)

And then there is that I know too much. It makes it harder. I know a lot about rape. I study it. I read about it. I think about it. I listen to rape victims. I engage with prosecutors and lawyers and legislators. I write about it. I was raped. I remember being raped. I can't count how many times or think now about in which circumstances. I say that we're fighting back. I give speeches and say women and girls are being raped and we need to do this and this and this. I'm an expert. I know hundreds if not thousands of raped women. I know about every kind of rape. I know everything but this drug rape is new. Young women, I thought. This happens to young women. The date-rape drug, you hear. Yes, these girls were out and about and someone slipped them the date-rape drug. They say it's worse but what can they know? There's no better or worse. There can't be. But they're right. It's worse.

The drugs erase the mind. The drugs shut down the brain. The drugs put you into the equivalent of a coma. The drugs are cheap and easy to get. Rohypnol or roofies as the scum calls them. They're supposed to be used in hospitals. They have no taste and no color. They work. They put you out. You can't remember once you're out or even when you're conscious but gibbering and out of control. There's GHB—Gamma hydroxybutyric acid, a little salty so it's used in sweet drinks, like liqueurs and champagne, and Ketamine, an animal tranquilizer used for elephants. This isn't an aspirin in your drink. It's not like getting drunk. It's not like getting high. This is so easy for the boy. This is so simple for the boy. This is foolproof rape. The gang who can't shoot straight can do this kind of rape. You can do this hundreds of times with virtually no chance of getting caught. I think how easy this evil is to do.

I think about what marks women are, what suckers, but *I wasn't* suckered, I wasn't. I didn't do anything to make this happen. I was there, okay. I was a woman alone in a hotel, okay. So if I had been somewhere else this wouldn't have happened or if I had been with someone this would not have happened. How can I stay away from everywhere? Maybe I could go to Afghanistan or Saudi Arabia and get them to build a wall around me. Maybe I should wear a chastity belt. I don't know what to do.

I can't sleep. How can I close my eyes? I have had this argument with God. Why, I ask, did you make it so that we had to sleep? How could you build it in that we would have to be so vulnerable, find somewhere dark and sheltered to sleep, not be able to protect ourselves? I don't think I will ever sleep again. When I do I have nightmares. My worst dream always is about my ex-husband. He is very friendly and I try to be friendly because I don't want him to hurt me and in every agonizing minute I'm smiling and being nice and I'm so afraid that he will turn on me. It can happen in a split second. I can't stand the nightmares. I feel as if I've lived through whatever I was dreaming. I feel as if I have a life that takes over when I sleep, a life of fear and terror, and I have a life when I'm awake, and both are poisoned now by this. I wake up exhausted and either sweating or ice cold.

I remember the worst thing I've ever done in my life.

(5)

I beat my dog. When I was married I beat my dog. She was a beauty and she was my heart and soul. He wanted the big dog. He got her but she was too small and sensitive for him. Big dogs, guns. It's a cliché, I guess, but that's what he wanted, big dogs and guns. I don't know why I hit her. It made me want to die. It's not as simple as he hit me, I hit her. Sometimes I was afraid, the way women are with children, if the kid does this, he will hit me so I have to stop the kid no matter how. It presents itself as an emergency when everything is overwhelming, when there's nowhere to turn. The awful thing is that the dog will keep loving you. It's so awful. She'll keep her faith in you. She'll be happy to see you. Her tail will wag. It doesn't matter what you did. It's so unbearable to see her eyes. I can't think of anything I don't deserve, any punishment, but the worst is her, I couldn't undo it, I can't undo it. At night I see her, I see her eyes, and her fragile, delicate skeleton curled in a half circle with her long-nosed head on her front paws. People don't know how delicate big dogs can be. I loved her so much. I was cruel in desperation but it doesn't matter why, it really doesn't. Don't feel desperate around animals or children, no one has the right. Don't hurt them. Zero tolerance. Zero tolerance for me. It can't be bad enough, whatever happened to me. How could anyone be so stupid and so mean?

I can't bear it. I can't. I can't bear it. I thought I could walk away from anything. I thought I had a real cold heart. I wanted one. It takes a cold heart to survive. Survival's the trap. One wants to live.

If you want to kill yourself, though, you have to strike while the iron is hot. Every delay leads back to life. Every minute of hesitation pulls you back. Nostalgia pulls you back. You just want to see the cats one more time pulls you back. You want to hear Paul's voice on the phone just one last time. Any remnant of interest in anything pulls you back. You have to be in the kind of pain that keeps you from feeling anything else. If you want to leave a note it pulls you back. This is a note. The problem is that once I stop writing the new rape is all I have, all I know. I can't be in a room by myself, I can't read a book or even anything, like watching television or going to a movie, without the presence of the new rape in me, filling every-thing, spreading, polluting, poisoning.

What will happen to the girls with this new rape, if they have to bear it? How can they coexist with it? How can anyone promise them anything if they have to bear this and any ordinary moment of life can become this? I was reading a book. *French Literary Fascism.*

(6)

I love a man. Paul. This is not easy for me. He's on the rapist side. He comes from there. That's his place of origin. He's gendered and so am I. I don't want to be but I am and he is too.

I think about Paul. I worry about him. I like to see him. I think his jokes are funny. I like his stories. I like to touch him. I like talking to him. Sometimes I light up when I see him. Usually I do.

This time I asked him to look at the marks on me, the appalling scratches, the bruise on my left breast. He said that what was there could not be there. The scratches were not made by nails attacking my skin or anything like that. He didn't know what it was but it wasn't that. The bruise couldn't be what I thought. I remember hoping he was right. I remember wanting to believe what he was making himself believe. He wanted to console me and he tried. He listened. He'd nod his head. I thought about every piece of furniture—had it scratched me? I thought about every single place my left breast might have bumped into— did the bruise come from a wall or a door or a person I had bumped into? No, these were human-inflicted marks.

I asked Paul if he thought the body knew even if the mind didn't. He said he didn't know, which was fair enough. He never said anything villainous or stupid like, well, you were out during it so how bad could it have been, which isn't so much beside the point as the direct opposite of the point. That was the essence of the violation. I was a dead body. Someone had fucked me dead.

I had understated the internal pain. Not wanting to exaggerate it, wanting to be absolutely fair to the maybe rapist, I had just said I had felt internal pain, not how bad it was or how unwelcome or how inexplicable. I said the awful scratches were scratches, not how deep and long and bloody they were. I didn't want the only person who believed me not to believe me so I held back my horror as best I could. I had to be reasonable, not hysterical or insane. I couldn't afford to make a mistake. I couldn't risk too much emotion.

I was also completely numb. I tried to remember my priorities and my routines but I didn't care. Everything was an act to get through a minute and then another minute and the one following right after that. Life goes on, Paul said, and I nodded concurrence. But it would be better if it didn't, if everything stopped. As long as I was numb I could get by. Once I knew it had happened the numbness was replaced by hell, a constant emotional disorder, a continuing reconstruction of events with my inner eye acting as a microscope going back over and over it without respite or relief. I just want to sleep. (. . .)

(8)
(. . .)
My ex-husband launders money. He's been charged with malicious wounding, causing grievous bodily harm, burglary, theft, fraud, embezzlement, attempted murder and manslaughter. I got him young and he practiced on me. He's in with the Russian gangs and he's as brutal as anyone they produce. They weren't girls or women he was charged with hurting—that's all free, a bonus you get if you are both violent and vile enough. No one's going to step between him and a woman he's beating up on. He's never been convicted of any of the things he's been charged with, he's free as a bird, a flying dinosaur, a raptor with wings. I'm not reckless, I'm saying this now because I just don't want to die, even by my own hand, without anyone knowing this. This is my note in a bottle. I was his beginning. You can see his heel marks on my face but especially on my breasts with their odd scars. He was a virgin. What did I do? How did I do it, create the monster. Any fear I have is fear of him, transmuted and transformed. When I have flashbacks I'm a prisoner of his brutality. It happens again and I can't by an act of will stop it. I see it, I see him, and I'm paralyzed with fear and I can't stop it. Intrusive thoughts is one euphemism for being pursued by harsh, indelible memory.

And now I have the equal and opposite problem: I'm pursued by absence, not even forgetfulness, no repressed memory because there is no memory at all. It happened to me, but what and by whom and how many, were there two as I thought? The boy. I came awake for maybe two minutes, he was in the room already, he was delivering the food, I got up from the bed and he had a look of horror on his face, a look I've never seen before, and I keep thinking that it was as if I arose from the dead, he expected me to be out cold but somehow I roused, I was nearly out again when he closed the door behind him and I couldn't get up to lock it but they have pass keys anyway, which is how he got in in the first place. When the boy grows up will he say he raped a girl when he was a kid or he saw a rape when he was a kid? That's what my ex-husband says but it's not true. I was his first. I couldn't imagine being fifty-two back then. I remember turning twenty-five and thinking I can keep doing this day by day for the next twenty-five years, I just have to put one foot in front of the other, try to stay out of his way. I thought, I can do this. A year later I was on the streets running, hiding, moving, in a cold sweat, then I got a way of leaving for good and I did. Even gone, I kept in hiding, because he could find anyone, he had a predator's special instincts.

I feel culpable because he's still a monster and there's a trail of violent crime. I think I should have stopped him, it was my special responsibility. I think that since he hurt me beyond my own under-standing I should have shot him dead. I think that would have been honorable.

I wish someone would help me out. Isn't there women's secret police who could find him? Isn't there a secret world of women assassins or fighters or revengers? I'm pathetic. I can't do it myself. I call that pathetic. I'm treated like the world's hardest bitch but I can't finish off that particular beast even though my name is written all over him, he's mine to kill. I can do me easier than him, even at fifty-two. I call that pathetic.

I wonder if the beauty I saw in him had any truth to it. It's not there now but way back was it really there or did I fill in the blanks, make him up, imagine him? I hope it was really there. I want to think that what I saw in him was true.

I would like him to be dead because then I might be able to stop suffering. I'd like that before I die. I've been very selfish. People think too well of me. They don't see the trembling piece of shit I am.

(9)

Everything I read about these rape drugs talks about young women and date rape. I knew it was important but it was on rung two, not up front. I thought, maybe this is different, this kind of rape, and if so I should try to figure out how and why. I left the thought to simmer on a back burner. I wasn't facing it straight on, because what did it have to do with me, I'm too old.

Once you really think about it, that logic couldn't be more wrong. Just as now people are thinking that it's if you drink alcohol when anyone could put it in anything, coffee or tea or anything and there's nothing that says you have to be in a bar, they only drug and rape women, young women, in bars. Everyone wants to think that it's punishment for cheap or hedonistic behavior. No matter how many times I say that God made the hangover—not rape—to punish getting drunk, I don't even assimilate it myself. Everyone wants to think it's because of something the woman did, banal stuff, how she dresses, where or when she walks, she shouldn't be at a bar, she shouldn't be out after dark, she shouldn't be being raucous with men or being where men are, she shouldn't, she shouldn't onto ad infinitum. It's as if the woman enters into a contract to be raped just by walking outside or opening a window or what clothes she wears or by liking men at all.

It's the rapist, stupid. It's always the rapist. He decides how, when, where, who, why. He decides by what means. He picks the target. He creates the opportunity. He puts the drug in the fucking drink, hello. He knows and you don't. He decides what to do, you can't stop him once you're out.

Most rape victims need to face what happened but with drug rape you can't face it because it's not imprinted on your brain at all, it's not that it's lost, it's not as if you have to recover it, it was never there.

This rape makes my life a lie, everything I care about, everything I fought for, it's all a lie or a laugh. I can't give another speech or write another book. Saying what? Saying fight back? Saying they hate you? Saying rape is about power? Saying that for the rapist the rape is sex but not for the victim? Saying that rapists are ordinary men, nothing to distinguish them, you can't buy a little decoder ring and see anyone's real intentions. It's hard enough to look young women in the face with how much we have all failed them. They have grace and they fight a good fight but how to tell them that thirty years can go by, forty years, and the rapist gets new weapons and the rape victims can barely keep up.

There are dozens of studies of college men who are asked if they would rape if they could get away with it. Consistently, thirty percent say yes. Well, now they can. Is the drug rapist different from the overt physical force rapist? Do we start longing for the good old days when the violence was overt and explicit? Do we wish we were in Bosnia or Kosovo where the rape is military, a straightforward act of war that is not in dispute? Where someone might mourn what's happened to you? Where there is a collective memory, a history, a record, a crime scene, where each woman doesn't have to make the case herself?

The worst thing is how they rape us because we're part of a group but we have to fight back as individuals. I can't do it for you, she can't do it for me. The rape itself isolates you, because who can you tell, how can you make it real even though it was real?

(. . .)

(11)

These rape drugs are an advance in war weaponry. They are a new day in sexual assault, a new front line, a new moment for women and girls. Memory is all the rape victim has. Memory is required by law. Memory and language are everything. Together they are human intelligence and human will and human history. What would have happened if the Nazis had had Rohypnol and had used it strategically? Would any survivor remember? Would the human history of 1939–1945 in Europe exist? Suppose the Serbs had had it and used it in the Bosnian rapes? It is inevitable.

Then the question becomes, what kind of rapist wants no resistance, doesn't want to use physical force, wants muscles relaxed, including vaginal muscles? Who is the guy who prefers coma to intimidation, dead weight as opposed to terror? Have rapists just wanted to masturbate inside women all this time? Is it true that it doesn't matter to them if we're dead or alive? Do they just want to ejaculate in the presence of a female form?

Doesn't anyone care that this is not a world girls and women can live in? I can see the defense lawyers. She consented because she didn't "protect" herself. I can hear him asking, did you tell your girlfriend to watch your drink, well, if you didn't but you knew about the possibility of being surreptitiously drugged doesn't that suggest that you wanted it? It's hopeless. How can we survive this? What will happen to all the girls?

(. . .)

(12)

(. . .)

I thought I'd go to Paris to write a first chapter for a new book, because I love Paris, I walked a minimum of two miles a day, I went to bookstores and movies, I saw a friend several times and had dinner with a prospective publisher, then I was drugged and raped, and I was too tired to walk, I just couldn't find any energy at all, there was time missing, I was confused, I had been reading in what seemed to be a Zen garden, I had been drinking champagne with kir, the drink didn't taste right, I decided to go to my room to lie down, I remember standing in front of the elevator and praying in my mind, just let me get to my room, just let me get there, I remember my feeling of relief when I got in the room and locked the door behind me, I ordered room service and apparently conked out, I opened my eyes and the boy was in the room delivering the dinner and I got up but couldn't really stand up, I signed the room service bill while having to use the wall to hold myself up and then I went back to the bed, the boy went out, I couldn't get up to lock the door behind him, when I came to it was dark, it had been light out when I came into the room, I didn't know where I was, there was this pain inside me, internal pain, I went to the toilet, I found blood on my right hand, it was bright and new red blood, I found gashes on my right leg and I saw a huge black and blue bruise on my left breast, it was like a big hickey, not a regular bruise, I said to Paul over the phone, I feel like Linda Blair in *The Exorcist*, I have marks all over me and I don't know why, I had been working every night on my chapter but now couldn't, I had no energy, I sat, I stared, I took pills to go to sleep, oh, the irony of it.

I want to live but I don't know how. I don't want more violence to my body, even by me. But I can't bear knowing what I know, in all regards. I ask God to forgive me. Please forgive me all my stupidities and my cruelties. Please don't let there be karma because I don't want to have to do this again. Please take care of Paul and my cats. Please help the women. Please let me die now.

Notes

Introduction by Johanna Fateman

1. Andrea Dworkin to Harry and Sylvia Dworkin, 7 April 1969, folder 9.9, Papers of Andrea Dworkin, 1914–2007, MC 540, Schlesinger Library, Radcliffe Institute, Harvard University (hereafter cited as Dworkin Papers).

2. Photographs of Andrea Dworkin's wedding to Cornelius "Iwan" de Bruin, February 1969, PD.23–PD.24, Dworkin Papers.

3. Ellen Willis, "Hearing," *New Yorker*, 22 February 1969, 28.

4. Andrea Dworkin to Harry and Sylvia Dworkin, 10 September 1971, folder 9.11, Dworkin Papers.

5. Andrea Dworkin to Harry and Sylvia Dworkin, 3 April 1973, folder 9.13, Dworkin Papers.

6. We have not included excerpts from Dworkin's *the new woman's broken heart: short stories* (1980), *Scapegoat: The Jews, Israel, and Women's Liberation* (2000), and *Heartbreak: The Political Memoir of a Feminist Militant* (2002), nor from two books she coauthored with Catharine MacKinnon, *Pornography and Civil Rights: A New Day for Women's Equality* (1988) and In *Harm's Way: The Pornography Civil Rights Hearings* (1990).

7. Andrea Dworkin, *Pornography: Men Possessing Women* (New York: Plume, 1989), 69.

8. Passages of this essay are adapted from Johanna Fateman, "Andrea Dworkin," in *Icon*, ed. Amy Scholder (New York: Feminist Press, 2014), 33–65.

9. Andrea Dworkin, "My Life as a Writer," in *Life and Death: Unapologetic Writings on the Continuing War against Women*. (New York: Free Press, 2002), 20.

10. Ibid., 23.

11. William E. Farrell, "Inquiry Ordered at Women's Jail," *New York Times*, 6 March 1965.

12. Andrea Dworkin, *Notes on Burning Boyfriend* (unpublished book manuscript of writings, 1963–68), n.d., folder 64.12, Dworkin Papers.

13. Andrea Dworkin, *Our Blood: Prophecies and Discourses on Sexual Politics* (New York: Perigee Books, 1987), xi.

14. Photographs of Andrea Dworkin and John Stoltenberg, 1975–81, PD.26, Dworkin Papers.

15. Andrea Dworkin to Lily Tomlin, 7 January 1976, folder 11.6, Dworkin Papers.

16. For the most part, we have avoided internally editing our selections. In some cases, notably in "The Rape Atrocity and the Boy Next Door," we have omitted lengthy citations of now-outdated research and passages that echo ideas expressed at more length elsewhere in the collection. Bracketed ellipses denote where we have condensed the text in this way. In some cases, our excerpts do not start at the beginning of the original text, beginning after section breaks or omitting epigraphs.

17. Dworkin, *Our Blood*, xvii.

18. Andrea Dworkin, "Pornography: The New Terrorism," in *Letters from a War Zone* (New York: Lawrence Hill Books, 1988), 201.

19. For a comprehensive history of the groups Women Against Violence Against Women and Women Against Pornography, see Carolyn Bronstein, *Battling Pornography: The American Feminist Anti-Pornography Movement; 1976–1986* (Cambridge: Cambridge University Press, 2013).

20. Andrea Dworkin, "Pornography and Grief," in *Letters from a War Zone*, 19.

21. Ellen Willis, "Nature's Revenge," *New York Times*, 12 July 1981.

22. Dorchen Leidholdt, "Invidious Comparison," *New York Times*, 23 August 1981.

23. Andrea Dworkin, *Ruins* (unpublished manuscript), 1978–83, folders 75.5–75.7, Dworkin Papers.

24. Andrea Dworkin, "Reviewing Andrea Dworkin," *New York Times*, 24 May 1987.

25. Carol Sternhell, "Male and Female, Men and Women," *New York Times*, 3 May 1987.

26. John Stoltenberg, "Living with Andrea Dworkin," *Lambda Book Report*, May–June 1994.

27. Dworkin, "My Life as a Writer," 13.

28. Wendy Steiner, "Declaring War on Men," *New York Times*, 15 September 1991.

29. Dworkin, "My Life as a Writer," 13.

30. Huey P. Newton, *Revolutionary Suicide* (New York: Penguin Books, 2009), 3.

31. At John Stoltenberg's request on behalf of the Estate of Andrea Dworkin, the playwright and director Adam Thorburn edited Dworkin's manuscript of *My Suicide* for the stage, shortening it to a 90-minute theater piece titled *Aftermath*. The piece was first presented as a staged reading May 1–3 and May 8–10, 2014, in the Willa Cather Room at the Jefferson Market Library in New York City. The text of *My Suicide* that appears in this book is an excerpt from *Aftermath*.

32. John Stoltenberg, "Andrea Dworkin's Last Rape," *Feminist Times*, 14 July 2014, http://archive.feministtimes.com/andrea-dworkins-last-rape.

33. Andrea Dworkin, "Andrea Dworkin: The Day I Was Drugged and Raped," *New Statesman*, 5 June 2000, https://www.newstatesman.com/comment/2013/03/day-i-was-drugged-and-raped.

WOMAN HATING

Woman as Victim: *Story of O*

1. *Newsweek*, 21 March 1966, 108.

2. Pauline Reage, *Story of O* (New York: Grove, 1965), xxi.

3. Ibid., 80.

4. Ibid., 93.

5. Ibid., 187.

6. Ibid., 32.

7. Ibid., 106.

8. Robert S. de Ropp, *Sex Energy: The Sexual Force in Man and Animals* (New York: Dell, 1969), 134.

OUR BLOOD

Renouncing Sexual "Equality"

1. Kate Millett, *Sexual Politics* (Garden City, NY: Doubleday, 1970).

2. Sophie Tolstoy, diary entry, 12 September 1865, in *Revelations: Diaries of Women*, ed. Mary Jane Moffat and Charlotte Painter (New York: Random House, 1974), 143–44.

The Rape Atrocity and the Boy Next Door

1. Sigmund Freud, "Femininity," in *Women and Analysis*, ed. Jean Strouse (New York: Grossman, 1974), 90.

2. *The Jerusalem Bible* (Garden City, NY: Doubleday, 1966), 243–44.

3. Ibid., 245.

4. Cited by Carol V. Horos, *Rape* (New Canaan, CT: Tobey, 1974), 3.

5. Cited by Andra Medea and Kathleen Thompson, *Against Rape* (New York: Farrar, Straus & Giroux, 1974), 27.

6. Horos, *Rape*, 6.

7. William Matthews, *The Ill-Framed Knight: A Skeptical Inquiry into the Identity of Sir Thomas Malory* (Berkeley: University of California Press, 1966), 17.

8. Medea and Thompson, *Against Rape*, 13.

9. "Forcible and Statutory Rape: An Exploration of the Operation and Objectives of the Consent Standard," *Yale Law Journal* 62 (December 1952): 52–83.

10. Ibid., 72–73.

11. Medea and Thompson, *Against Rape*, 26.

12. Mary Daly, *Beyond God the Father: Toward a Philosophy of Women's Liberation* (Boston: Beacon, 1973), 8, 9, 33, 37, 47–49, 100, 106, and 167.

13. New York Radical Feminists, *Rape: The First Sourcebook for Women*, ed. Noreen Connell and Cassandra Wilson (New York: New American Library, 1974), 165.

14. Ibid.

15. Medea and Thompson, *Against Rape*, 16.

16. The Institute for Sex Research, *Sex Offenders* (New York: Harper & Row, 1965), 205.

17. Sgt. Henry T. O'Reilly, New York City Police Department Sex Crimes Analysis Unit, cited in Joyce Wadler, "Cop, Students Talk About Rape," *New York Post*, 10 May 1975, 7.

18. Horos, *Rape*, 13.

19. Menachim Amir, *Patterns of Forcible Rape* (Chicago: University of Chicago Press, 1971), p. 200.

20. Medea and Thompson, *Against Rape*, 34–35.

21. Robert Sam Anson, "That Championship Season," *New Times*, 20 September 1974, 46–51.

22. Ibid., 48.

23. Angelina Grimke, speaking before the Massachusetts State Legislature, 1838, cited in Gerda Lerner, *The Grimke Sisters from South Carolina: Pioneers for Woman's Rights and Abolition* (New York: Schocken Books, 1971), 8.

24. Eldridge Cleaver, *Soul on Ice* (New York: Dell, 1968), 26.

25. New York Radical Feminists, *Rape*, 164–69.

26. George Gilder, *Sexual Suicide* (New York: Quadrangle, 1973), 18.

27. Ida Husted Harper, *The Life and Work of Susan B. Anthony: Including Public Addresses, Her Own Letters and Many from Her Contemporaries During Fifty Years* (Indianapolis and Kansas City: Bowen-Merrill, 1898), 1:366.

PORNOGRAPHY

Introduction

1. Roger Manvell and Heinrich Fraenkel, *Himmler* (New York: G. P. Putnam's Sons, 1965), 105.

2. Terrence Des Pres, *The Survivor: An Anatomy of Life in the Death Camps* (Oxford: Oxford University Press, 1980), 61.

3. George Steiner, *Language and Silence* (New York: Atheneum, 1877), 65–66.

Power

1. Arthur Rimbaud, "A Season in Hell," in *A Season in Hell and The Drunken Boat*, trans. Louise Varese (Norfolk, CT: New Directions Books, 1961), 3.

Pornography

1. Kate Millett, *The Prostitution Papers* (New York: Avon Books, 1973), 95.

Whores

1. H. L. Mencken, *In Defense of Women* (Garden City, NY: Garden City Publishing, 1922), 187.

2. William Acton, *Prostitution* (New York: Frederick A. Praeger, 1969), 118.

3. Jane Addams, *A New Conscience and an Ancient Evil* (New York: Macmillan, 1914), 40.

4. Sigmund Freud and C. G. Jung, *The Freud/Jung Letters: The Correspondence Between Sigmund Freud and C. G. Jung*, ed. William McGuire, trans. Ralph Manheim and R. F. C. Hull (Princeton, NJ: Princeton University Press, 1974), 503.

5. Rene Guyon, *Sexual Freedom*, trans. Eden and Cedar Paul (New York: Alfred A. Knopf, 1958), 239.

6. Guyon, *Sexual Freedom*, 198.

7. Ibid., 200.

8. Ibid., 204.

9. John Wolfenden, *Report of the Committee on Homosexual Offences and Prostitution* (London: Her Majesty's Stationery Office, 1957), 80.

10. Alberto Moravia, *The Woman of Rome*, trans. Lydia Holland (New York: Manor Books, 1974), 88.

11. Otto Weininger, *Sex and Character* (New York: G. P. Putnam's Sons, 1975), 219.

12. D. H. Lawrence, *Sex, Literature and Censorship*, ed. Harry T. Moore (New York: Twayne, 1953), 69.

13. Ibid., 69.

14. Kate Millett, *Sexual Politics* (New York: Avon Books, 1971), 119.

15. Max Lerner, "Playboy: An American Revolution of Morality," *New York Post*, 10 January 1979.

RIGHT WING WOMEN

The Promise of the Ultra-Right

1. Cited by Norman Mailer, *Marilyn: A Biography* (New York: Grosset & Dunlap, 1973), 17.

2. Terrence Des Pres, *The Survivor: An Anatomy of Life in the Death Camps* (Oxford: Oxford University Press, 1980), vi.

3. Leah Fritz, *Thinking Like a Woman* (Rifton, NY: Win Books, 1975), 130.

4. Anita Bryant, *Bless This House* (New York: Bantam Books, 1976), 26.

5. Marabel Morgan, *The Total Woman* (New York: Pocket Books, 1975), 57.

6. Ruth Carter Stapleton, *The Gift of Inner Healing* (Waco, TX: Word Books, 1976), 32.

7. Ibid., 18.

8. Morgan, *Total Woman*, 8.

9. Ibid., 96.

10. Ibid., 60.

11. Ibid., 161.

12. Ibid., 140-41.

13. Anita Bryant, *Mine Eyes Have Seen the Glory* (Old Tappan, NJ: Fleming H. Revell, 1970), 26–27.

14. Ibid., 84.

15. Bryant, *Bless This House*, 42.

16. Bryant, *Mine Eyes*, 83.

17. Bryant, *Bless This House*, 51–52 .

18. "Battle Over Gay Rights," *Newsweek*, 6 June 1977, 20.

19. Phyllis Schlafly, *The Power of the Positive Woman* (New Rochelle, NY: Arlington House, 1977), 89.

INTERCOURSE

Occupation/Collaboration

1. Octavio Paz, *The Labyrinth of Solitude*, trans. Lysander Kemp (New York: Grove, 1961), 22.

2. Shere Hite, *The Hite Report* (New York: Macmillan, 1976), 196.

3. Anaïs Nin, *In Favor of the Sensitive Man and Other Essays* (New York: Harcourt Brace Jovanovich, 1976), 8.

4. Ellen Key, *Love and Marriage*, trans. Arthur G. Chater (New York: G. P. Putnam's Sons, 1911), 82.

5. Hite, *Hite Report*, 141.

6. Franz Kafka, *Diaries 1910–1913*, ed. Max Brod, trans. Joseph Kresh (New York: Schocken Books, 1965), 296.

7. State v. Hunt, 220 Neb. 707, 709–10 (1985).

8. *Id.* at 725.

9. Iris Murdoch, *Henry and Cato* (New York: Viking, 1977), 262.

10. Paz, *Labyrinth*, 13.

11. Don DeLillo, *White Noise* (New York: Viking, 1985), 29.

12. Norman O. Brown, *Love's Body* (New York: Random House, 1966), 133.

13. Sigmund Freud and C. G. Jung, *The Freud/Jung Letters: The Correspondence Between Sigmund Freud and C. G. Jung*, ed. William McGuire, trans. Ralph Manheim and R. F. C. Hull (Princeton, NJ: Princeton University Press, 1974), 265.

14. Marguerite Duras, *The Lover*, trans. Barbara Bray (New York: Pantheon Books, 1985), 63.

15. Ibid., 63.

16. Ibid., 62.

17. Victoria Claflin Woodhull, *The Victoria Woodhull Reader*, ed. Madeleine B. Stern (Weston, MA: M&S, 1974), 40.

18. Wilhelm Reich, *The Sexual Revolution*, trans. Theodore P. Wolfe, rev. ed. (New York: Farrar, Straus & Giroux, 1970), 15.

Acknowledgments

Without John Stoltenberg's tremendous generosity and vision this project would have been impossible. We are also forever grateful to the impeccable and gracious staff of the Schlesinger Library; to Hedi El Kholti and Chris Kraus for their support and enthusiasm; and to our friends. We especially thank Jeanann Pannasch and Elizabeth Koke, and David Geer for his invaluable insights.

Andrea Dworkin (1946–2005), was an American radical feminist author associated with antipornography, antirape and battered women's movements of the 1970s and 80s. She wrote more than ten books, including nonfiction works, anthologies, and novels; and she coauthored, with feminist law professor Catharine MacKinnon, the highly controversial Antipornography Civil Rights Ordinance in 1983.

Johanna Fateman is a writer, musician, and co-owner of Seagull Salon in New York. Her art criticism appears regularly in *The New Yorker* and *Artforum*.

Amy Scholder is an editor and writer. She is currently producing a documentary feature, *Disclosure: Trans Lives on Screen*, and serves as board president of Lambda Literary.